Horse Trek
Into the Mystic

Books by Jaime Jackson

Equine
The Natural Horse: Lessons from the Wild (1992, 2020)
Horse Owners Guide to Natural Hoof Care (1999)
Founder – Prevention and Cure the Natural Way (2001)
Guide To Booting Horses for Hoof Care Professionals (2002)
Paddock Paradise: A Guide to Natural Horse Boarding (2005)
The Natural Trim: Principles and Practice (2012)
The Healing Angle: Nature's Gateway to the Healing Field (2014)
Laminitis: An Equine Plague of Unconscionable Proportions (2016)
the Hoof Balancer: A Unique Tool for Balancing Equine Hooves (2019)
The Natural Trim: Advanced Guidelines (2019)
The Natural Trim: Basic Guidelines (2019, 2022)
Navicular Syndrome: Healing and Prevention Using the Principles and Practices of Natural Horse Care (2021)
A Closer Approximation of ⊙ on the MATW Using an Infrared Thermometer with Laser Pointer Gun (2021)

Other
The Canvas Tipi (1982)
Guard Your Teeth: Why the Dental Industry Fails Us A Guide to Natural Dental Care (2018, 2022)
Buckskin Tanner: A Guide to Natural Hide Tanning (2019)
Cheyenne Tipi Notes (1903): Technical Insights Into 19th Century Plains Indian Bison Hide Tanning (2019)
Living Behind the Facade: Memoirs of George Somers – A Gay Man's Journey Through the 20th Century (2019)
Platform: A Humanitarian Model for an Egalitarian Society (2019)
Zoo Paradise: A New Model for Humane Zoological Gardens (2019)
Horse Trek – Into the Mystic (2023)

Horse Trek
Into the Mystic

Jaime Jackson

Natural World Publications

Natural World Publications
naturalworldpublications@gmail.com
www.NaturalWorldPublications.com

ISBN-13: 978-1-7333094-7-9

Into a strange desert I am beckoned to go,
    by a Calling in the shadows I do not know.
A seeker of a Vision, not chosen by me,
    into the mystic, 'twas my destiny.

Chronology I

Chronology II

Chronology III

Chronology IV

Foreword

I've been a professional "hoof man" for most of my adult life. In the 1970s and 80s, I was a farrier — one who nails metal horseshoes on to the horse's foot. I learned from experience and observation, shoeing corrupts the integrity of the hoof and the vitality and health of the horse that wears them. Less than a decade later, and ever since, I metamorphosed into America's first "natural hoof care practitioner" — no shoes, just naturally trimmed hooves which favor the health and vitality of the whole horse.

Going "natural" was inspired by my studies of wild, free-roaming horses living in the U.S. Great Basin during the years 1982 to 1986. These are horses living outside the domain of human domestication and self-serving exploitation. Their exemplary hooves, like the animals themselves, are healthy and sound as a result. Just as nature intended when any animal is fitted to its adaptive environment.

Many people have asked me what it was about me that, as a farrier, not a scientist, I would go among these wild animals to learn about them, spend as much time doing it as I did, and then take it upon myself to write *The Natural Horse: Lesson From the Wild*

(*Facing page*) That's a Suffolk stallion I'm about to trim. This was around the same time that I was finishing the second edit of *The Natural Horse*. Northland Publishing in Arizona published it a short while later in 1992.

1

(1992), not being a writer either. Guilty as charged on both counts. Others just assumed that I had grown up with horses, was some kind of "child of nature," and that's what such children do.

But neither was the case. I did not grow up with horses nor was I raised in a wilderness setting. In fact, I have no recollection of ever having seen a horse in the flesh — nor do I recall a single conversation about them — until several years after I left the U.S. Army in 1970 as a young adult. My parents really couldn't afford a horse either, nor could our neighbors, come to think of it. Horses were simply out of sight and out of mind. I knew nothing at all about the species, wild or domesticated.

🐎

Ironically, my path to horses — and wild horse country in the U.S. Great Basin, in particular — was inevitable. A story I decided to tell in this book, *Horse Trek: Into the Mystic*. Yes, there was an extended horseback ride across part of the southeastern United States, a "Horse Trek" as I shall refer to it throughout this book, and it was a mystical experience, to say the least. But I've never thought of myself as being a mystic, nor one who seeks or pursues mysticism as a lifestyle. It just happened to me. All of this begs the question, "What is mysticism?

Arguably, mysticism has no tenable home in common words or other existential expressions of common human life. Its detractors and skeptics, thus, define and relegate mysticism to "belief without basis." If this brings them psychological and emotional comfort, then I am happy for

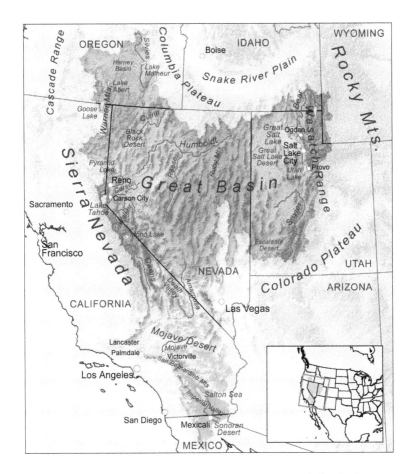

them. No one should delve into mysticism with both feet on the ground.

Nor am I given to the "occult," or metaphysics and its epistemologists and borderline atheists, nihilists and solipsists, who academically must wall off the unwieldy, shadowy, and at times frightening pathways of mysticism. I'm more of a free-thinker and a pragmatist. If I can see it, hear it, or touch it, then to my way of thinking, it exists. Even if you can't see, hear, or touch it, and swear it doesn't exist.

But Horse Trek also taught me to reject the pedestrian entrapments of being a simple "realist," because mysticism will have no part of such limiting, armchair intellectual denialism. I was enveloped in mysticism through unexpected paranormal experiences, which brought into question the very fabric of reality as I once understood it to be. Genuine paranormality, however, doesn't seem to drop in everyone's lap. The paranormal does better at creating skepticism than believers.

In fact it was a steady stream of paranormal experiences entering my life before, during and after the Horse Trek that influenced, if not commanded, my destiny among horses, both wild and domesticated. In this sense, I came to realize that a "higher power" had worked upon me, sometimes viciously so, to change the direction and substance of my life. To be perfectly clear and honest though, my vision as a young man had been to become a physician, not a horseman or hoofman. Which is to say that mysticism aborted one vision, and birthed me in another.

In writing this book, I found it necessary to embed the paranormal events within the realm of their native home in mysticism. But to be more specific, if not chronological, their mystical elements occurred just before and within what is known as a "Vision Quest." So, one may also ask, what is that? While my story will detail what that is from my perspective and experiences — not others — a few words here about it are in order.

A Vision Quest is certainly not the adventures of one possessing an aimless, wandering mind. I would say it is one of a questioning and probing mind. Such a "quest" is one's personal journey to seek and understand the meaning of a Vision — a dream state — which first comes into their mental consciousness, and then takes form in life. It requires the individual to suffer extreme personal deprivation in their journey: hunger, extreme weather, extended periods of solitude, nature's mischievousness, fear, danger, and uncertainty. A Vision Quest, to say the least, is no "cake walk." If you are afraid of the dark or living at the edge where you will question your own sanity, or are unable to endure the castigations and humiliations of others, in either case going alone in the unknown, you might wish to seek another path to personal enlightenment!

Many of the titles of this book's chapters reflect the very troubling nature of the Vision Quest. Indeed, from the onset, I did not think my Quest would be a funzie terpsichorean jaunt through a magical forest in search of bed-set depressives to kumbaya with around the campfire. What it was, as I've said, was an exhausting ordeal of seeking to understand not only the Vision's meaning, but also its purpose. For sure, the initiating Vision did strike me as being profound and worthy of more serious ruminations, including my taking counsel with trusted friends as I describe in my story. But another part of me understood that the whole thing was a bit crazy. I am also a skeptic.

Of the Vision itself, I eventually came to understand that it was to prepare me in such a way as to pursue a new direction in life, from which evolved a new "foot on the ground" pragmatism doused with spiritual enlightenment, mysticism, and the paranormal. While the Vision's meaning and purpose to improve the lives of horses has been well-known among many horse owners for decades, the existence of the Vision Quest and its origins behind all of it, I've held in secreted abeyance to this very day. Even to this precise moment that I am typing these words.

The story behind *Horse Trek: Into the Mystic* took place more than ten years before I wrote *The Natural Horse* in the late 1980s. Both books are autobiographical about events in my life with horses in nature. In my mind, as stories, they are inseparable, albeit linked together by a strange, if not an unlikely, continuity of eerie life-changing paranormal experiences rooted deeply in mysticism. So, after 50 years of secreting and disguising that journey in embellished lie after lie, and with no other "category" of thought and experience but mysticism to put it all into, I've decided to tell the story as I recall and lived it. And let the chips fall where they may among skeptics and believers alike.

Nevertheless, and on a lighter note, if you have found your way to *Horse Trek — Into the Mystic*, and horses are important in your life, then surely it will be an easy "trek" forward 10 years in time to join me in its sequel, *The Natural Horse: Lessons From the Wild.*

Into the Mystic

Towards the end of infantry training, Ft. Lewis, Washington, March 1968.

U.S. Army, 1967–1970

I was drafted into the U.S. Army straight out of college in late 1967. I protested my induction by letter to the local Selective Service Board in Orange County, California, making my case for a college deferment. For whatever reason, my request fell on deaf ears and it was rejected. At that time, I was scarcely aware of our country's involvement in the war in SE Asia, the Vietnam War. I really knew nothing about it. It was far away, out of sight, and out of mind. As were horses. We were all busy with our studies. And of war protestors, if active on our campus, I never saw any.

I was living with my uncle in San Francisco at the time, and since he had no TV, news about the war wasn't reaching me from that source either. Ditto local newspapers, which I never read. They were full of the same meaningless, trashy shit then, as they are today. Before continuing I want to say a bit more about my Uncle George.

George, who passed away in 2015 at the age of 101, was gay. He was a talented artist with many gay and "straight" friends in the Bay Area and elsewhere. He owned a grand three-story Victorian home on Bush Street in the city, which he had renovated himself as he also possessed carpentry skills. George was given to hosting these extraordinary parties for his gay friends, who, like himself were talented professionals in their own disciplines. I was awed how these men, who worked in the shadows of the gay façade by day, but who took great comfort in sharing each others company at George's parties, which were held monthly in George's home. The numbers varied, but as many as twenty were not uncommon. There were also two lesbians, a couple, who often came, friends of George since the 1940s, post WWII. Interests varied among those who came, and George afforded his guests with opportunities to listen to classical music, opera and jazz, while conversations drifted between gossiping about this and that, amid serious conversations that gay people face in the world. Most were socially conservative, were successful in their professions (doctors, lawyers, artists, businessmen), came as couples with relationships that spanned decades, and many traveled widely around the world which influenced their cultured lives. I could go on, but for me, it was a time of inspiration and insights that few "straight people" I imagined possessed concerning the lives of homosexuals. A joke had been cracked more than once, "Jaime's the only straight guy in the house." But I was accepted and respected as a young man making his way in college. Why I brought all this up has a purpose, which we will get to shortly.

I was to report in late January (1968) to a government office serving Fountain Valley, Huntington Beach and out-lying areas of Orange County. Some two hundred or so of us were picked up by these dark, unmarked buses at about two in the morning. It was creepy, to say the least. As the bus doors opened up all at the same time, as though on cue, out came these middle-aged soldiers in Army uni-forms, yelling at us to "shut the fuck up" and get on the buses. Those were the friendliest words most of us would hear for the next several months — and beyond.

The buses drove off in tandem in the dark of night. None of us knew where we were going, and no one dared to ask. We all just sat in dead silence. About an hour later, the buses arrived together at a federal courthouse somewhere in Los Angeles, where I had never been before.

Our army escort stood up in the front of the bus and shouted out in a nasty stream of *accented* threats, "*You are* going to get up and head out this door. *You are* going to walk straight down that sidewalk to that door in the side of that building. And *you are* going to get your fucking asses inside."

I'd never heard this kind of dialect before, asking myself, "Is this *how you* talk in the Army?"

"Now," he growled in a second wave of Army jargon, "*there are* going to be people standing along each side of the side walk. *They will* be saying things to you. *You are* going to look straight ahead and not at them. *You are not* going to pay them any attention. And, I repeat: *You will* get your fucking asses inside that building."

He then took a deep breath and shouted at the top of his lungs, "Now get the fuck up and get your sorry asses in there!"

So we did.

And all along the way on both sides of the sidewalk, were rows of men and women holding these lit candles. They were telling us over and over and over in a chorus of soft voices, "Don't go, don't go, don't go."

Years later, I was told they were probably Quakers, a

pacifist religious order I knew absolutely nothing about.

Once inside, we were threatened by more military types to remain standing. With their mean looking faces, they were even less friendly than our bus escorts, if you can imagine.

We all stood in silence in what was a huge and stately old courtroom. The architecture and woodwork was stunningly ornate and beautiful. Funny I would remember that.

Moments later, a surprisingly undersized door opened in the vast wall to the front of us, and out came a small, elderly, white-haired man in a black robe who took his seat at the judge's bench. He looked irritated, probably because we got him up in the middle of the night. Maybe he was on night duty or something, sleeping in a bed behind that wall?

One of the soldiers towards the front then yelled out, "Raise your fucking right hands."

"Can't," I asked myself, "they say anything without deploying the 'F-word?'"

The judge, speaking into a microphone, read a short oath of allegiance to the United States Constitution and other things I can't remember. When he was done, he declared we were now members of the U.S. Armed Forces. He then got up, and left out the door he came through.

I don't think we were in the courtroom but five minutes before being ushered right back into the buses, of course, under another barrage of threats accented with F-words. To this day, I can't understand why the whole lot of our inductors had to be such "fucking assholes" themselves.

As we were being marched back to the buses, I couldn't help but notice that all the protestors were now gone. I wondered, "Were they out here every morning before dawn doing this, as though on a schedule? Like the judge? Did they light candles for him too? And how did they know we were coming here and at what time?" College had reinforced my predilection to question anything and everything. That would get me into trouble with military types in the years ahead.

We then caravanned northerly along the California coastline on the Cabrillo Highway. But I still had no idea where we were going. And our nasty escort didn't offer us any clues. The whole affair seemed surreal to me. Only days before I was sitting in one classroom or another at the college where intelligent discussion was encouraged. Now I found myself in a darkened, unidentifiable bus sitting in silence with our Army escort's eyes glaring at us in the bus's rearview mirror if our searching eyes just happened to land there.

Later that day, we arrived at Fort Ord, an Army infantry training camp where we were to be garrisoned. We were hustled into these old barracks by another soldier, a sergeant, amid more yelling, threats, and copious F-words thrown in for effect. I recall someone else arrived with sack lunches, since we hadn't eaten anything all night and all day. We were warned — also under threat — not to leave the barracks.

Night time finally arrived and still no orders or explanations, nothing. Everyone eventually just laid down to rest on these old vintage-style military style beds, probably from WWI, or maybe the Civil War? Giving us no peace, yet another sergeant we'd never seen before came into the barracks to harass and threaten us one more time before calling it a night.

"Get the fuck up out of your bunks!" He shouted at the top of his lungs.

Everyone quickly jumped up and stood at the end of their beds along this long aisle dividing the room in half lengthwise, bunks on either side. All except one guy, who stayed laying down, yelling back, "Go fuck yourself, asshole." A declaration of war, if not a call to a rebellion.

The sergeant came hurrying down the aisle to his bed, then, screaming at the guy to get up, reached down for him. What happened next scared the shit out of all of us.

The guy pushed him back, and got up. He must of stood 7 ft. tall, and not an inch less. And, worse for the sergeant, he was muscled up with a rough face to frighten a ghost. He grabbed the sergeant by his throat and crotch, lifted him up, and threw him right out the window behind his bunk, shattering every pane of glass along with the window's old wooden muntins.

We all looked on in horror. But the show wasn't over yet. He then headed for the door leading out of the barracks, stopping long enough to yell out, "I'm getting out of this shit hole. Anyone want to go with me? I'm heading to Canada."

At least have a dozen guys headed out the door with him. That was the last I heard of him, or them. As for the sergeant outside, I assumed he was humiliated and licking his wounds. And, from my perspective, maybe he learned a lesson in life too. Nothing was ever made of it. And, thinking back, I think the Army also lost a real "fighting" warrior to Canada.

Someone near the door turned off the lights. I fell asleep, only to be awakened in the middle of the night by a lot of rustling and bustling within the barracks in the dark. No one said anything to me about it, so I just laid there falling back off to sleep again.

I woke up a few hours later at the first hint of daylight only to discover that the barracks was emptied out except for me and five other guys. I didn't know what to make of it. Nor did the others. So, we just sat and waited for something, anything, to happen.

It wasn't long before an officer, an Army captain as I recall, came in to talk with us, one by one. I was closest to the door, so he started with me, sitting down next to me on my bunk.

Speaking in a surprisingly friendly and gentlemanly voice with no F-words, he asked, "What is your name?"

I told him, and looking at a clipboard with a bunch of names, he found mine, and then asked, "Did you know that all the others that were in here with you were going AWOL?" – explaining what that meant: Taking leave without permission, a serious offense in the military.

I told him I heard a bunch of noise in the dark but didn't know what was going on.

"Why didn't you leave with them?" he asked.

"Well, again, I didn't know what was happening. But that would have been wrong, wouldn't it?" I asked him, and he seemed satisfied.

I learned later that a lot of men were going AWOL during the time of my stint in the Army. Many were going to Canada and other places like the big guy in our barracks, so I had thought, to escape going to Vietnam. My uncle had served in WWII in both Europe and the Pacific, and had impressed upon me the importance of "service to country" when I got the draft notice.

"When you get back," he tried to comfort me, "you can return here to go back to college, finish up, and then go to medical school." And that became my future plan.

Continuing . . . the captain got up and said he would be right back.

A few minutes later he returned with a folder that had all my information, including my educational records. How he got all of that and so quickly was beyond me.

"I see you were planning to go to medical school when you finished your upper division studies," he said.

"Yes," I explained, "It's been a dream of mine. In fact, I worked in a hospital during the summers to help pay my way at the college. Working there taught me a lot about the medical field."

He then asked, "Are you willing to go to infantry training, if I can arrange to send you afterwards to train as a medical corpsman?"

I told him, "Well, yes, and I have no problem using a gun to protect myself or others, if need be."

He continued, "Thank you, I'll see what I can do."

He then got up and headed to the next guy.

♘

I was shipped out by bus the next day for training at Ft. Lewis, Washington. True to the captain's word, after I finished infantry training, I was sent to Ft. Sam Houston, Texas, the Army's main training center for the medical sciences, medical corpsmen, x-ray technicians, and so forth..

Once there, they trained me to be a field medic, a "Medical Corpsman." But seeing how well I did at their school, they sent me on to train in the operating room — to assist in surgeries. It was during this phase of my training at Ft. Sam, as it was called, that I came in contact with Vietnam returnees suffering the worse kind of skull and brain injuries imaginable. An enormous ward, it seemed like the size of a gymnasium, was filled with these soldiers, everyone of them unconscious with shaved heads, laying on tables with IV's poked into their arms and other cables taped to their bodies that attached to nearby machines measuring vital signs. I began to dread this kind of work, and even doubt my decision to go to medical school.

Following that I went on to train at various Army hospitals around the country. This went on for an entire year.

Along the way between training sessions, I always got orders to go to Vietnam, but they were always canceled the next morning. I want to think this happened at least three or four times. It wasn't clear to me, or ever explained to me, why this kept happening.

By now, I had seen more of the devastating impact of the war on soldiers returned to stateside Army hospitals to be near their families for long term care or life-saving surgical procedures, in which I assisted. This had the effect of reinforcing in me the sacred Oath of Hippocrates, "Do no harm." To me, that meant that war is nothing but terrible.

"What in heaven's name has humanity come to?" I began asking myself again and again. "Surely, there's a better way to resolve differences between people?" Such was my naiveté at the time. But a belief I hold onto to this very day.

♘

My last training assignment was at West Point Army Hospital in upstate New York. I was beginning to believe I would never leave the states, sparing me, I pondered, the same fate of those I had helped save in the operating rooms of Army hospitals. That might have been the case had I not screwed things up for myself.

As my fate would have it, there was this very attractive Army nurse working in a ward right off of the operating room suite (we called it the "OR"). We had taken a mutual fancy to each other, and so I invited her to come visit me one night while I was pulling the graveyard shift. Several of us in OR rotated through that duty in case emergencies requiring surgery arrived in the middle of the night.

I let her in and, it wasn't long before we were having a time. Too much time, as it turns out, because we both fell asleep in one of the operating rooms. I was awakened to loud banging on all three of the doors leading into the OR.

Totally groggy, and not really awake or knowing what I was doing, I yelled out, "Would you cut out the fucking racket, we're trying to get some sleep!"

Exhausted, I closed my eyes and started to fall back asleep, when more banging then really woke me up and brought me to my senses. "Oh shit," is all I could say when I finally came to grips with our situation.

No one could get in because I was required to lock those doors from the inside. I woke up my companion. Both of us were now in full panic mode. God save us!

I cracked the door open just enough to look across the hallway to the elevator door which had a window in it. And staring me in the face was the Colonel, an older, controlling, career Army nurse in charge of all OR operations. Making matters even worse, both of us had left all of our clothes in the cubicle down another hallway in the OR — where I was supposed to have slept, alone. I had broken all the rules, and I was had. The Colonel's dagger eyes and boiling blood summed it all up.

"Soon our blood," I lamented to my partner in crime.

Not only had we overslept — how about two hours worth of it? It was my job to have all the rooms ready for the next day's surgeries by the time the surgeons, nurses, orderlies, and everyone else arrived. But nothing was ready. The entire OR was a complete friggin, stained disaster.

Now you are probably asking yourself, what of the naked nurse and the naked me trapped in a room with no way out except in full view of the Colonel? And others probably also trying to get a sneak view from the elevator window?

Well, I had no choice but to walk naked straight across the hall and open the elevator door so the Colonel and half a dozen of the others could get in. But this may not have been the first time this happened. Because the Colonel asked me right off, "Who's in that room with you?" Like it was commonplace.

"Well, uh," I stammered.

Ignoring me, she turned to one of her subordinate surgical nurses, and said, "Grab a sheet, take her to his cubicle, get her dressed, and get her out of here."

Then turning to me, "You go get your clothes on and stay in your cubicle. I'll deal with you in a minute."

I knew what that meant. A court-martial was as good as on the way. I was done for, and all the evidence was literally there for everyone to see (and clean up).

"Would it be jail time, a dishonorable discharge, or maybe a firing squad?" I asked myself.

After 30 minutes or so, the Colonel returned to my cubicle showing me with relish a sheet of paper with numerous "infractions" on it detailing my purported poor behavior under her command. She clearly had it in for me all along and had kept an ongoing roster to document it. And now, I had handed her exactly what she needed to get rid of me.

I was to wait there, as she was going downstairs with her list to report me to "the General," a physician who headed the entire hospital's operations. My goose was to be cooked thoroughly, and I knew it. In fact, everyone else in the OR knew it too, and at least a few gung-ho types in there wanted me extra-seared too.

One stopped by the cubicle to let me know just that. "Jackson, I've waited for this day to come, so they will throw your sorry ass out of the Army."

True, I was a "difficult personality" in that I didn't like taking orders from anyone. And Army nurses did appeal to me (another major infraction). But, on the other hand, the work I was doing in surgery was my calling and I loved learning and helping. Too much so. More than once I had worked all night long with the hospital's two staff surgeons on fairly major cases. The colonel would arrive in the morning and tell me to leave, and I would refuse.

I would argue my case with her, "Colonel, the surgeons have been here all night long and they're going to be here a whole lot longer. I'm not leaving, I'm going to go the distance with them." This recalcitrance infuriated her, because it's called "insubordination" in the military.

The surgeons, on the other hand, took note of my dedication but advised that maybe I should leave, and not face reprisals from higher-up authorities running the hospital. I relented, begrudgingly, and let the Colonel know it. In fact, I had the audacity to joke with her about it in my present circumstance, fanning the flames for my impending execution, "You've only got one sheet of infractions on me?"

No sooner than the Colonel went downstairs with her list, than the head physician in the OR, an anesthesiologist, came in to talk with me.

"I talked with the other doctors," he explained, "and we're going to stand up for you the best we can, because you actually are very dedicated to your job."

At least in the operationg rooms. I thanked him and he left.

But I knew the offense was serious enough to bring charges against me. So, I waited in my cubicle for the indictment followed by a death sentence.

The call came and I was to report to the General's office.

I was met by a tall, handsome strapping of a man, a colonel, just outside the General's personal office.

"Have you ever been before a General?" he asked.

"No, sir." I said.

He then reminded me of the protocol for doing so, which I had supposedly studied in the Army's Handbook back in boot camp, but which I had no memory of. Besides, what are the odds of a low level draftee ever coming before any general?

In less than a minute I was called into his office.

I went in and was not half way across the room to his desk to do the saluting thing, when he got up from his chair — with the Colonel's list in his hand — and, ignoring me, turned to her sitting next to his desk, saying "Colonel, you can leave now," as he walked to the door, opened it, and effectively escorted her out.

I don't know who was more stunned, her or me. In fact we both looked at each other with confusion. She — why I wasn't being reprimanded and charged then and there in her presence. Me — why I wasn't being reprimanded and charged then and there in her presence. Part of me wanted to say, "Now, hold on General, don't I have the right to face my accuser?"

He shut the door behind her, looked at me and said, "She's such a bitch," and threw her list in the trash.

"I heard you're a dedicated worker. So get back to work," he ordered me, "and don't worry about any of this,"

But I decided to stay and gamble a chance. Instead of leaving I sat down in the chair next to his desk.

The General looked at me, pondering what the hell I was doing.

"General, may I ask you a personal question?" And this was the gamble. The Big Gamble lie just ahead.

To my relief, he said, "Go ahead."

"General, forgive me for asking, but, are you gay?" Of course, I knew he was. I learned every gay trait and mannerism known to man at George's.

While flabbergastered, he confessed, "Yes. And how did you know?"

I told him his honesty was safe with me, and I poured out my life with George and all his gay friends, half of whom or more were WWII and Korean War vets. This took twenty mintes straight, and the more I talked, the more he loved hearing about it with great interest. In turn, he shared with me the gay scene at West Point, which didn't surprise me.

I then offered him George's phone number, and told him to call him to verify my story. And that if he were ever

23

in San Francisco (there was a major VA hospital there), be sure to pay George a visit, that he would be in good company.

Later, when I returned to George's while on leave, George told me the General had called, that they had a delightful talk, and that he would enjoy the opportunity to visit George if his military responsibilities made time.

I thanked the General for his time, and he thanked me for being open and trusting. I then got up and left, with a salute by the way, which he returned.

Back down in the OR, everyone, and I mean everyone in the operating suite — and across the hospital too as it turned out — was begging me to tell them how I got out of it.

I said, "It was simple. Be dedicated to your job."*

I then walked out of the OR and went looking for the nurse to make sure she was okay. I found her downstairs in the hospital's rather nice military dining hall eating breakfast.

"Can I join you?" I asked, "I've been looking for you."

"Sure," she said.

"What happened when you left the OR?" I asked.

"Nothing. All the nurses just wanted to know if it was good." she shared.

"Well?" I probed.

"I'll see you tonight, and we can talk about it then," she said with a smile.

---

*The "other" reason has remained a secret for over fifty years to all but me, my gay uncle, and the General. I waited until both men had passed.

U.S. Army, 1967–1969

❧

Several months later, amid wintry weather, orders came to send me overseas. I was to be assigned to an evacuation hospital, not in Vietnam – but in South Korea. I knew very little about this country, other than the U.S. had been there fighting Chinese and Korean "communists" during the early 1950s. That was the Korean War, which ended in 1953. My father had taken me to a parade in Long Beach, California, that final year, to celebrate returning GIs from that war. Thousands of Americans lined the streets along the parade route to cheer the troops on.

But exhiliration soon turned to darkness as the soldiers came through in mixed formations. The military saw fit to show the troops as they were: many in wheel chairs, laying on gurneys, with crutches, bandages around their heads still showing blood. Drum and bugle corps were spaced between each unit, blazing away inspirational muscial scores I'd never heard before. Still the crowds clapped their hands in appreciation. Many stood at attention, some even saluting, many in tears, others stunned by the spectacle. I found it inspiring, even though I was only six or seven years old at the time. Today, they and the war they fought in seem distant and even forgotten by Americans. Shadowed by WWII and now the war in Vietnam.

Korea

I entered the country at night by plane, and was immediately shuttled away to some barracks where we — men on their way to different units — were all given vaccines to spare us every disease known to man. All of us got sick to our stomachs as they restricted us to the barracks to wait it out under the watchful eyes of attentive Army orderlies and nurses.

There was this place on the backside of the barracks, an enclosed patio with a large drain in the middle. Here, they told us, we were to go to "puke your fucking guts out." A Korean national stood by with a hose to wash the gunk into the drain. This state of misery went on for two days, after which time they hustled us off to different assignments, never to see each other again.

I was sent straight away to the 121st Evacuation Hospital just south of the DMZ. It was a relic left over from the Korean War. I believe it is gone now, dismantled or possibly converted into something else. Within days I was reassigned to the hospital's "Mobile Blood Team," a squad of about eight medics all trained to do nothing but travel around the country taking blood from soldiers stationed here and there. Blood that would be sent to Vietnam, where it was badly needed. I thought, "What a strange assignment. All that training in the OR gone to waste."

We became a fairly close-knit group, armed part of the time with 9 mm handguns because there were still ongoing skirmishes between the North and South Koreans — and the 50,000 American soldiers stationed all over the place. Especially along the DMZ, a "no man's land" spanning much of the 38th Parallel dividing North and South Korea. There were U.S. units bunkered all along the edge of the DMZ and we went to them to get their blood too.

We would hit the back roads for weeks at a time in jeeps, Army ambulances, and helicopters, returning to our base camp at the evacuation hospital to rest and then go back out again. It was on one run near the DMZ that the first of many paranormal events in my life occurred. I've kept these secreted from others my entire life, until now. But they are all pertinent to the rest of my story, *Horse Trek*, so it is logical that I take the reader here first, the others in later chapters as they occurred.

Across the Metaphysical Curtain to Vietnam

[Somewhere along the DMZ east of Panmunjeom, South Korea, Late Fall, 1969]

Our squad had been sent aboard a UH-1 "Huey" helicopter to the Joint Security Area (JSA) at Panmunjeom. This brand of chopper was also used extensively in Vietnam for troop deployments and as armed "killing machines." We were to take blood from an Army infantry unit stationed there. JSA was the place where North Korean and United Nation negotiators faced off with each other to sustain what was and has been a tenuous armistice since 1953. The atmosphere around the whole place was eerie and palpably unfriendly. Bad, bad energy was everywhere.

By the time we were done, it was nightfall and getting colder by the minute outside. In fact, it was beginning to snow. We loaded back into the chopper and took off to return to our field headquarters, not far from the DMZ. After 10 minutes or so, not long it seemed, the pilot sent his crew chief, a sergeant, back among us to ask if any of us knew where we were. The pilot was lost. But so were we because it was pitch black outside. Not good at all.

As it was, we were all gulping because we had been straddling the southern border of the DMZ, and if we crossed over it, the North Koreans would have no problem shooting us out of the sky. Which they had done with others before, and I believe after I left country too. The pilot decided to put us down, wherever we were, and take our

28

chances on the ground rather than stray any further into the unknown.

We learned he had no radio contact either. And apparently, he was also low on fuel. None of this made any sense to anyone, and panic began to set in. We had been issued a single 9 mm pistol for protection. Although we were medical corpsman, not riflemen ready to engage hostilities, we all had been trained with high powered rifles, pistols, grenades, and other killing instruments. It's just that we were basically unarmed in this situation. Not good either. This compromise reflects the arrogance of some (not all) "uppers" in military and political command circles who seem to think they know better than those on the ground facing adversity.

The pilot, or co-pilot, thought he had seen lights off in the distance, possibly a village. He told us to stay put while he checked it out. He seemed gone forever, and it was cold enough that we had to huddle together inside the chopper to keep warm.

A little later, we heard another helicopter overhead. In a minute, it landed a ways off behind us to one side. We couldn't tell if it was American or North Korean, when out jumped its co-pilot, an American, yelling at us to get out and run for our lives to his chopper. We knew what that meant and out we went.

I couldn't see a thing in the darkness and falling snow, as the other chopper cut its lights for obvious reasons. We seemed to be scattering in different directions. Two guys followed me towards the rear when I ran right into what I thought was the rear propeller or the rear horizontal stabilizer (a fixed wing-like structure made of steel located towards the tail of the chopper). It caught me right across my upper lip and nose, and I dropped to the ground, out cold.

I recall seeing a galaxy of colorful stars in what seemed like Outer Space, apparently all in my mind's eye. But in the next moment, like a split second, I was standing on the top of a steep hill fuming with smoke everywhere. It smelled like gunpowder or some kind of detonated bomb or bombs. The ambient air seemed hot and very humid. I was in a daze, blood dripping from my nose (and mouth as I learned later) and had no idea where I was.

Suddenly, my mental fog cleared and I realized from military debris scattered all about, this was a small, remote, but abandoned forward American military base. From some markings on the debris, it appeared to have been occupied by U.S. Marines. Clearly, something terrible had just happened here. But what? And where was I?

Something inside me, like an intuitive voice, told me to go towards the edge of the hill and help someone there. This voice would remain with me for years to come. It was a strange experience, one unfolding as though in a dreamscape from which you cannot escape. For reasons at that time I could not explain, I became immediately responsive to the voice. But the dream state, if that is what it was, felt like no dream at all. I could smell the smoke, feel the ground beneath me, hear every sound, and see everything in front of me.

I headed quickly to the steep edge of the hill in the direction the voice indicated. I noticed that the base was surrounded as far as the eye could see by rugged, heavily forested mountains. But the immediate area around the hill had been scorched clean of any living thing. I sensed I was in a war zone. Yet, there were no bodies that I could see laying all about, suggesting there had been no close-range fighting or rocket-like aerial attack with many casualties.

As I neared the edge, swarming up and over the sides of the hill, and hurrying past me, were many Vietnamese soldiers. I suspected they were a mish-mash of Vietcong and some kind of special forces, maybe a North Vietnamese version of U.S. Army Rangers? I wasn't sure. They couldn't see me, like I was invisible. Moreover, they seemed confused and appeared to be investigating what had just happened on the hill — as though what had gone down was not of their doing. There was much chattering among themselves, and what appeared to have been their field commanders barking orders to hurry up. Perhaps they feared a return of

American forces that surely had occupied the hill but had left unexpectedly in a great hurry. I had no idea. But what I did know is that I wasn't in Korea along the DMZ, but I was (so I learned later) near the DMZ in South Vietnam.

I also wondered if my "invisibility" could flip at any moment, exposing me to the Vietnamese. I would take no chances, and searched the area before me. I then noticed there was a hole or bunker nearby, and perhaps others. It had been blown wide open. But laying in there was a soldier, a Marine, in tattered combat fatigues, with terrible injuries. I thought to myself, "He's dead."

The inner intuitive voice suddenly spoke, "Take his hand, lift him up, and lead him up the hill. When you reach the top, escort him across the invisible curtain to the other side."

I had never heard of an "invisible curtain" before. But my intuition and the total bizarreness of it all led me to believe it had to do with one's afterlife.

"But he is not alive," I countered the inner voice within me.

"It is his soul, not his ravaged body, that you will be escorting."

All of this seemed as crazy to me as it would to any mortal soul. But in my state of mind, it also seemed logical.

Doing as directed, I reached down for his hand.

He opened his eyes and stared at me, asking, "Who are you?"

"I'm a soldier from another place who's come to help you." I explained. "That's all I know."

Still he stared.

I asked him, "What is your name?"

He answered, "James W. Jackson, Jr., United States Marine Corps."

"This *is* crazy," I thought to myself. He's got the same name as me.

I continued, "You must come with me, now. There may be another explosion, and there are enemy Vietnamese all around us."

He took my hand, but what arose was like a living, three-dimensional translucent version of him. His mangled body remained on the ground.

He then protested my exhorting to leave, "There was another Marine next to me, we cannot leave him here."

I didn't see anyone else near him. I tried to comfort him anyway, "I think he was led away too. He's not here."

"That way," I pointed with my finger, "we must go to the top of the hill now."

As we reached the top, I noticed that the Vietnamese were now scurrying back off the hill. I'm not sure what they learned, if anything. Seconds later, they were all gone. Then all of a sudden, a massive explosion occurred in the bunker where we had just been. To this day, I'm not sure if the Vietnamese detonated an explosive there, or it had already been there and for whatever reason went off. But I also wondered why Jackson was alone here and hadn't been evacuated with the others, even if just a body, in his unit.

I told him, "We are going to walk through an invisible curtain. Others will be waiting for you on the other side.

They will guide you from there." All of which he accepted calmly.

Together we stepped forward, each of us disappearing into thin air. Or so it had to have been.

In exactly that same moment I was being lifted off the ground next to our chopper in the cold night air along the DMZ.

"What happened to you, Jackson? Are you okay?" It was the two men in my squad.

"I don't know. Something strange just happened to me." I said.

They added, "To say the least, you ran into something, because it knocked you back flat on the ground. You were out. We thought you were dead."

They continued, "We've got to get out of here and over to the other chopper. They're going to fly us out. So far as we know, the fucking North Koreans could be here any moment."

When we got back to the evacuation hospital, an Army nurse took a quick look at me, "You're going to be okay. You can go."

I noticed a commotion in the emergency room behind her. "What's going on in there?" I asked her.

"You don't want to know," she warned.

I went around her and into the room and there laid four U.S. Army soldiers, infantry from what I could see, all shot up to hell. And I mean their entire bodies were literally riddled with bullet holes, blood everywhere. I sensed whoever did this were filled with rage and hatred.

"They were ambushed by North Koreans coming down through the DMZ, infiltrators we're told," she continued, "but they got away, and we don't know where they went."

She added, "You guys were lucky, it could have been you."

I nodded, shivering inside in shock.

I headed to our barracks and then into our communal bathroom, which was empty of others. I looked in one of the mirrors over a wash sink and saw that the tip of one of my upper front teeth had chipped off. My nose, which had bled a little but was dried up, felt like it might have been broken, but was stable enough, so I just left it alone.

My thoughts turned back to my "disappearance." Whatever it was that just happened to me and that marine on that hill in Vietnam has remained a mystery. I decided to say nothing more of it to anyone. But with each passing day, I began questioning my sanity. Then, it happened. I returned to Vietnam again, and again — the second time putting blood on my hands and conscience by willfully killing "enemy combatants," as they were called. That excursion across the curtain may have earned my place in hell. A third, and final time, occurred on the very day I was to leave South Korea and return to the U.S. In fact I was boarding the plane that was to take me and others home, when I crossed over and back into Vietnam for the last time.

Vietnam Again

Months earlier, I had put in for an extension to go to Vietnam, thinking I could find out what had happened to me there, to right a wrong if I could by crossing into enemy lines. But it never came through. But as it turned out, I was destined to return to Vietnam again anyway. As I took my seat in the jet airplane, it happened again.

This time I was alone, touchable in the flesh, and clearly visible because I just scared the shit out of a goddamned monkey sitting on the ground in front of me that screamed and took to a tree. It and me were in the middle of a South Vietnamese jungle! I had no idea where I was, and I was unarmed. I transitioned immediately into survival mode. Looking about, I noticed a nearby fresh water stream that came down through the understory. I headed over to it. I then noticed a well-worn path alongside it. I decided to take the path downstream.

I hadn't gone far when I heard voices coming upstream. They were Vietnamese, and I didn't know if they were friendly or otherwise. I headed back upstream, only to run into more voices coming down from where I had been. What to do? I decided to do nothing. Whatever this force was that brought me here, certainly not to die, would deal with it. My panic turned to calm.

In a minute they closed in on me from both directions. I stood there closing my eyes, come what may I thought. They had gone silent, when I felt the cold steel of the end of a rifle muzzle against the back of my neck.

I was now surrounded and captured by combined squads of Viet Cong. To my surprise, one spoke enough English to ask me what I was doing here alone, and unarmed. I tried to explain what had happened, but he would have none of it. I noticed that he was missing one of his hands, which had healed into a stump.

I was pushed and dragged off upstream and not long after put in a wooden cage that sat in a clearing. He and several others were clearly trying to decide what to do with me, when he turned towards me and signaled one of his men to release me. Whoever he was undid the latch, stood back with the others, and they all just stared at me. Seconds later, they all turned and headed out, disappearing into the jungle.

I didn't know what to make of it, and apparently they didn't either. The voice from within said, "You are done here, and one day you will learn something from it." I did, and the rest of Horse Trek says as much in its stories of personal transformation and redemption. As I pushed the slatted wooden door open, and stepped forward, I found myself on that airplane leaving South Korea for the U.S.

Stateside

[Aboard a plane full of soldiers whom I did not know, approaching Tacoma and nearby Ft. Lewis Army Base, Washington State, January 16th, 1970.]

We were all returning home from our tours of duty. The dull, incessant roar of the plane's jet engines had given me a giant headache that wouldn't let up. We all sat in silence. We had served our time in different units in different places, some entrenched in more violence and death than others. So, we were not compatriots who actually knew each other. We could only wonder what others had gone through and what was going on inside their heads. And, also, what lay ahead for each of us — now that the military was done with us, or at least me (I hoped).

But for now, inner silence prevailed, like a solemn ceremony in which no one is celebrating anything. And that no one is interested in celebrating either. To be alive was enough, or so I ponder within myself, having come to believe that life, like death, is nothing but a fleeting, mystical illusion. I wondered if any those around me had experienced the same thing as me . . . the invisible curtain thing.

The nose of our plane suddenly dipped towards the ground, signaling our descent and return to the common homeland. All in the shroud of nighttime darkness, two years after I was drafted into the U.S. Army — also in the middle of the night if you recall.

Minutes later we were hustled off the plane, into

buses, and taken into an old building and "debriefed" by a snarky, smart-ass sergeant full of himself. He made me reflect back to the big fellow in the barracks at Ft. Ord, and what he might have done to this jerk given a crack at him.

The briefing event, not more than 30 seconds long, was a total farce. But no one really gave a damn what he had to say anyway. Everyone just wanted "out" and as quick as possible. To get on with our lives was our silent mantra.

So, this sergeant steps up to the front of the room, and belts out, "I'm here to debrief you."

And then not a second later, "There, you guys are debriefed and can go."

Not a word of thanks, nor another word period. And that was it.

A few minutes later, and what was for me a *déjà vu*, we were loaded for the last time onto a caravan of — guess what? — dark, unmarked Army buses waiting outside, and shuttled back to a nearby commercial airport where I thought we had landed not many hours before. Seemingly out of nowhere, we were handed tickets to go our separate ways on different flights leaving throughout the night. The Pentagon had this all figured out, like clockwork.

I wondered, "Are we being secreted back into society?" It felt that way to me, for sure.

♞

I landed back in San Francisco, my last known address — a friend's — even though I never had a residence there. My uncle had sold his place in the city and moved away across the San Francisco Bay in the Oakland Hills. I had decided before leaving Korea, that I would not return to live with him again. In fact, I was done with college too. So, I really had nowhere to go to.

Backing up a bit in time before I was drafted into the Army . . . my parents had long since divorced, my mother leaving for another man, my father a violent alcoholic too crazy and dangerous to be around. Before my uncle invited me to come live with him in SF, I had left home going on 17, found my way to a community hospital where I lied about my age to get a job. The man who did the hiring in Human Resources was on to my lie from the start. But he gave me a chance anyway, advancing me enough money up front to rent my own apartment a block away. He sent me where he had also sent others needing lodging. A year later, my gay uncle had located me and invited me to live with him and his partner in SF. So, that's how I ended up in SF.

Long before my return from overseas, I had become acutely aware of the now full-on, nationwide raging anti-war movement against the bungle in the jungle of Vietnam. But I also had witnessed first-hand the devastation wrought upon those who bore its wounds or had died, violently so. While overseas, I had used my academic prowess to study the origins of the war, concluding that a toxic mix of ignorance, racism and war profiteering facilitated by politicians and industrialists, lie at the bottom of it all. And I was quite vocal about it with other members of my squad.

Not surprising, the sergeant in charge of our squad, an avowed "lifer" and alcoholic, and I got into it one day when

I said to the others we were on the wrong side of history. That we had no business in Vietnam or Korea. That we should get the fuck out now, and let the peoples of those countries work out their own future. That they didn't need us for that.

Well, that was one too many antiwar pontifications for him, and he blew a fuse and came for me!

"You're going to get what you deserve now you fucking Commie bastard." He yelled out.

I burst out laughing at him. Couldn't help myself!

But before he could advance another step, the other guys grabbed and restrained him. I just stared at him. He eventually calmed down and tried to explain himself. I said it's okay, it goes no further.

So my new purpose in life was now to become a part of the resistance to the Vietnam War, and any war, for that matter. While I could say it would be an important part of my character development as a person trying to right a terrible wrong, I began realizing within myself that it is was only a stepping stone to something else. Maybe a greater purpose in life, or maybe just a way to save my soul for having been a naive instrument of war. Even as a Medical Corpsman and a phantom intruder in the back country of Vietnam.

So, with nowhere called home to go to, an alarming sense of being homeless began to set in upon me. It meant, in the rawest sense of uncertainty, finding myself with boots on the ground in a strange new world I could never have contemplated nor envisioned in my former self. That self was now dead as a doornail.

Words Held Within

Within weeks of my release, nature, a directing force acting upon all of earth's creatures (whether we're aware of it or not!), did in the most strange and mysterious of ways, begin to move upon me. Stripping me down as a person to some base level I had never known. In retrospect, it was to prepare me for life-changing experiences that were soon enough to come.

I found myself totally out of character, suddenly engaging in a stream of unwitting and reckless behaviors. Each entangled in misguided decisions for which there was no plausible justification or rationale I can offer the reader. This take down of who I once was didn't take long. In the span of less than a month, I found myself in a spiraling social collapse. I became friendless, jobless, and more or less homeless. So isolated, I had become unrecognizable of my former self, alienating every person I once knew or came upon.

So I was stuck in a kind of mental paralysis that made no sense. I suppose it was a state of mind — one without goals for a future — that would terrorize any mortal possessing a lick of common sense and direction in life. The reader will just have to imagine it. And yet amid this bizarre psychological calamity I began to sense within myself that larger forces of nature — a "higher power" — were at work.

I saw that my isolation was not the prison of a tormented soul. Nor a punishment for some wrong doing.

Not even a cruel avenue for self-destruction set out like a welcome mat by some dark force. I began hearing about many returning vets who were so alienated from "society" as to kill themselves to end their mental torture. But, for me, as my story will reveal, it was an awakening to provide me with unfettered clarity and extrasensory perceptiveness with which to recognize and negotiate a future that was to be completely out of my control.

Slowly, under a paranormal guiding force that took me three times into Vietnam, I came to realize that there was a higher purpose in all of what was now happening to me, but which I could not rationally put into words — that which must be held within by the mystic. And no less frustrating than for the infant crying out in the darkness, demanding to be seen and heard, but unable to utter a single comprehensible word as to why.

I was entrenched in this state of mind amid truly precarious circumstances. I was now living in an old 1947 Chevy pickup truck I purchased for next to nothing with some savings I had from my Army pay. That truck and I were both born in the same year, the year of Roswell. Together we roamed the streets of the San Francisco Bay Area — a man metaphorically carried by his trusted steed of steel with rubber tires for hooves! We parked wherever we could, like nomads, just long enough to nap or take on fuel and food. And then keep moving without a contrived destination.

One evening I returned to my truck that I had parked

near a lake tucked away in the higher forested hills of the
East Bay. Street life at night in the inner cities seemed dangerous. So I took to these hills, as far from the wandering
and depraved night people as I could manage. The hordes
of homeless that we know today, ensconced in every nook
and cranny, day and night, in every city, were back then
still small tribes of the desperate. I had started to become
like some of them — more inclined to roam furtively to the
furthermost outskirts of the cities at sunset, returning by
daylight to scavenge and eek out an existence. Those like
me at the edge seemed to pose no threat to others sharing a
common plight, some even inviting me to their campfires
including this very night. But towards outsiders I wasn't so
sure, as some were armed with knives, and maybe guns. I
was well-trained to kill in the military, but promised myself
not to "carry" for any reason upon my return to the states —
a pact I was later compelled to break, revealed later in my
story. It was now getting late, and I returned to my truck.

It was a moonlit night, darkened only now and then by
wafts of maritime clouds drawn from the ocean and moving over the forested hills. A great redwood forest once
stood here before meeting the mighty, cruel axe of civilization. Half a millennia earlier, its tallest member, 33 feet
across at its base and over 400 feet high, served as a sylvan
lighthouse for Spanish galleons seeking to enter San Francisco Bay. Sawed off at the base, it became a 19th century
dancehall before being rooted out and turned into firewood.

As I began to unlock the door to get in, a figure suddenly rose up from the bed of the truck. It was a bearded man with long, darkish, and straggly hair. I had scared him as much as he did me. But in the voice of a soft-spoken gentleman that surprised me, he spoke out to break the impasse, "I apologize sir, I didn't mean to frighten you, I needed a place to sleep for the night."

I saw that he was a veteran like myself, maybe ten years my senior, though fully worn down by the elements like other homeless living in the hills and down in the cities. He was still wearing his dog tags. And his Army issued field jacket suggested he had been an officer.

"No, no, it's okay," I countered, "I'll be sleeping inside the cab. Please stay where you are."

He laid back down without another word.

I got into the truck, locked the door, and readied myself to lay across the bench seat, covering myself with a blanket I kept for that purpose. I thought better a moment later and got up, returning to my guest with the blanket.

He had fallen soundly asleep, perhaps comforted by my invitation to stay with me. But he laid open to the elements, and the cold ocean air coming across through the Golden Gate was a bit much. So I laid the blanket over him and returned to the cab to make the best of it.

I roused myself from a lousy night of "near sleep" at the first light of dawn, and got out of the truck. He was gone, but the blanket lay neatly folded in the bed of the truck. I wondered what demons or voices wrestled with his mind to bring him to such dysfunction? But then, what of my own?

I decided to leave the Bay Area and travel north along the coastline to a fairly remote stand of virgin Redwood forest that extended down a steep gulch to the turbulent Pacific Ocean below. You would think these giants of the world's forests intended to mingle their roots with the waves of the sea! Here, where tree met sea, I set camp, reminding me of my earlier military bivouacs in the dense conifer forests of Ft. Lewis and elsewhere. But it was a welcome retreat in the bosom of nature, far, far from the incessant roaring sounds of civilization's machines that numb and grate away at the human soul.

As I lay down to sleep on the first night, I was startled by the infiltration of a mysterious entity within my mind in the form of a voice — at first, just a whisper, but growing louder in intensity as if to purposefully wake me up. I then realized, it was the same voice that was with me on the hill and in the jungle back in Vietnam.

"Why," I asked myself, "had it returned?"

It was a voice that over time I would learn to trust and act upon as though in a trusted relationship. As I had done on the hill, and during my brief capture by the Viet Cong. So, as before, I relented and deemed it my Guide, like a compass pointing my way forward. Not as a tyrant ordering me what to do under duress — to comply or else, like a towering and intimidating Army drill sergeant. But in a good way, though I will confess here, it would become difficult to see and appreciate it as "good" on more than one occasion!

47

Eventually, it also conveyed mystical powers, as I came to understand them. Powers of healing and intuitive insight that provided me with a defensive means of survival in the face of adversity, coupled to a window into nature's astonishing web of life. It was also harnessed to a Vision of personal purpose with significance. None of which I had ever contemplated, pursued, or asked for, let it be known. As I have prefaced in this book, mysticism, the occult, and New Age Incantations to the Spirit World, have never been a pursuit of mine.

The Vision would be revealed in time to me, but not this night here in my primitive sylvan encampment. Nor did it say in what form it would take. I would simply have to wait it out for its arrival — like the faithful dug-in for the Second Coming. But I was by now well accustomed to that type of "waiting for Gadot" treatment. The Army was notorious for its infamous indoctrination, "Hurry up soldier, and wait."

You can imagine, hearing stuff like this in one's head out of the clear blue, was just plain weird. Well, it gets weirder yet. And I often questioned my own sanity as a result of its intrusions. Suddenly, I blurted out loudly like a madman and enough to scare off the nearby wildlife in the forest: "Is this the penance or indoctrination of a homeless soul that has lost its way? Or a person simply 'going off the deep end?'" Of the latter, I was partly comforted by the words of a soldier overseas who told me, "If you're able to contemplate the idea that you're going crazy, you probably aren't."

This invisible entity also commanded discretion from me, as was its way through intuitive messaging. That if I were to talk openly about its "Voice," it might very well pave the way for my incarceration in a mental ward!

Even writing these words now seems grounds for such an indictment with a straight-jacket for my wardrobe! One, arguably, I might even levy against another person professing the same exact thing as me! So be it, and not that I really care what others may think. Not at this point in my life. But proof to myself of my own sanity was that, over time, I had mustered the wisdom to use discretion when deciding who, and who not, to talk about it with. A truly crazy person possesses no such discretion or inhibition and will openly preach, howl and fulminate from the nearest park bench to anyone, whether they're paying attention or not.

But to be clear, of the Vision itself, I was free to confide it in whomever I might trust. Not a problem during that point in time as I was pretty much down to just myself and the truck as explained above by my "nutty" behavior.

I decided that the words of this Voice should probably be held within in secrecy, at least until the purpose of the Vision was fulfilled at some unknown later date. Or maybe never.

I humored myself at one point, "Get it all done, then talk about the Voice, and then get myself incarcerated!"

Not so funny really, as some people I met during the Vision Quest, or whatever we wish to call it, damned well would have rounded me up and put me away if given the chance!

But I will confess in advance, I even breached this decision to conceal the Voice. But only because I learned later that I wasn't the only person being guided by such a thing. And "hearing an imaginary voice" is not actually what was happening. It is my intent, if not my hope, that the reader will understand what it is and why such things happen to some people before this book ends.

After several days, maybe a week, I returned to the Bay Area, invigorated with the prospect of purpose. Upon my arrival, I reflected once more on the experience I had with the other vet in my truck, and my close encounters with other homeless souls. What would become of them? I felt a streak of compassion pass through me. One I've never been able to shrug off to this day. These lost souls are casualties of an apartheid of the haves from the wandering haves-not in our world, a descent of the human spirit shackled to corrupted voices within — crazy talk that makes no sense at all in any reality. But I have mused more than once with a twist of trepidation concerning myself, "What of my own words held within?"

As I regained my footing among the living, I learned from a new acquaintance that my uninvited visitor is what is known among psychics, healers, and contemplators — including tribal shamans though by another name — as a "Calling." That what was happening to me was neither schizophrenia nor some kind of PTSD. Nor a hallucinogenic, magical mystery head trip induced by drugs or the frightful delusions born of alcoholism. For I've always been a teetotaler, and I am leery, if not fearful, of any mind altering substance. Nor was it a pathway to spiritual redemption. Because I'm not religious in any orthodox sense and I feel no need to beg of any purported extrasensory divinity who may come down from above for forgiveness on any account. In fact, what was happening was not about me at all, which I found liberating, thus, sparing me the indictment of a sociopathic narcissist.

I was to be simply an instrument wielded by a greater force than I was able to fully comprehend, and for the singular purpose of accomplishing something well out of the ordinary. A force that did secure me with immunity from certain death on more than one occasion in an unfolding future I was destined to enter. And soon enough, it armed me with the Vision that would point me in the direction of my unknown destination. And, finally, enable me to recognize its temporal significance upon arrival through that Vision.

That's all I knew, or at least had come to expect and faithfully follow at that point in my story. Unless! — I had stumbled upon a way to shake it all off and exorcise the entire frigging thing from my life. And then go get a job or a profession or something a bit more sane than "Vision Seeking." But there would be no such luck. I was harnessed to it like a pack saddle strapped to a mule.

Being a resourceful and pragmatic person by nature and habit, I took stock, applied my talents and intelligence in various ways, and lifted myself out of my present purgatory. So accomplished, I proceeded to let the Vision unfold as it may: Whatever it was to be exactly, when and where it was to happen, and in whatever form, so be it I resigned myself. But, to be honest, such faithfulness was not without my questioning it time and again. "Why me of all people?" had been chosen or entrusted to pursue it on this Calling's behalf.

Anti-War Radical

I left the U.S. Army with an honorable discharge. But with a dishonorable conscience. Within months of my release, I became one of those returning vets who was self-conscripted into the antiwar movement opposing the conflict in southeast Asia. In fact, opposing U.S. militarism anywhere in the world. Battle lines were drawn at colleges and universities, city halls, banks, the U.S. Capitol, on bridges and other major thoroughfares, and in the streets of nearly every major city. *There would be no business as usual.*

At first, this dissidence irritated over half of the American people, while an indifferent fourth of the population could care less and probably weren't even aware that a war was going on. The rest, a minority, "got the message."

It was a tumultuous time for renegades like myself, positioning ourselves "up against the system" as we saw it. But for damned good reasons! Our drum beat focused on what Eisenhower had warned Americans of not a decade before: The emergence of "an immense military establishment and a large arms industry," and that the people "must not fail to comprehend its grave implications." It wasn't hard for disobedient vets and other incorrigibles to draw a straight line to Vietnam, where nearly a trillion dollars and tens of thousands of American lives had been given for nothing — except war profits. And what of the horrific toll taken on the Vietnamese people who wanted nothing more than to determine their own future?

Leaving the homeless life behind me by now, I ran with a bizarre mixture of vets, draft resisters and draft dodgers, AWOL soldiers who'd seen the light like those who fled the barracks in the middle of the night at Ft. Ord, liberals, radicals, housewives, students, students' teachers, and even some of the homeless. Possibly even the vet who slept in the bed of my truck! We were a spectrum of personalities who otherwise had little or nothing in common in civilian life. Only the one we all shared: At all costs, ending our military involvement in North/South Vietnam, Laos, and Cambodia.

On any given day of a planned march and protest, crowds would form and join in. Things would then get really weird. Mixed in were others with totally extraneous agendas who didn't really give a shit about the war — opportunists as I thought of them: Self-styled socialists, communists, Maoists, anarchists, hippies, pseudo-American Indians with eagle feather bonnets, chanting Hare Krishnas with finger cymbals and dirty bare feet beating their tablas, half-naked poets, artists who painted their naked bodies, druggies who had no idea what was going on, musicians with blazing bongos, dropouts, street drunks, religiosos, men looking for crazy women, women looking for crazy men, gay men looking for men, lesbians looking for women, transgenders trying to figure themselves out, fascist vegans, people who badly needed to take baths, gawking tourists with cameras, university professors trying to lecture everyone in sight, politicians begging for money, and even

FBI agents! Almost any kind of gig was in on it from all sides. And it was crazy. I wouldn't have been surprised if Jesus Christ had showed up. And why not?

At one point I remember asking others during a protest, "Can anyone tell me just what the fuck is going on here?"

I even began to think, "Maybe the Calling will get me out of this."

In one incident, we entered classrooms on a college campus to disrupt numerous classes at the same time. I took one, a sociology class, and took a seat in the back of the room. It wasn't long before students, and then the teacher, didn't recognize me as a registered student. Five minutes after all the classes began with their "business as usual," our orchestrated disruptions began.

I stood up and started pounding on the top of my desk with my fist, speaking loud enough to get everyone's attention, "How can you sit here while your fellow Americans your age are being killed at this very moment in the jungles of Vietnam. Shame on all of you for carrying on with your lives as normal. You need to get up and get out of here and tell others, 'No business as usual. Bring this senseless war for profits to an end.'"

This tirade brought the expected range of responses from shouts of anger at the disruption, to faces of guilt, to some getting up and leaving, some crying, to calls of "right on."

With disorder established, and having made my point,

I left and headed out to join the other protestors who did the same thing. Everyone would have to disperse quickly in every direction to confuse and escape campus police that would be chasing after us. As I went out the classroom door the instructor chased after me, calling me to stop.

Catching his breath he confessed, "Thank you so much for doing that. I wanted you to know that I'm right with you. But what can I do?"

I said, "That's good, now just change the discussion to the war and educate your students why it has to be ended."

Actions by "outside" agitators is what helped fuel the massive movement of "Teach-ins" led by brave, renegade instructors and professors who put their careers on the line by defying university administrators. Many of those universities were heavily involved in different ways supporting the war. As anti-war protesters became aware of them, those colleges and universities became targets for disruptive protests. This led to clashes with university law enforcement, blocked traffic on bridges, and other acts of open defiance. The movement couldn't be stopped. The situation was growing increasingly out of control. TV stations focused heavily on the disruptions. And more and more Americans began to be swayed to pressure their politicians to bring the war to an end.

But the antiwar effort wasn't exactly a 24/7 battleground with the American establishment — and let me add here that the same thing was going on in other countries too. Anyway, there was a bohemian eatery and hang out over in the Mission District of "The City by the Bay," (San Francisco) called "The Island." It seemed like everyone in the "counterculture" went there at one time or another. The food was culturally diverse and admittedly great. They served three meals a day, and the days usually extended late into the night.

I went there often to eat and get in on the dialogues going on about every radical cause across the country. The building was a giant converted warehouse or something akin. Inside there was a huge eating hall with a series of platforms rising in stages from the bottom floor to near the ceiling. You sat down, and servers with menus came out of nowhere. I don't recall any conventional tables with chairs, just low lying tables and you sat on the floor or pillows or someone's lap.

A staircase went up the center. Somewhere midway up the stairs there was a small stage with a microphone and you never knew who was going to perform or rap on it. I remember a famous poet, a chubby gay guy with a great beard dressed in some kind of an oversized African dashiki or Hawaiian muumuu This guy brought the house down with his theatrics, booming voice, and prose that attacked the "system" we all cajoled in one way or another.

In another moment there might be a folk singer or trio, Hare Krishna drummers, Black Panthers protesting police violence, Native American radicals with nothing kind to say about the Bureau of Indian Affairs (BIA) and corruption on reservations, a juggler, even a howling mad man who wandered in off the street. Crazy as it was, a lot of debating and insightful discussions took place there.

And the food was always worth coming for. All kinds of exotic foods were served, made from flesh to plant. I think the radical vegan movement might have begun there, because I recall many being very vocal about it. What if a piece of meat happened to touch a vegan or vegetarian's plate accidentally? The servers, begging forgiveness with religious fervor, made it right and brought the incensed victim a new untainted serving on a fresh plate. Kajeezzzzzzzzzz!

🐎

On another occasion, a radical "gang" of Marxist-Leninists — if there ever was one in this country — invited me to go to one of their public gigs. There was always something about them that made me uncomfortable, leery may be more accurate. But they had a plan to take "wholesome foods" (that's what they called it) to the Pine Ridge Indian Reservation where dissident Ogallala Indians and armed members of the American Indian Movement (AIM) were holed up in a church located in the reservation hamlet of Wounded Knee. They were surrounded by armed federal agents and tribal police. That commotion made the international news. It all had to do with Indian treaty rights, self-determination, corruption in the reservation's tribal government, and other battle-cry issues. More on this a bit later in my story.

So, I pissed off the whole bunch when I said, "There better be lots of pork and beans, white flour, white sugar, and grease 'cause that's the sort of shit they're used to eating on the Rez."

Two white guys in dark suits across the aisle from me laughed. I turned and said, "You guys look like FBI agents?"

"We are!" they said with another laugh.

I told them this was a bullshit meeting and I'm getting out of here. I think the meeting's facilitators were about to escort me out anyway. When one white gal in particular opened her mouth to lecture me, I headed for the door.

Well, the two agents joined me outside and we had a pretty interesting talk about the problems in society, including the issues at Pine Ridge and other reservations. They were surprisingly very much up on what's going on, and were actually sympathetic with the plight of Indian people still subjected to oppressive American laws. I told them that the reservations are really military style internment camps from the 19th century disguised by the BIA to look like something else they aren't. I also told them that Hitler was aware of them and there were rumors that he modeled his concentration camps after them along with the Bolshevik interment camps Lenin created following their 1917 Russian Revolution. They nodded. It was weird, but I felt I had more in common with these FBI agents than the nasty Commies full of whole wheat flour back inside the meeting.

What none of them knew inside is that an anthropologist I had recently met by the name of Louise Revol — who was in charge of Native American artifacts and displays at a city museum in the East Bay city of Oakland — had con-

Showdown at Wounded Knee. Assistant US Attorney General Kent Frizzell and other Nixon Administration reps, at right, listen to AIM leaders in a sit-down inside the tipi prior to signing a peace settlement, April 5, 1973 in Wounded Knee, South Dakota. Kneeling at center with his goodwill pipe is Wallace Black Elk (1921-2004) and to his right are AIM leaders Russell Means (1939-2012), Dennis Banks (1937-2017), and Carter Camp (1941-2013).

tacted me to meet a Sioux Elder from the Rosebud Reservation, which is only a couple of hours from where the Wounded Knee incident was occurring on the Pine Ridge rez. His name was Wallace Black Elk, a tall and striking man, and a good friend of hers.

At the time, to support myself, I had opened this workshop where I made all sorts of things from canvas and hides that I tanned the "Indian Way." More about this later. So, one day Louise brought Black Elk there to meet me. We sat together and talked about many things. He was of my father's generation. I remember him as being very tall, soft spoken and very kind in his words. He wanted me to make him a tipi to take with him to Pine Ridge, where it ended up at the Wounded Knee fiasco! I'll explain later in my story how this connection came about, so that this interaction with Black Elk makes sense as it is a bit out of context at this point.

🜍

Anyway, Louise, also of my parents' generation, was a good friend of many Indian people in California and elsewhere, and she always tried to cast their histories and cultures in the best light possible at the museum. But she was also as an advocate for the "old ways" that were shared with her by older Indian people still alive then, not a few of whom she introduced me to. I had done traditional tanning for one of her exhibits at the museum, for which I was paid, and which is how I had come to meet her in the first place.

🜍

I continued with my anti-war involvements until it was brought to end by President Nixon about the time of the Wounded Knee incident. Now, more about myself leading up to the Vision.

Canoe

I was born in California right along the ocean near the Mexican border. To make a long story short, I grew up going into the sea almost on a daily basis. So water was part of my cultural upbringing. With the war protesting over with, I thought about doing something that would put me back in contact with water, but not in a bathtub. So, I made a canoe out of canvas and wood in my shop.

The wood formed the frame, and the canvas the "skin" which I varnished to keep it from letting in water. I laid a deck of redwood slats across the bottom on the frame to support my weight. I also added slatted Redwood strips for the gunwales. It was 16 feet long. I modeled it after the Ojibwa Indian bark canoe with upturned ends. The closed ends of mine were longer and more roomy though than the

Ojibwa women in canoe (1896).

Ojibwa, and in them I stored supplies I would need for longer canoe trips. They also shed water off to the sides if I ran into rapids in a river. A sturdy wooden thwart held the beam (widest part of the canoe at its middle), and I attached a broad wooden strip running lengthwise down the bottom of the canoe (the keel) to minimize damage to the skin if I hit bottom. I carried patching materials if I got a tear, which was often in some places. Paddles were easy to come by and buy ready-made. I was set to go.

I ventured to many places around the state. And I would like to digress a bit to describe just a few, not just because they were great adventures, but because the Calling was involved.

Once you get on a river in the back country you see things otherwise not possible, and you know you're "in the remote." Some lakes I visited gave me the same sense of remoteness. It also brought me into contact with wildlife living in the water, along the shores, from the sky, and even things dangling from low-hanging branches (like snakes). The disconnect from civilization felt good. So, life with the canoe was good too.

One memorable trip took me to this beautiful lake in the middle of a national forest in northern California. Later, I would return often for the welcomed solitude it and the surrounding forests offered. This lake was east of the great Redwood forests along the coast, where the Calling had come upon me earlier in my story. It was here that my next paranormal experience occurred.

Canoe

The lake in the mountains that I frequented with my canoe. Here is where I connected with a Bear Spirit that infused me with the strength and resolve to endure the hardships of the forthcoming Horse Trek that was yet to be revealed to me.

It was a ways, a bit over a mile, to reach the far end of the lake. That's where I set camp on a cutbank that rose up just above a river where it entered and fed the lake. It was a great spot, and the rushing of the river below over rocks was spell-binding and nurturing of the soul housed within me. I planned to stay 3 days on this visit, exploring the upper reaches of the wild river by foot.

Nightfall came quickly upon me so I made fire within a ring of river rocks to stay warm as it was now wintry in the mountains that surrounded the lake. Sometime later as I was gazing into the fire, I felt the earth rumble beneath me as something large ran behind me not a meter away. Out of the corner of my eye, I saw it was a large black bear.

I got up to investigate, and it sounded like it was heading up this steep hill behind me, thrashing its way through a ton of brush in the understory of the forest. Since it didn't attack or threaten me, which it could easily have done, I assumed it intended no harm. I believe it knew I was there all along.

As was my custom, I made a bed inside the canoe, using the paddles to form a center ridge from bow to stern, using the thwart as a midway support and brace. All my belongings were returned to the closed endings of the canoe for storage. I draped a large oil-tanned cowhide over the gunwales to seal the top above me, and so ensconced, I was prepared for sleep.

Minutes later, a light rain began to fall over the mountains, river, lake, and me in the canoe. I slept well and dry to the soul-nourishing pitter-patter of rain falling on the hide and canvas walls throughout the night.

The next morning, I arose to light snow coming down. The rain was transformed by freezing temperatures during the early morning hours. Anticipating inclement weather, I had kept a supply of dry tinder and wood within the canoe to start a new fire in the morning. From my supplies, came utensils for boiling water to make good coffee, for which I've had a lifetime addiction to this day.

I tilted the canoe on its side at 45 degrees to form a canopy with the hide slanted above me by means of the paddles — a makeshift tent! Soon the coffee blended with the scent of the forest, and I couldn't help but think how blessed my life was in this serene moment. But soon my curiosity turned to that bear. Where had it gone to up there? Did he or she live up there?

The Calling came upon me, "It is a female and her spirit guide will serve to give you strength, courage, and resolve for what lies ahead. Go to her now."

There was nothing left to do but take the hill and find her. Seeking a spiritual connection with her seemed dangerous, as common sense would dictate. But my quest had become not one to question but to seek.

Tracking the bear was easy, until I neared the top of the hill. The understory of brush got so thick I had to crawl on my gloved hands and knees. After several minutes of this, I ran into a solid wall of broken twigs and other flotsam of the forest. And by now my body temperature had risen to a boil from the labor of getting just to this impasse.

So I laid there on my belly as though snared in a giant spider's web. I decided to go to my right and began to crawl "on my belly" along the wall's edge, which now turned into a circle. I kept crawling, deflecting lower hanging branches of the Fir trees that guarded the path I was on. It began to feel like an eternity as I made my way forward and around.

I finally reached what appeared to be half way around a circular mound of forest debris. I turned my head towards what was a small opening in the mound, which reminded me of the entrance to the traditional Inuit's igloo. I peered into the opening, but it was too dark to see anything.

The Calling came upon me, "Reach inside the opening."

My sense of fear was overshadowed by the will to fulfill the Calling's command. I slowly reached in and at arm's length, my hand came upon a warm wall of body covered with fur. It was the bear.

"This bear is a female." the Calling reminded me. "She is in a deep sleep and will not harm you. Keep your hand in place and her spirit guide will enter you."

And so there I lay with my body connected to the warmth of this powerful female entity of the forest. The connection and energy flow was extraordinary.

The Calling once more: "Now go and return to your camp. It is time for her winter sleep."

Another memorable canoe adventure occurred, not in the mountains on a serene lake or even going down a challenging river, but in the middle of the San Francisco Bay! It turned out to be a daring voyage because the water in the Bay can be turbulent and rough, and its cross-currents powerful. Worse, its surface can rise from calmness into threatening waves at any time. And, as I was about to learn, it is generally pretty tricky at times to navigate due to oil tanker shipping lanes. Regardless, I wanted to give it a go. Such was the lure of this great body of water. If not a reckless voyage to embark upon, one could rightfully argue it was foolish. So be it. The "call of the wild" was upon me.

I decided to cross from where the cities of Berkeley and Emeryville meet at the Bay's edge, and end up at Angel Island. It would be an eight mile trip to get there, and an-

White line and arrows trace the path of my canoe voyage, an 8 mile journey to Angel Island, and another 12 to get back to my starting point in Berkeley.

other 10 to 12 to get back — if I took in a few other sights in the North Bay. And barring any unforeseen problems along the way.

The first problem I ran into was a visibly turbulent and

powerful current just north of Treasure Island and the Bay Bridge. It was impossible to cross without being swept away in the wrong direction, and too powerful to resist with my paddles. So I decided to cut across it on the diagonal going the wrong way, then back track on the other side of the current. It worked and soon I was on my way across the bay.

But then out of nowhere came a huge oil tanker straight at me. I was stunned by how fast it moved. The pilot was blasting a warning horn and made a last minute decision to cut to the north to prevent a disaster, meaning running me over. But this put me against his flank, and facing a powerful wave left in his wake. I took it straight on like a surfboard, and over the wave's crest the canoe and I went. On the back side of the wave I was almost looking straight down, thinking, "This will be the end of me." But the sheer lightness of the canoe kept us buoyant and above water, and the closed bow cleaved the water to the sides like a waterfall. To be honest, it was as much a fool's paradise as it was exhilarating. Several smaller waves followed, which we moved over with ease as I took aim again for my destination.

🐎

A mile or two shy of the island came the next surprise. To one side of the canoe the water suddenly became turbulent, but no more than several feet wide. I looked down and saw what I thought was a seal coming up. Instead, a hand came out of the water and gently took a gunwale! It was a diver out in the middle of the Bay! He lifted his mask and let go of his mouthpiece and hose which led to a tank on his back. As quickly he engaged me in light conversation. He said he was scouting for shrimp down below when he caught eye of a strange looking vessel up above he wanted to check out. That was the canoe, of course.

As he marveled at the design, he asked, "You made this out of wood and canvas? Never seen anything like it out here before. Where'd you come from?"

I told him the East Bay, and then a bit about the current crossing and the near collision with the tanker. He just half-nodded, probably thinking I was out of my mind. But a frogman looking for shrimp out in the middle of the Bay, miles from shore? Figure that one out. We said our goodbyes, and down he went as I aimed for the south side of the island.

🐎

As I began turning northward, Alcatraz Island came into view. I decided to make an excursion over to the island. Once there, I stopped the canoe off shore and reflected on what I knew had been going on there a year or so earlier.

All these American Indians decided to occupy the island and claim it under vague treaty rights going back a century ago. I think close to a hundred Indians were out there at one point. It all had something to do with treaty rights dating back to the U.S. government's land grab of Sioux Indian lands in the 1800s. But the occupation failed as did Sioux treaty rights a century earlier. Sioux were eventually confined by military force to reservations that are still there today. The Indians were removed from Alcatraz by

Just a year or so before I embarked on the canoe voyage to Angel Island, Native Americans (Indians) occupied the abandoned federal prison on Alcatraz Island, not far from Angel Island. It ended in June of 1971 as a force of federal agents removed the Indians — a failed attempt to secure treaty rights to unused federal lands. Today, the prison is managed by the National Park Service.

federal agents, and the island and prison were both absorbed into the National Park Service.

⌂

The remainder of the paddling to my destination on
the south side of the island was uneventful. Small waves
coming off the Golden Gate carried me into a cove with a
sandy beach. It was pretty windy as I steered the canoe onto
shore. When I finally landed I looked up to find myself
staring into a crowd of naked men and women sunbathing.
Being scantily clad myself, I almost fit in. But instead the
spectacle of a stranger arriving in a canoe right out of the
sea was a bit too much, and the looks weren't exactly
friendly. I guess you could say I was also intruding on their
privacy. But a nudist camp run by the California State
Parks? That was a new one on me. So, I left immediately.

I decided to skirt the eastern flank of the island. To get
there I had to round Pt. Blunt, the most protruding salient
of the island facing towards the south. On the east side of
the Pt., there were many large rocks rising above the sea. I
decided to navigate between them. The rocks, I soon discovered, were covered with sea lions and seals, basking in
the sun like the nudists on the other side of Pt. Blunt. As I
wound my way between the rocks, I was literally staring
them in the face. But here and there, a whiskered face
would also pop up out of the water, brushing up against
the side of the canoe. The whole lot of them were just as
curious as me, but none showed any fear or aggression towards me. I soon passed through the rocks and paddled
northward along the east side of the island.

Angel Island. Learning about the island's history from a park ranger also made the journey worth the effort. The Tiburon Highlands was then far less developed than today.

🐴

Angel Island has had other human visitors besides the nudists laying in the sand back in the cove. Miwok and Ohlone Indian tribes hunted and fished here before the arrival of the Spanish explorer Juan de Ayala, whose ships set anchor on the opposite (west) side of the island in 1775. But the Calling said this was not the case. That another Spanish fleet had entered the Bay over 200 years earlier. That is a story I will tell in another book.

During the first half of the 20th Century, immigrants coming from everywhere were sequestered here before being allowed entrance to the United States with the promise of eventual citizenship. A park ranger who greeted me when I decided to come ashore on the east side of the island told me over 1 million Chinese were held up here during that time. The military was also stationed here dating as far back as the War Between the States (U.S. Civil War, 1861-1865) and on up until WWII. Back then, it was a Nike Missile base, and finally a public park just a few years before I arrived by canoe.

I paddled north across the upper Bay to a beach with an adjacent forest near the Tiburon Highlands. By now, it was getting late, and, worn out, I decided to spend the night in the canoe, falling asleep to the lapping of the waves on the shore. At dawn, I paddled back across the Bay to my pick-up truck and headed home to an old and abandoned canteen I rented for $25/month.

Canteen

The canteen, as it was called, sat on an acre or two of dusty land. It was part of a "company town" called Clyde that was created in 1917 for ship builders and their families. The town was located just south of where the great Sacramento River poured into a series of bays, marshes, and canals, eventually flowing into and mixing with the ocean waters of the northeast corner of San Francisco Bay.

I'm not sure what the townspeople did in the canteen, which sat by itself at the edge of town. It was a two-story building stripped of anything from its earlier days. It sat vacant for as long as anyone then living in the town could recall, with the exception of an elderly lady who lived alone in a small house across a small alley from the canteen. I think I recall her saying it was a small railroad station at one time, maybe later becoming a town community hall. That's probably why people took to calling it the Canteen in later years. I believe it was torn down several years after I vacated it.

Inside the canteen I had a workshop, actually a downsized version of my sewing shop, which I had moved not long before from the East Bay. I'll have more to say about that sewing shop a little later in my story.

Around the grounds of the canteen I grew a garden, which produced a ton of produce. I would take sacks full and share it with neighbors. But only one neighbor, that older woman, is the only person I can remember much about. She was in her 90s, meaning she was born in the 1870s, and had lived in the town since its inception. Her husband had passed away 20 or more years earlier. During one produce drop-off she wanted to gift me this small and very ornate pendant made of silver in gratitude for all the food I had been bringing her.

She was born and raised during her early years in a small village of homesteaders called Moccasin, located in what later (1889) became the State of Montana. This was a time when great hostility still existed between Plains Indians living in the region, and the U.S. military and local pioneers.

So her story went, "One morning an Army officer and a small contingent of soldiers on horses came to Moccasin, which had a main street and one row of houses and merchants on each side. [Main street, of course, was just a dirt road back in those early days! - JJ] The officer told everyone to get in their homes and stay there until we were told we could come back out."

She then related that everyone in Moccasin hung out by their doors and glassless windows with open shutters to see what was going to happen. The air, she said, "was filled with both excitement and dread."

She continued, "Hours and hours passed by when suddenly a cloud of dust began to appear just beyond the far edge of town. Out of the dust came the sound of many hoof beats, and soon the beginning of a long caravan of Indians escorted by the U.S. Cavalry. We all stayed in our homes as the caravan passed by."

Cheyenne family using a horse-drawn travois, c. 1890

She told me the Indians were on foot or on horseback, but no wagons. Their goods, and even children — were carried by many horses using what is called the "travois."

She continued, "The Indians passed by all day long and throughout the night and all the next day, too. Finally, it came to an end, and the officer returned to tell us we could now leave our homes and go about our business."

I was trying to imagine the whole ordeal, asking myself, "Which Indians were they and where was the government taking them to?"

She then finished her story, "We kids returned to the road to play in the dirt like we always did. We began to notice that some of the Indians' belongings had fallen to the ground as they passed by. It was in the dirt that I found this beautiful pendant, which probably belonged to one of the Indian women. I've kept it all these years, but I'd like you to have it now."

I did keep the pendant for some time, but I think I gave it away at some point because I don't have it any longer. But the memories she shared have stayed with me all these years.

But back to the canteen. It was there and exactly when I got that pendant, as I think back in time from this moment, that my future was about to unfold in the most profound experience of my entire life.

The Vision

By 1973, with 58,000 Americans dead and over 300,000 living casualties, the fighting was nearly over, both abroad and at home in the streets. Nixon, amid his presidential demise from the Watergate scandal and sanctioning illegal bombing raids in Laos and Cambodia, found a way to end it militarily. Gerald Ford, Nixon's successor, tried to refund it, but politicians in Congress under public pressure refused. The American people had had enough of the killing. For me, it was time to pick up the pieces and move on.

♞

I knew then that my life would never be the same again. There would be no turning back to my earlier years, no comfort in what I once was, no returning path to tread upon. It was then that something really strange happened to me on the heels of the anti-war thing. It was the Calling surfacing again. It all began one early morning at the Canteen, as I lay alone half-awake upstairs in my bed.

Time began to slow *down,*

down,

down, eerily so. So much so that I began to take notice. Then *Fear.* It is hard to explain. Then time soon seemed to stop all together, like I was in some kind of vacuum state where nothing is happening. And no sounds either. A strange dream — what I came to recognize and appreciate as the long awaited Vision —

then came upon me.

I saw myself riding a horse whose coat was splashed with a mix of brown and white colors, what I later learned is called a "pinto." We were moving and climbing upwards upon a narrow ridge trail, or so it seemed, towards a peak. Steep cliffs streamed ever downward on each side, almost like a waterfall, forbidding a dark abyss somewhere below. It struck fear in me, so I did not look downward, just forward. I hate heights, they make me dizzy, even though I spent over half a year overseas riding around in Huey choppers without a flicker of concern. This was also weird because I had never ridden a horse before, and I knew nothing about them as I related at the beginning of my story. Nor would I ever put myself so precariously upon the spine of a mountain ridge on the back of any animal.

"So why all of this?" I thought to myself, suddenly realizing that this dream wasn't really a dream but more like another reality I crossed over into. Just like on those excursions into Vietnam.

We continued up along the trail until we reached the very pinnacle of the peak. Suddenly, a strong wind came up and the horse's mane and my own long black hair, which stretched nearly to my waist in those days, began to mingle. The horse stood solid with great patience and was seemingly indifferent to our situation. I didn't know what to do, as it was the horse that led us up the mountain, not me!

Not exactly sure how to get myself out of the situation, I scanned the horizon ahead from left to right to figure out what was going on and where I was. As I did, I saw or sensed the world before me as a very troubled place, which was really a no-brainer given what I had just been through in recent years. I then turned in the saddle to my right to look back, and still the world was troubled. But, then, as I began to turn to look forward again, the wind began to calm. And as it did, what now began to unfold before me was a world of great peace, serenity, harmony, and beauty. Below the peak, as far as the eye could see in the distance were great numbers of beautiful horses of all colors and types.

Startled by this, I opened my eyes, and the Vision ended. As quickly, the passage of time that had been altered in the Vision, was now familiar and normal. And all the familiar sounds of life also returned. What the heck?

Somehow, I had been awakened to a new path in life that was not at all logical. Not that I didn't want to shake it all off as just a weird dream. Believe me, I probably would have if it weren't that another part of me said more convincingly, "This Vision is good and is inevitable. I will find my way to this peak and discover the meaning of the Vision."

I realized also that the Calling put it before me intentionally. But why?

I began pleading with the Calling, and I suppose myself, "I have no idea where to find this peak, and what am I to do exactly if I did find it? And why are all these horses even involved?"

I decided to take the Vision to two very close and trusting friends, a husband and wife whom I had met a year or so earlier. I explained to them what had happened. The Calling, as the inner voice, would be left out of my descriptions of the Vision, less they diagnose me as a schizophrenic and call the men in white jackets to take me away!

They listened attentively as I told them about it. I then told them I was going to follow it. Moreover, that I felt like I had no choice, strange as it sounded to them. Which even sounded crazy to me as I said it. Though still a mystery to me, I knew within me, like an instinct, that it was a good thing to do, or at least keep pursuing at this point in time.

But their interest soon turned to frowning faces of concern, when I confided that I actually had no *exact* idea what to do. Seeking justification, I told them that I was convinced I was in some strange way a "marked card," destined to seek the purpose and path of the Vision — but, again, not mentioning the Calling as the source of it all. Nor had I told them about my forays into Vietnam.

I rationalized to them, "The suggestion of the Vision representing a transformation of the world, or some part of it, from troubled to something very positive that was going to happen, is enough for me to follow it."

The husband spoke out, "Jaime, the purpose you see in it may be good, but maybe it's not such a good idea to take too seriously at this time."

"Why not?" I asked.

"Not enough information to go on," was their logical comeback.

We left it at that for the time being, and I returned to the Canteen.

Not to be deterred, I felt that the Vision, however illogical, would soon unfold in its entirely. And then reveal to me its purpose and what I was going to do about it and why. "There will be a sudden Great Awakening of purpose and enlightenment," I now rationalized to myself.

But that never happened, at least not all at once. This "Calling," my story will tell, required that I be slowly prepared for what was to come. I would be humbled, stripped further of my past self, and made to suffer the throes of uncertainty, deprivation, and even danger. It was the price I would have to pay to fulfill the Vision.

As though coming to my rescue, within days I was drawn back into a second Vision. And this time the horse was not there. Just me alone walking the path to the same pinnacle the Pinto and I had ridden out to.

Time had again slowed and then stopped and there was no sound — all as before. But this time around I had no fear as a strange darkness came upon me. I entered into a deep sleep. From within me came the Calling again, not spoken in audible words as was usual, but as an understanding delivered as a thought wave.

It was a directive: "Sell or get rid of everything you own. Be prepared to leave the west coast of California for a new location."

The Calling continued, "There you will find the horse in the first Vision, and you will then travel together towards your destination." I then awakened and, as with the first Vision, all was normal again.

Even I had to admit with the same frown of concern as my friends following the first Vision: All of this was crazy, the stuff of lunacy. A charge that could easily be brought against me, bringing back the ominous warning of incarceration in a mental ward!

I pondered, "I'm to get rid of all my belongings? Then leave the west coast? But not know exactly where I'm supposed to go and find this Pinto?"

That last part was almost the deal breaker because it really made me challenge my sanity. To save myself, I decided to take council again with these same friends.

The husband, a Canadian French-Cree Indian (known historically as the Métis) on his father's side, was, like me, part Indian, or so my father told me one day when I was a young teenager. A drunk until the day he died, my father never brought that up with me again. Not that it mattered to me, anyway. I'm simply a human being who happens to be a man. But my father did bring me into contact more than once with Indian people and that must have rubbed off on me, for I felt a connection to them. One that carried over to my Metis friend. We could talk all sorts of Indian jive that he was in the middle of — spirits, the Indian Way, Red Power, Metis sovereignty, all of that. Naturally, my Vision fit right in.

"Maybe," he spoke, "we will simply have to wait and see what happens."

I knew what that meant, "Indian time." One doesn't

worry about time, being on time, or thinking about anything in relation to time. The seasons, the sun rises or sets, or when the deer meat looked cooked, stuff like that. We would wait and give it no more thought.

But almost as quickly as our jive-ass Indian talk ended, elements of my path forward began to present themselves.

Oakland Intertribal Friendship House

Back then, about the time I met the Metis, I had supported myself making things, all kinds of things, out of canvas and Indian-style tanned leather. I had created a sewing shop in the East Bay and recruited a dozen or so young men and women I had met in the Bay Area to help me. This was the same shop that I eventually moved to the Canteen in Clyde several years later, located in the North Bay area.

I want to digress a bit into that whole experience, because they were an interesting bunch and we all had great fun working together and going on outings too. I taught myself to fix all our industrial sewing machines, and even considered becoming a sewing machine mechanic as a "career." Maybe I will go into some of that later in this story. Or maybe not.

But, to digress a bit further, the shop is how I met my Métis friend. He came wandering in one day and asked if I could make him a bed, a large "comfy" pad he requested, for their old dog. So I did. And thinking back from a future my story has not yet taken us to, a time when I always slept directly on the earth, that comfortable dog bed is something I thought a lot about.

We got to know a lot about each other, including a lot of stuff about Indian culture that I knew about, a welcome relief from his incessant Indian jive talk. I taught him a bit about hide tanning, fire-making, weapon making, how to take a scalp (only kidding). He saw that I was pretty busy in my shop and maybe needed more help from local Indians he knew, or knew about.

In fact, there were a lot of Indians who had left their reservations to move to the Bay Area. This was due, in part, to the Indian Relocation Act of 1956,* but also WWII which I'll talk about later in my story. The U.S. government wanted them off their treaty lands and assimilated in the cities. Here, they were told, they would get trained for jobs and no longer be dependent on the BIA (Bureau of Indian Affairs) for their survival. By the time I opened my sewing shop, over half a million Indians were relocated and leading new lives among non-Indians in major cities across the U.S. But the removals didn't go exactly as hoped for.

Those Indians often faced racial discrimination in housing and segregated schools, got low paying jobs, and struggled to live just like generations of African Americans and Latinos were having to put up with. But also poor whites, come to think of it. Many turned to alcohol to fight depression — what Indian activists called the "wino wars." Intertribal friendship communities formed to help each other.

The Metis suggested we go to the local East Bay Intertribal Friendship House,** where Indians of any tribe could come and meet each other, and get help. He said maybe some of the Indians there would need work and I could

*Signed by President Dwight D. Eisenhower on August 3rd, 1956.
**Founded in 1955 by the Quaker organization, American Friends Service Committee.

hire them or even get them involved with the business somehow. I was skeptical, but went along with his idea.

When we arrived, the Indians running the place were blatantly suspicious and just stared at us, saying nothing at all. The Metis attempted to strike up a conversation why we were there. Which got us only more stares. But it seemed that most of the Indians there were dealing with alcohol and drug problems, and maybe that's why there were no takers.

We weren't there five minutes listening to the dead silence when I said to the Metis, and loud enough that our gawkers could hear, "Man, this place isn't exactly 'friendly' (a play on the 'intertribal friendship'), "Let's get out of here."

We took off and never returned. I learned years later that the Metis' wife and her family were Quakers. I wonder now if they weren't somehow involved with founding and supporting this particular Friendship House. And that's why the Metis took me there.

Ironically, not a day later, a Navajo Indian showed up at my shop. He came from a drug rehab program run by the BIA to get him away from pushers feeding Indians narcotics on his reservation in New Mexico. They put him in a graphic arts school held upstairs in the same building as my shop. He was curious what we were making, so I invited him in to see what we were doing and introduce him to the others. How he ever got involved with drugs was beyond me. He was a gentleman, kindly, polite, intelligent and likable. The opposite of the tight-lipped Indian bureaucrats at the ersatz "friendship house" — the last place I would have sent the Navajo to for help.

Everyone in my shop took to him immediately, and we invited him to join us on some of our outings on his day's off from the school. Maybe he was on some kind of parole, because going with us required permission from the school upstairs that, in turn, answered to the BIA.

It wasn't long before we learned the Navajo was quite the horseman back on his rez. And I began to suspect that maybe the Calling had something to do with his arrival in my shop. The horse connection excited the ladies in the shop, because all females on our planet love horses and can't help themselves.

We found a ranch somewhere in the countryside north of San Francisco across the Golden Gate Bridge that had horses to ride. The Navajo offered to give riding lessons. We all went and everyone but me got on a horse. I just watched and let him know that everyone appreciated his friendship and the riding lessons.

For whatever reason, the Calling had held me in check, "Do not ride."

"Gladly," I shot back in my inner voice.

The truth is, I was afraid to get on one of these half ton beasts. I knew nothing about them, and really had no interest: "In the Vision, okay," I comforted myself, "In life, no way." I was actually more nervous about the others noticing the yellow streak beaming down my back.

But back to the doings with my crew in the sewing shop.

American Freedom Train

On reflection, I thought it might interest some readers to hear a bit more about my sewing shop and the people in it. I met most of them before I created the shop. It was about half men, half women, all about my age. All but one lady were unmarried and single, coming from all over the U.S., eventually ending up in the East Bay (Richmond, Berkeley, Oakland). Most were attending one of the local colleges, looking for part-time work. One was a gay physicist working at the Lawrence Berkeley Laboratory at the University of California Berkeley, who met me through one of the ladies working in the shop. Another was the estranged son of a dean of a famous Catholic university. Unemployed until he came to work with me part time, he literally took living quarters wherever he could. But he had one of the most brilliant minds I had ever come across, and was a blessing to work on designs with me for some of my more challenging projects. I could go on, but they were all interesting persons and I grew to love them all.

One day I got a call from a man who saw an ad about my business in a local paper. I can't remember his name to this day even though we eventually became friends and had dinner together more than once. He was a veteran like myself, but of my father's generation, and had served in the medical corps in Europe during WWII as a captain. He'd seen a lot in terms of casualties and, by that I mean what happens to the human body when it takes a hit. But so had

Freedom Train traveling through California. The converted boxcars are so far back you can't see much. The passageways were added when the train stopped at various locations and the museum cars were opened to the public.

I, so we both understood what that meant. You can't forget it, and you lose sleep over it for the rest of your life.

He called because he wanted to know if I could help him put together a large order of flexible, accordion-like covered passageways that would stretch between baggage cars on a train. It turned out this was a major project being put together as part of the United States Bicentennial celebration sanctioned by the U.S. Congress. The passageways enabled people or workers to move between the cars without getting rained or snowed on.

This train became known as the 1976 Bicentennial American Freedom Train. It was going to criss-cross the country in celebration of the nation's 200th anniversary.

The vintage baggage cars had been brought several years earlier to what was the old Butler Steel yard in Point Richmond, located along the northeastern side of the San Francisco Bay. Here, the ends of the baggage cars were being retooled by engineers and welders for attaching these passageways.

The baggage cars were also being converted into mini-museums for displays of things related to U.S. history. I recently found the following description of the trains in an old article, which is better than I could ever do since I never actually visited the converted baggage cars when they took off for their historic journey:

> The train itself consisted of 10 display cars, converted from New York Central and Penn Central baggage cars. They carried more than 500 treasures of Americana, including George Washington's copy of the Constitution, the original Louisiana Purchase, Judy Garland's dress from The Wizard of Oz, Joe Frazier's boxing trunks, Martin Luther King Jr.'s pulpit and robes, replicas of Jesse Owens' four Olympic gold medals from 1936 (one of which was stolen somewhere along the way), a pair of Wilt Chamberlain's basketball shoes, and a rock from the Moon.

Butler Steel was active during WWII building warships for the Kaiser Shipbuilding Company. But it, and related industries, closed down sometime after the war ended. When I arrived at the factory in 1973, it had been converted into this massive warehouse for converting the baggage cars. Remnants of the old building still remained, including parts of large cranes and other massive structures designed to process and move heavy objects made of steel down an assembly line.

I was taken on a tour of the operation by the Project Manager (the veteran who called me at my shop). There were hundreds of men working in shifts around the clock — welders, machinists, electricians, and other technicians.

I overheard one floor manager remark about this army of men, "These guys are like animals, completely out of control."

I don't know where they recruited them from, but as a whole, they were an interesting looking bunch. Somehow though they eventually got the job done!

I finally reached the Manager's office, which looked down upon everything going on. He brought out detailed plans for what he wanted. These helped me to see what was needed, and I could see it was going to be quite the challenge. I've decided to explain what happened because I suspect there's a possibility that some of my readers may have toured the converted baggage cars and walked through the passageways and remember them. Now you will learn the rest of their story!

The end doors of the train were re-framed by machinists and welders into a protruding rim of steel that formed a flange in the shaped of an upside down letter "∩". The idea was that my shop crew would encase lengths of crowbars that his welders bent at an angle to slip over the door's flange. Clamps would be added at the bottom to secure the open legs of the ∩ below the flange. Now knowing what to

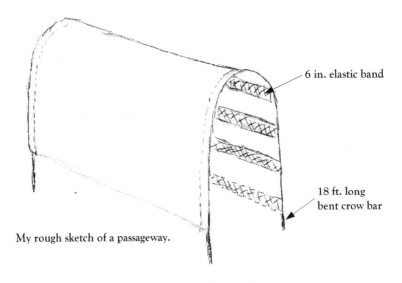

6 in. elastic band

18 ft. long
bent crow bar

My rough sketch of a passageway.

do, we then set to work to get the job done.

I had already built a work table 50 ft. by 12 ft. when I created the shop a year or so earlier. It had passageways leading into the middle of the table where I put various industrial sewing machines and chairs for whoever was going to do the piecework. The machines did different jobs and one of the guys and I created devices for folding the material into different kinds of seams. The machines were so powerful they could literally pull heavy lengths of canvas into and past the needles. Maybe even a clumsy hand too (never happened)! Some of the machine heads used two and even three needles at a time. The train's Project Manager had visited my shop and saw that we had the technology and space to do the job. That's probably why he took a chance with us.

I decided to make one passageway as a template to make sure it could even be done as planned. It was a gamble for sure, but my sewing buddies didn't care, so we all gulped and took the risk together.

First we cut the heavy material — sourced from one of my industrial suppliers, the old Kronke Company founded in 1910 in the South Bay — into lengths that would stretch between the baggage car doors, so as to form a covered passageway. The bottom edges were folded and hemmed for strength. The ends that would fit around the flange were sewn into pockets into which the bent crowbars would be inserted. Or so we hoped!

To keep tension across the passageway, we sewed 6 inch wide bands of heavy duty industrial elastic. This took several people working together to keep the materials laying flat when passing through the machines. And with the right amount of tension on the elastic so that it gathered up the material evenly from band to band on the back side of the machine. Sound confusing? It was a pain in the ass to do, but everyone pitched in to make it work. We ran three machines to get this part of the job done.

Last, we had to insert the 18 foot long bent crowbars into and through each of the end pockets. The task seemed impossible and I recall it took four of us to slide the pockets over the crowbars which were anything but smooth. But we figured it out and, in the end, working night and day (they were a dedicated bunch), we got the first one done and took it to the old Butler facility to confirm its fit.

It did, and the Project Manager was impressed enough

to order two batches of 17 units. He also ordered what he called "end caps" of the same material plus the crow bars. These also slipped over the flanges but sealed off the doors when the passageways were removed. They were to be used when the trains were moving from one location to the next.

We were all proud of our accomplishment, but agreed we never wanted to see another cap or passageway ever again.

Fortunately, other big projects were to come.

Our 20 ft. tipi being pitched at the "Freak Fair," in Berkeley, California. I'm standing on a makeshift crossbeam in order to lace the front of the tipi together. Just beyond the trees in the background is the San Francisco Bay where I had launched my canvas canoe for the voyage to Angel Island. That's John below who helped me gather tipi poles in the pine forests of the Sierra Nevada.

First Annual Counter Culture
Convention and Freak Fair

There were other fairly major sewing jobs we took on, and after completing one project, we'd often celebrate together on camping trips in a "house tipi" we all made. Some of those tipi adventures were really something. A more memorable one occurred on the shores of Berkeley, a walk away from where I had coincidentally launched the canoe voyage.

This tipi outing occurred at what was called the "First Annual Counter Culture Convention and Freak Fair!" But, as I recall, it was not only the first but also the last. Yet, it was an enormous success: Every hippy, redneck, back to the lander, real Indians with fry bread, fake Indians with war bonnets, crafters of every sort, tourists with cameras, musicians, jugglers, comedians who would insult you to your face for $1, artists, and all of us from the tipi shop. There must have been thousands of people coming through over several days to see it all, including local politicians, at least one famous British musician/songwriter, and several movie celebrities, and news reporters.

Given the times, I was surprised that pot and drugs weren't evident anywhere. The once popular Haight-Ashbury district across the bay in San Francisco, known for its phony love-ins and street bands, and air that wreaked of marijuana and street garbage, had festered and descended into a decadent scene of drug addicts, pushers, and lost

99

souls.

There was much curiosity about our tipi, which stood nearly 20 ft tall, and we constantly fielded questions from onlookers. It was large enough that all of us could sleep inside at night in our sleeping bags with a fire going to provide warmth. We were setup right alongside the San Francisco Bay that was known for its cold winds coming across from the Golden Gate Bridge. Possibly some of my older readers are long time Bay Area residents were there and remember the event?

All of this "sewing shop talk" is making me a bit nervous as I've really strayed far off the "Horse Trek" trail. But all of this in one way or another actually ties together.

The Indian connection thing happening wasn't over yet either. There are several more I want to share, one of which will bring us back into the sewing shop for the last time, though I can't promise. One occurred right near Butler Steel within months of making the train's passageways. Let's go there first.

Boxcar Indian Village

Not long after being introduced to Black Elk, the same museum curator, Louise, invited me to meet some other Indian acquaintenances of hers in the Bay Area. She said she would drive us there as their location was very secretive and that I would have to agree to tell no one of their whereabouts. I agreed, and we left for Point Richmond, just north of Berkeley.

We went past Butler Steel and entered what was the Santa Fe Railroad yard. There were tracks everywhere going in every which direction. I imagined that Santa Fe was somehow involved with the shipbuilding that had been going on during WWII. The road we were on was more like a well-worn path as it crossed over the tracks. Where we were going wasn't exactly clear because the perplexing maze of criss-crossing tracks were full of massive, industrial type train cars.

Eventually we reached a place at the far western end of the railroad yard that skirted the San Francisco Bay. I was shocked to see a small neighborhood of boxcars converted into tiny homes. These were the homes of Indian people brought here by the Santa Fe Railroad Company. I also noticed that each home had a beehive-shaped oven made of bricks and adobe.

Louise explained that Pueblo Indian people from the Laguna and Acoma Indian Reservations in New Mexico had been given jobs with the railroad in exchange for letting the railroad come through their tribal lands. That was in the 1920s. The Santa Fe railway terminated right here in Point Richmond. A decision was made to house the Indians, maybe 30 or so families, within the railroad yard in all these boxcars. By the time I was brought here, many of the Indians had left and their boxcars had fallen into ruin. But the ones still occupied by just a few remaining families were neat and in good shape.

I was introduced to the White Cloud family, who were from the Laguna Pueblo in New Mexico. There were no children living there, as their children had grown and moved out. I had met their daughter later, who was a single mother living in Oakland. So, it was just the parents, who were of my own parent's generation. They were very friendly. I can't recall all the details but I had brought them a deerskin I had tanned as a gift, and in return, they would show me how they made their ovens outside.

These unique ovens were traditional among the Pueblo Indians. I was eager to try something they made in them. I recall that I received some bread made in the White Cloud's oven. The ovens were made and used by the women, so the wife explained their construction and use to me. Apparently, the men did the tanning as a traditional role back at the Pueblo, so he showed me what he did and I shared with him my method in return. It was a good exchange overall and the experience deepened my understanding and appreciation of traditional Native American cultures.

10 years or so after I visited the village, the Santa Fe

A Pueblo oven. A fire is made inside the oven. When the proper amount of time has passed, the embers and ashes are removed and bread is inserted to be baked. In the case of corn, the embers are doused with water and the corn is then inserted into the oven to be steam-cooked. When cooking meats, the oven is fired to a "white hot" temperature (approximately 650 °F or 343 °C), the coals are moved to the back of the oven, and the meats placed inside. The smoke-hole at the top and the door are sealed with mud for this purpose. A large turkey will take 2½ to 3 hours to cook. I was treated to some bread in the White Cloud's oven.

Railroad Company closed it down and many of the Indians were returned to their reservations. I recall Louise telling me that the White Cloud's boxcar home with all their belongings inside were coupled to locomotives and pulled back to their reservation! Some of the youth of the Boxcar Village, educated in local public schools and having become adults, remained behind and made their lives in the Bay Area.

The end of Indian Village

Old boxcars were converted into housing units for the families of New Mexican Indians who worked for Santa Fe

Last two families have moved

By CATHERINE SCHUTZ
Staff Writer

Years later after my Horse Trek, I decided to drive out there to see if anything remained. Nothing remained. The entire area had been paved with asphalt, a giant parking lot as I recall. Apparently, the news media caught wind of this Indian village at Point Richmond, and reporters tracked down some of the Indians who once lived there for a story. But by then, it was gone as the Indians held it in secrecy until the end. I heard somewhere that there were other Boxcar Villages around the U.S., and not all of them were inhabited by Indians.

I feel comfortable talking about that village now though, nearly 50 years later, as it is no longer held secretively by the Indians who once lived there. The senior White Clouds and others who once lived there would be centenarians-plus by

Laguna Pueblo c. 1879

now and may have gone on to walk among the stars above their ancient homeland. But maybe not. I read recently there are nearly 90,000 centenarians still living in the U.S.

Not long ago on a cross country trip by car with a friend, we passed through Laguna Pueblo, stopping briefly at a tribal fuel station. By chance, pumping gas next to me was a young tribal policeman serving the Pueblo. We talked briefly and I mentioned the White Clouds. I told him about their lives and others in the Pt. Richmond Santa Fe Boxcar Village. He said he had heard something about that, but really knew nothing more. I think he was lying, just being secretive. He was surprised that their name didn't ring a bell having been born in and lived his entire life on this reservation. So, who knows? Maybe those White Clouds are still walking about somewhere in their ancient homeland.

San Quentin State Prison

It seemed like a lot was happening in the year I visited the Boxcar Village. Within a month of meeting the White Clouds, I got an unlikely call from the warden of San Quentin State Prison! The prison is located on the northern edge of the San Francisco Bay, a bit further north of the Tiburon Highlands where I landed the canoe after visiting Angel Island. The prison is noted for housing some of the State's most hardened and notorious criminals.

There were all these Indians in there, convicted of this and that, some of it pretty serious stuff. Many I learned had been in there and other prisons for much or most of their adult lives. Anyway, the warden — an older man, small in stature and soft spoken, and a real gentleman by my standards — told me that he and several of the incarcerated Indians were organizing a pow-wow for all the Indians in the prison. I recall this was related to the forthcoming American Indian Religious Freedom Act (eventually passed by Congress in 1978). The movement to make this happen began a decade earlier in 1967, and Indian activists involved no doubt influenced Indians everywhere to get involved, including in the Bay Area and at San Quinton Prison.

The warden wanted to know if I would be able to make an Indian tipi for the event. He explained that I would have to come inside the prison to see the location

Behind this prison wall is where I set up the tipi for the Indian prisoners.

for the tipi, to make sure it would fit in there. He added he was going to bring in all these Indian dancers from somewhere else to add to the effect of the event. The press would be invited too, along with local politicians whom I'm sure were also involved to make it happen. I agreed and a date was set for me to come.

I brought my Métis friend along to check it all out. Neither of us had been in such a place before, although I thought I had a close call when I got caught with that Army nurse in the OR that I told you about. So off to the prison the Metis and I went.

The place was like a giant medieval dungeon built

107

above ground. We could hardly wait to get out of there, just looking from the outside. Charlie Manson was in there at the time, I was told later. Due to security, my Metis friend unfortunately had to wait in the visitor's office. I was taken inside and introduced by the warden to the "head Indian" in charge of the celebration. He was a Sioux Indian whose name was Buffalo Boy Canoe. He was old enough to be my father. Like the Freedom Train Project Manager, he was also a WWII veteran. It was then I began to realize that I was increasingly being put in the presence of older Indian (and non-Indian) men and women of my parent's generation. No doubt the Calling had everything to do with it. I will talk about that further at the end of my story.

Buffalo Boy was polite almost to a fault and I immediately liked him. He took me on a tour through a maze of halls, with guards escorting us. Along the way he introduced me to some of the other Indian men, who were somehow involved with putting the event together. Somewhere deep within the prison, we exited into a large open area, a yard with grass surrounded by high walls. There, I was told, they wanted the tipi pitched. It was to be a large one, like one of the old ceremonial lodges the Sioux used when they lived on the Great Plains before the reservation period began.

I thought to myself, "But all these Indians in this prison surely aren't Plains Indians whose ancestors lived in tipis?"

It didn't seem to matter as I'm sure they were all acculturated to putting up with the white man's stereotypes, including the one that all Indians lived in conical wigwams, wore eagle feather war bonnets, and slept on soft buffalo robes.

Knowing now what they wanted, I thanked the Sioux for his guidance and said I would return with a large tipi soon. I located the Metis and we left.

༄

Sometime later, I ventured up into the Sierra Nevada, the enormous mountain range that divides California from Nevada — and wild horse country — to gather poles for the tipi. There was a vast pine forest on government land that had many young trees from which I had sourced these lodge poles before (including that Freak Fair). I selected the straightest, removed their bark with a draw knife on the spot, and returned with them to the Bay Area, where I had rented a small lot. Here the poles

A draw knife like I used for stripping bark off of the pine saplings.

would be cured in the sun on racks I made for this purpose. To keep the lodge poles from warping, I turned them daily so that all sides received the warm sunlight equally.

My sewing shop team and I then got together to make the tipi "skin" using marine canvas treated to prevent mildew. I learned tipi making from accounts by those who had visited or lived with Indian people. That's another long story I won't go into here. Eventually, I wrote a book about tipi making (*The Canvas Tipi*) many years ago, which is now out of print. Anyway, the prison system paid me for

I wrote this book many years ago, now out of print.

the tipi, and I volunteered my time setting it up.

🐎

The day of the celebration at the prison came, and I was invited to attend. I had seen professional Indian dancers in colorful outfits before, and I recognized some of them from previous pow-wows I had attended and even participated in around the Bay Area. Half of the dancers were women, who crossed several generations. The dancing didn't last long, and they were all whisked away as fast as they had arrived.

Soon, the tipi sat alone in the prison yard. I can't recall for sure, but I believe I helped several of the Indians take it down, and whatever happened to it after that is beyond me. Maybe it's still there at the prison. But that was 50 years ago and I have no idea.

After the dancers and other guests had left, I was invited to have dinner with the Indian prisoners in one of the prison's huge mess halls. It had a stage at one end, and I was told there would be announcements made there and some entertainment. As before, guards were everywhere.

Buffalo Boy stayed at my side the entire time, and we took seats at one of the dining tables. A hundred or more

Indians were seated around us. Servers (all Indian prisoners) came out with plates and eating utensils. I don't recall anything that could have been turned into a shank! But there were only Indians present, and I think that would have lessened racial tensions and prevented violence if white supremacists had been let in there too.

Next came things to eat, brought out on these wheeled carts by more Indians. The "special" was buffalo meat, but I can't remember to this day how it was cooked or what it even tasted like. There were vegetables too, I think Indian corn and some greens. Finally, a dessert but I can't remember what it was either, maybe pudding?

As I looked around at all the tables, it was clear that these Indian men were enjoying their food and time together. Yet, their faces reflected very hard times in their lives, and I felt compassion for them. I could see also that prison officials had gone out of their way to try to make the meal and the day's events special for them. Acts of kindness and opportunities for self-improvement surely would go a long way towards making the world a better place.

After dinner, several speakers came on the stage to talk about the forthcoming American Indian Religious Freedom Act that would allow Indians the right to practice their respective tribal religious practices. Many of these had been banned during the early reservation period by federal and state laws. All of this in violation of the U.S. Constitution which prohibits government from interfering with religious practices — the separation of church and state clause. I didn't need the Calling to tell me that what I had just participated in had served in spirit the objective of the new religious act.

Last came the entertainment, which was a young Indian guy with a guitar who was going to sing a song he had written. He was nervous and reeked of self-confidence issues. Once they got him on the stage, he made excuses, demeaning himself as not worthy of performing. This brought a wave of protest from his audience, me included, telling him he can do it at the top of our voices. I could feel his agony, and it nearly brought tears to my eyes. He finally caved and began to play and sing his anthem about being an Indian and being proud of it. He got a great round of applause with whistling and war whoops Indian style when he finished!

The celebration was now over, and the prisoners were marched back to their cells. I was thanked by some of the Indians, and escorted to the entrance by Buffalo Boy, where prison guards took over and let me out. I returned to the Metis' Berkeley home, where I related to him what had happened inside the prison walls.

Some time later, I received a letter from the prison, signed by my Sioux Indian guide Buffalo Boy thanking me for my contribution.

🐎

Buffalo Boy and I became friends, at first by letter from the prison, later by phone, and then in person. To my surprise, they were to release him shortly from the prison after many years locked up in there. They moved him to an Indian "half-way house" tucked away somewhere in the

City of Sacramento, California. He had my phone number and called to ask if I would care to come visit him. I did and we met up at that facility.

It was surrounded by a tall cyclone fence, and you had to ring a buzzer with an intercom from outside the fence at a gate to get the supervisor's attention inside. I asked for Buffalo Boy. That got him out of the place right away.

Inside the fence were all these Indian men chain-smoking cigarettes and roaming around, I thought furtively so, looking very anxious, you know, like you're afraid that something bad is about to happen to you. The Sioux told me that all of them, he included, were nervous about returning to public life. They didn't know what to do. How to behave, stuff like that. So the prison system gave them a safe haven as they tried to figure out their forthcoming lives "on the street."

I was allowed by the state government agency in charge to take my Sioux friend out for one hour, but no longer. It was his first time out, and I had to bring him back on time. We drove down this inner city road with all sorts of stores, fast food restaurants, and God knows what else. I recall him looking nervously out the window as I drove along, taking in the sights.

I ask the reader, "Can you imagine what decades of incarceration with some of society's most dangerous felons does to a person, who is then suddenly set free?"

After a short while of just driving nowhere in particular, he asked me if I was hungry, which I was, and so was he. So I asked him where he wanted to go. He said

"Macdonald's," the famous burger chain, which he heard of but had never seen before. Hard to believe, but the company was not but a decade old at the time, and I don't think the chain existed when he went in the Big House. We went in to sit down and eat.

As I started to pay, he stopped me. "Let me do this, please. It's important to me."

I understood immediately and said, "Sure, thank you."

The prison system gave the Indians at the half-way house a small allowance to help them transition. I think maybe it was earned from years of working inside the prison itself. But that is speculation and I wasn't comfortable asking him where he got it from.

I got him back on time. I took him on several other outings, and finally an "over night" stay at my place, as he and the system authorities had both gained my trust. During this visit I learned more about his beliefs, what it meant to be a Sioux, things that happened that got him into legal problems and eventually into prison. I also introduced him to several people in the area who would be contacts for him to move forward with his life.

After returning him from the overnight at my place to the Sacramento halfway house, I departed and never saw or heard from him again. I suppose both of us had to follow separate paths. Indeed, the Calling was about to send me in an entirely new direction. And as for Buffalo Boy, I learned in recent years that he had passed away some 30 years after we first met at the prison. I'm not sure what all he was involved with during that time, but apparently he stayed clear of further trouble with the law.

Transition

As quickly as the entire San Quentin connection with Buffalo Boy ended, the Vision finally began to unfold in rapid motion. This time I was told by the Calling that my destination would be in America's Deep South. And that my move was imminent. But that once there, I was to return towards the west with the horse.

To me, this was further evidence that either I had lost my mind altogether, or that I was a babe in the woods about to get a major lesson in life. A shellacking that might not be pleasant.

I pondered again, "Why go east only to return to the west? And why the Deep South? And what horse?"

These cryptic messages I kept getting were beginning to drive me crazy. I decided to take council with the Métis once again.

I explained that there was a second Vision. This time with me riding a horse back across the country from the Deep South. He agreed that was strange, maybe even crazy, but in any case, possibly dangerous.

"What do you mean by 'dangerous'?" I asked him.

"The Civil Rights movement in the Deep South is still in force due to racial violence there." He cautioned. "And a 'long haired' semi-dark-skinned man riding through the region alone might not sit well with some folks down there."

To which I gulped.

"Are you sure you want to do this?" He entreated as

only a true concerned friend would.

We agreed that more information was needed in yet another Vision before I could logically take any action. Of course, I couldn't reveal that it was the Calling's words within that were directing me, not some dreamscape. We would wait, but not for long.

A Tragedy

I recall that last conversation with the Metis occurred late at night, typical for us. Sometimes I just stayed over and slept on their sofa, getting up early and leaving at sunrise. We had spent hours talking about the Vision and what it meant, including the potential risks if I followed through with it.

It was now an early hour in the morning, maybe two hours past midnight, when I left to return to the canteen. Their house was located high up in the Berkeley hills near the university of the same city name, where the Metis's wife worked as a scientist. I finally reached the lowlands near the San Francisco Bay and headed down a long boulevard that was normally full of traffic during the day, but completely empty at this hour.

As I drove along, my headlights picked up a person walking straight at me in my lane. I put on the brakes as they kept walking toward me. I then stopped altogether.

It was a young woman, who couldn't have been much older than a teenager. Her clothes had been ripped off her body so that only a few shreds hung from her arms. She kept walking towards me and I could see she was in shock. Her mouth was agape like she was going to cry, but couldn't. It was clear she had been abducted, raped and God knows what else, and dumped on the road.

But by now, I was already out of my truck and running to her. She stopped and looked at me with eyes that pro-

jected both terror and a cry for help. I took off my three-
quarter length leather jacket and wrapped it around her.
She continued to stare at me.

I implored her, "Please come with me to my truck. I'm
not going to hurt you. I'm going to take you to a safe place.
Will you come with me?"

She moved towards the truck. I kept my arm around
her and we walked to the passenger's side. I saw also that
she was barefoot and there were scrape marks on her legs
and feet.

I thought to myself, "Who would have done such a
thing to another human being, especially a female?"

She climbed in with my help and I locked the door behind her. She followed me with her eyes as I circled around
the front of the truck, and then got back in myself. She was
looking at me with pleading eyes.

I continued, "Okay, you're safe in here now, and I'm
going to take you to that safe place. You'll be okay."

The fact is, I didn't know she was going to be okay.
But I didn't hint that at all. I had a human being in great
distress in my care, and I didn't really know what to do. So,
I took her to an outlying station of the Berkeley Police Department. On the way, she kept staring at me with that
dreadful traumatized look on her face. Her mouth was still
wide open and I began to wonder if she had been abused
there and was unable to close it.

All I could think to say was simply to repeat myself
over and over, "You're going to be okay."

She wasn't bleeding anywhere, so I thought maybe it

was best to take her straight to the police instead of a hospital — because they were going to be involved soon enough anyway. And I had no idea where the local hospital was located anyway. Whatever the case, I didn't really know what to do. I'd never experienced anything like this before.

Then I began to think and doubt my actions, "What if I got stopped by the cops with her looking like this in my truck?"

There's no telling what they'd have done to me, but I'm certain they'd have had me cuffed and in lockup in minutes.

I knew where this station was, and we arrived without incident in less than five minutes. She continued to look at me.

I then told her in as calm and reassuring a voice I could muster, "I'm going to go inside and get you some help. I'm going to keep the door locked so no one is going to bother you. I'll stand right at that door there to keep an eye on you, and you can see me too, okay?"

In that moment, another dreadful thought occurred, "Since she can't seem to talk, are they going to arrest me as the rapist?"

There was no DNA testing back then, so anything was possible. But I'd come this far, so I bit the bullet and went to the front door and looked inside. There was a front desk, but no one was there. A long empty hall reached to the back of the building.

Still standing at the open door where she could see

me, I yelled out so someone inside could hear me, "Is anybody here?"

My loud voice was enough to stir an officer out of a room near the front of the building, and he came running. He wasn't happy with my tactics. I pointed to the truck, handed him my keys, telling him there was a young woman in there and that I found her walking down the main boulevard unclothed. I blurted out my opinion of what I thought had happened, only to dread that I sounded like I was guilty and trying to cover my ass in advance: "I think she was raped. I put my coat around her. She doesn't seem able to talk."

He immediately went into action, but not as I had hoped. He handcuffed me and took me to a room at the end of the hall. He removed my wallet from my back pocket and took my drivers license out, looking at the photo, then at me, then ordered me in this gruff voice, "Stay here in that chair, and don't leave."

Maybe he was one of those Army drill sergeants before he became a cop? He sounded like one. I didn't say a word as he left, leaving the door open behind him. He hurried to the front again, which I could see from my room, but then went into another room off to one side. He then came right back out with a woman dressed in street clothes. In seconds they were at my truck, and took my passenger back into the same room off to the side. I thought maybe she was a detective or rape victim's advocate or something. I'm not sure what was available to help rape victims back in those days.

For the next hour, maybe longer, I sat alone in that chair with my wrists cuffed and aching. He never came back to check on me or ask any questions. No one else seemed to be in the building either. Finally, he returned, uncuffed me, handed me my coat, keys, and wallet, but kept my drivers license. (A few days later, the license arrived in my PO Box.)

"You can go," he growled in a rough tone, tainted with suspicion. He offered no word about the young lady, nor a hint of thanks for bringing her in. And then he escorted me back to the front.

There was little doubt in my mind that had I uttered a word, I'd have spent the night behind bars and charged with rape in court the next day. I was completely defenseless.

As I was getting up to go, I said to myself, "I wonder if cops treat rape victims the same way? So to protect women, had lawmakers put female advocates in there to take control?"

Since then, I've come to understand that's often the case. It's called "blaming the victim." But not to take sides against the cops, if what I brought into them in the middle of the night is typical, or worse, I can understand how jaded they could easily become. Best to do it the right way, though, and have female advocates "in house."

In the Lion's Den

I have one last story related to the sewing shop before we leave it behind once and for all. In an unpleasant way, it relates to the previous story. I'm bringing it up because it has left another indelible mark on my psyche and how I think and feel about women.

I can't remember the day of the week, month, or year that it happened, but one morning before any of my fellow workers arrived, three women whom I had never met before came into the shop. They were interested in purchasing one of my "tipi kits," a DIY where I provided canvas cut to size, sewing and assembly instructions, and the customer does all the sewing. A way for some to save money, for others a way to feel more connected to the tipi they were going live in. Back in those days of the "back to the land" movement, people were getting out of the cities and living as organically as possible, as much on principle if not necessity, I suppose. It wasn't clear to me yet what these ladies had in mind with their tipi, they just wanted the kit.

One of the ladies was older, taller and looked physically stronger than the other two. Her demeanor was of the alpha personality type: polite, clear-headed, in charge. The one mid-sized was also tall, slender, quiet, pleasant. The third, the youngest and my age, began questioning me about what I was doing, who I was, probing into this and that, and a bit sarcastic at the same time. Ironically, I was immediately attracted to her, not only by her outward manner which I like in women, but by her physical beauty. She saw this in me immediately and started to take offense, but I think more out of surprise than anything I said. Because I hadn't really said anything but to respond to her litany of unrelated questions. But the Alpha stepped right in to conduct business in the nick of time! She saw there was some mutual attraction at play, but understood the timing probably wasn't right. At least right then and there. But not wanting to quell anything entirely, the alpha changed the subject in a way that surprised me and the other two. It was her turn to question me:

"Did you set this operation up yourself?"

"I did, but I also listen to the others suggestions who work here with me, and occasionally we come with up with some innovations." I added, "Some of them will be here in a bit to work on some of our projects. You can talk with them if you like."

"Projects?" she asked.

"We make other things here besides tipis. Anything requiring industrial sewing machines, heavy materials, and custom work." I explained some of the other projects we had done, including ones I've already talked about earlier in my story.

"What do you yourself do here?" she questioned me further.

I explained, "Well, I do everything the others do. We're a real team. If a big project comes in, we have a meeting about who's going to do what on it, when, which machines, and so forth. I designed and built the table [I described earlier], repair the machines if something goes wrong, order the materials, do the bookkeeping, and help with the sewing."

Then came the question that took me by surprise.

"Who taught you to sew, your wife or girlfriend?"

I came back quickly, "I've never been married, and I live alone. I'm kind of married to my work." All true.

She then changed the subject abruptly to the tipi kit with specific questions. I answered them and she wrote me a check. The three of them then left. I didn't expect to see or hear from them again.

Two days later, the Alpha and the younger lady I had expressed interested in, showed up again in the morning.

"We're having trouble with our sewing machine." explained the Alpha, "It's not taking in the thread correctly."

"You're going to help us aren't you?" came an order from younger one.

The Alpha stepped back in, "If I pay you, could you come out and take a look and see if you can fix the problem?"

I wasn't quite sure what to make of it, being ordered and asked at the same time. I agreed to come at the end of the day, and they left.

I found their house in the flats below the Berkeley hills. It was an older, very large, two story Victorian house. I grabbed my sewing machine tools and headed towards the front door. As I approached, I heard a bit of commotion, like a bunch of people arguing inside. Hesitant, I knocked on the door.

More arguing, but no one was coming to answer the door, I thought, "Maybe I should get the hell out of here right now." But before I could make an about face, the door was opened.

It was the young one, and she started right in on me,

"What took you so long?"

Hell, I was a few minutes early. But thought better of pointing that out and just wait and see what was going to happen next. What happened next really scared the shit out of me. I was still standing outside the front door, but could see inside. I don't know how many women were in there but the place was full of them. And they were visibly upset and there was a cacophony of angry voices directed at me as though in a panic state!

"Who is he?"

"What the fuck is he doing here?

"Somebody tell that asshole men aren't wanted here."
I then noticed women, different ages, scurrying back and forth behind the door, glancing at me with mean faces as they passed by. As you can imagine, I was ready to run for my life. But before I could take one step, the Alpha arrived at the door and everyone inside went quiet. She clearly ruled the roost.

In a calm voice, she thanked me for coming and said "Come on in. The sewing machine is upstairs. Just follow me." The younger one followed behind me and I noticed she was kicking at the back of my ankles. Fortunately, I had my boots on, which helped a little. But I kept an eye on with what else was going on around me.

Apparently, it was the "dinner hour" because I noticed the women were carrying their plates laden with food heading in the opposite direction I was going in, and I mean with dagger eyes.

We continued up the stairs, down a hall and into what looked like their sewing room. The machine sat in the middle of the room. I took a seat in the chair next to it, checking the needle thread tensioner, working my way down to the needle and found that it was out of sync with the shuttle. I also discovered the needle was bent and ready to break off near the eye. I removed the needle.

I turned to the Alpha, "We need a new needle," showing her the problem. The bobbin here is okay, but the shuttle (pointing it out) will need to be adjusted. Once that's fixed I will check the feed (dog) up front to make sure the material passes to and fro the way it's supposed to."

I looked around and saw that the room was now full of women glaring at me. Surely, I thought, the Calling had not sent me into this lion's den to be murdered?

The needle was a fairly standard size for a home machine, so one of the ladies was dispatched by the Alpha to get a new one. That left me sitting there like a biospecimen being examined under a microscope.

"You know," came the young one, "now is when we all eat together. But you're not invited. And I won't cook for you. I don't cook for any man."

"Okay," I responded in a low voice.

She than began to repeat herself and kicking at me again.

I then told her, still in a quiet voice, "I wish you wouldn't do that. You're hurting my ankle."

I then put both of my elbows on the bed of the machine, held my face with my fingers, and closed my eyes. I didn't know what else to do. It was clear to me that the house was a home and refuge for women who had been abused by men. In that moment of awareness, I inexplicably felt a deep sense of compassion for them. I had just seen such a victim not long before — the young lady I picked up and took to the Berkeley police department.

It seemed like the lady returned with the replacement needle in just a few minutes. I attached it to the needle bar, adjusted the shuttle and tensioner, and asked the Alpha for a piece of scrap material to finish with the adjustments. Thinking better of it, I asked the Alpha if the tipi kit were nearby and I would set the tension to the canvas. It was brought to me and it went through just fine.

"I think you're good to go." I told the Alpha, and got up from the table.

She escorted me to the front door, and asked me if she could drop by the shop the next morning to pay me in cash.

"No need to. It's on me." I said. And left.

Several weeks later, the original three ladies came to visit me again at my shop. I sensed a bit of remorse in them.

Came the alpha, "We were wondering if you could show us how to pitch the tipi, and we'd like to buy some of your tipi poles."

"I'd like that," I said.

And a few days later I took them up into the hills where that veteran and I had slept in my old truck, which I still had. The four of us set to work and had it up in minutes. We sat down inside and I shared some stories of Indian women and tipi days of old, beginning with, "Tipis were once made of bison hides, tanned by the women who fitted and stitched them together with sinew. These beautiful structures were their homes . . . ."

Going East

Things then really began to take shape and move along. Enough to make a clear-headed person see that the Calling had its hand in all of it. But I still harbored doubts that I was that clear-headed person. I then got a phone call from a man whom I didn't know from Adam.

He was telling me that he wanted to buy my sewing shop. He had read about it in the Whole Earth Epilogue Catalogue, the sequel to its parent, the Whole Earth Catalogue, which was famous then, but today is lost to current generations with their noses stuck in electronic games.

I believe both catalogues are now long gone right along with the Hippies and the "Back to the Mother Earth" movement of trust fund adult babies. But those catalogues included, nurtured and promoted at no cost, a myriad of jugglers, artists, dancers, musicians, and crafts people like myself. The caller said he was in Alabama near the Florida panhandle. Which, as the Calling foretold, was in the heart of the Old South. Without hesitating for a moment I said I would sell it to him.

It was the Vision definitely coming alive. The time had arrived to head east. I sold everything else I owned except the clothes on my back, loaded my store goods and equipment onto a commercial mover he paid for, and headed to Alabama with a friend who offered to drive me there since

I also gave up my old 1947 Chevy pickup truck (like the one at left). That was the same truck I mentioned at the beginning of my story. I didn't really know what to do with it, so I drove it to the local police station, and left it in their parking lot with a note inside saying it was a gift and they could do what they wanted with it. You could imagine what they all thought. And no one ever tracked me down about it. My next form of transportation was to be the same horse that I saw in the Vision. At least the one I thought I saw.

Horsed

The sewing shop equipment, and my friend and I, all arrived at our destination at the same time. We unloaded everything into the new shop headquarters and that ended that. Fall had arrived, so we escaped the dreaded heat and humidity that deep saturates everything in the Deep South. I decided to rent a room until it became clear what was going to happen next. You might say I had become codependent with the Calling. So be it. I had come this far with it. But instead of waiting around to hear voices in my head, I decided to take action and just look around and maybe the connection to the horse would happen. Well, that's exactly what happened.

I read in the local paper that this fellow on the outskirts of Mobile had horses he wanted to sell. We drove out there, only to discover that he was a "horse trader," actually a hustler and an alcoholic with a full time career job on the side he never talked about. For some reason, he took an immediate interest in me and began to ask me questions. He soon learned I knew nothing at all about horses.

"Why do you want a horse then?" he began to dig.

Out of nowhere, I gave him the craziest answer that even surprised me. "I'm going to ride into oblivion. Me and the horse are going to disappear in a Vision that came to me."

In his mind, that meant I was some kind of Indian on a Vision Quest. Probably fueled by my semi-Indian looks.

Anyway, me and the Vision really got him going, because it seemed to genuinely interest him.

He continued to press me, "Do you know where you're going when you leave here?"

"Not really," I told him.

Skirting the Calling within, I told him, "The Vision is like a story that I have to figure out. It directs me. It's going to be some kind of horse trek."

To him, all that Indian jive translated to "freedom" in his mind. Freedom from work, certain responsibilities (like staying sober), his troubled wife, two troubled sons, and stuff normal people had to deal with every day. I sensed he wished he could go with me – as many others would along the way, some even begging me and showing up with their horses saddled and ready to go! Short of that, he really wanted to be a part of it in some way.

He then asked, astutely so, I thought, "What's the horse in the Vision look like?"

I gave him a description and it floored him.

He came back, half asking and half saying, "You're not kidding me are you? Well, follow me."

And off we went to a small covered stall he had just put together further back on his property.

"This horse just came in yesterday," he said, and to my shocking surprise, there was the horse in the Vision, a Pinto!

He then named his price, which I agreed to. Later, after my friend returned to California, he insisted, "I'm not gonna' charge you, 'cause this could be the Pinto in your

Vision."

I doubted that, but maybe he was right. To be honest, I didn't really know anything more than he did at this point in time. But then I reminded myself, he just wanted to be a part of what I had to do on account of the Vision.

So, I said. "Okay, I'll go with that."

He continued, "Now, I've got to get you a saddle, and other stuff you're going to need for the ride. And what did you say you called this ride, 'trek' something or another?"

I hadn't really crystallized it into a name, but decided to just repeat myself, "horse trek." And that was the first time I verbalized it as such to anyone; on reflection, it also seems a fitting title to this book joined with *into the mystic*.

I followed him to a nearby barn like he was my mother hen or something. I didn't know a damn thing about saddles, bits, and all that, and he knew it so he didn't waste any time asking me what I thought I needed. He just put it all together, and that was that. He wouldn't accept a dime for any of these things either.

"You don't know how to ride either do you — no you wouldn't," he asked and answered in the same breath and without a peep coming out of me.

He explained, "This horse will be good for you. She will teach you all you need to know, so why don't you just take her out in that field over there, get on her, and see what happens."

I asked him if this was a man or woman horse.

He said, "She's a mare."

"A mare?" I countered in thought only, "What the hell

kind of word is that?"

It didn't matter. She was a female and I figured she would teach me what to do. Because human females always seemed good at that, and, being a female too, why would this she-horse be any different?

Well, somehow I got on her, but immediately realized that I didn't know what to do once I was on board. So, I just sat there in the saddle until she did something. And then I would just hang on. Somehow.

I mused to myself, "Why couldn't the Calling have picked the Lone Ranger or some other gun-toting cowboy. Why the hell me? I don't even like horses. In fact, I'm at best leery of them." Scared was closer to the truth.

So I sat, and sat, and sat, and sat . . . until the horse, clearly bored, gave a deep and prolonged "sigh" that seemed to swell and then shrink her body beneath me, and walked off. So I just went with it.

Instinctively, I tried to move my seat and legs to match the sway of her back. I did this for mutual comfort if nothing else, because the horse was now in charge of everything and I felt I needed to make some form of contribution. A good move, and from then on, that's what I did and have always tried to do. Isn't doing what the female wants the secret to a good relationship?

Spurs, like the trader wore, seemed cruel, as I wouldn't want anyone jabbing them into my ribs. So I declined those when he offered them. I wasn't so sure about bits. But later on during one of my encampments, I dispensed with the bit (a snaffle) and replaced it with a braided nose band I made like Indians used a little more than 80 years earlier on the Great Plains. The horse seemed comfortable with that, so we went with it.

I tried to develop a vocal language with her. I would call her "Pinto," which means "spotted" in Spanish. But soon realized she didn't have any idea what it meant. So, we developed a way to communicate by using pressure (meaning, "move away from"), mainly using my legs, but also the reins moving against the side of her neck. It worked, but later the Calling opened new doors of communication I couldn't then even begin to imagine existed.

Next, I figured to stop her from moving I should pull back on the reins. I did and what I got in response was a violent jerk of her head, meaning, as I understood her, "Quit pulling on my fucking mouth!"

I carried on with her in the pasture until it was clear I felt trust between us and I had mustered enough confidence to take us out into the real world. That made me a bit nervous because there would be no fence, paddock, stall, or barn to take refuge in. I began to feel like those Indians back at the half-way house must have felt — living with uncertainty in the unknown.

The Horse Trader loaded the Pinto into his livestock trailer and delivered me to where I had decided I wanted to start the Horse Trek. This was just north of the Gulf of Mexico in bayou country. Lots of forest, government land, and very few people to contend with. He suggested I camp there for at least a week, at which time he would return to see how things went, or more like if I was still alive. I agreed, and so my journey in the Vision was to began here.

First Camp

What I thought would be no more than a week's stay soon turned into weeks, then a month, and then more than a month but "time" had also become relative. Meaning, I stopped trying to figure out what day of the week it was, and waited for further information from the Calling. "It got me into this place," I rationalized, "and it will get me out of here."

But amid all of this waiting around in "Indian Time," I had to change my location in the immediate forest several times. People were starting to come around, having heard that an "Indian" was camping or living in the woods. Curiosity from visitors who stumbled upon me — or who had sought me out — naturally led to many questions, which I fielded the best I could. But it became clear that my position was now actually vulnerable to troublemakers.

There was nothing left to do but move deeper into the forest along one of the many streams that flowed through it. Just before I made that move, there was an unusual encounter that I've never forgotten and wish to share.

🐎

During the first or second week, two couples arrived together to check me out. The husbands were friends and worked together at a major Intel corporation. Young, handsome, intelligent, and friendly, they were the perfect picture of the quintessential Ivy League success story in the mak-

137

ing. But equally so were their lovely wives who did not stand in their mates' shadows. We talked briefly and they were not at all put off by my bizarre presence and appearance, fused with campfire smoke. Viewed together, I suppose we made for a stark contrast in looks. But not so otherwise.

I was surprised to hear them say, "We wanted to tell you that we admire and are inspired by what you're doing. We actually have plans to get out of our line of work and move into the countryside together."

We wished each other the best and they departed. I've always felt certain that they fulfilled their dreams. At the time, I was less certain of my own future. Losing good company, such as the four of them, heightened my inner sense of isolation. But so too the increasing remoteness of my reborn sylvan existence — a reminder of my time among the homeless living in the East Bay forested hills after my release from the Army just a few years earlier.

The Horse Trader visited several more times.

On one occasion he brought a second horse — an Appaloosa — telling me, "You'll need a second horse to carry supplies along with you. Take this one."

But there was only one horse in the Vision, so I accepted this young male horse with reluctance. For the time being, the Ap kept the Pinto company, and me too for that matter as visitors were now scarce. Right away, I got the feeling that neither one of them cared that much for the other. Yet they seemed to get along, probably for lack of other more preferred equine company, and that was good enough for me if it was good enough for them.

To keep both of them from straying or running off, I fashioned a long line of rope strung between two Pine trees. I then secured each horse to the line with lead ropes tied to makeshift rope halters the Horse Trader had provided. They could move up and down the line at will, so they weren't stuck in one place. Although it only made for very limited movement, it was only temporary. There would be plenty ahead once the Calling gave the word to get going.

So, for more weeks upon weeks we lived in the woods together. The Horse Trader brought me oats for them to complement the scarce forage and strange plants that grew in small nearby meadows where I would turn them out onto. I kept each one alternately staked to the ground with that long rope, while the other nibbled on this and that nearby. This seemed to work well for them. I had stashed dry goods for myself and did some fishing, as I had not turned to hunting land animals from necessity.

One day I returned to the camp from a nearby river where I bathed, only to find both horses gone. Their halters and lead ropes were still hanging from the main line. Panic set in. Had someone breached my buffer zone from the outside world and taken them? I scoured the forest floor for hoof prints, but none led to the only path exiting to the outer world.

My attentions now turned to some of the nearby waterways that were homes for the many alligators that I shared the bayou lands with. I hadn't seen any yet, but now I wondered if the horses ventured into one of the bayous to drink and met their fate in the jaws of these powerful apex predators.

But what happened next was like a miracle and further proof to me that the Calling was in some mysterious way mediating events around me. Preparing me further for my role in the Vision.

I decided to let fate take its course. Either I believed in what I had given myself to or it was all just a delusional escape from reality. Night had now fallen and I laid down to sleep.

Some time during the night, I was awakened by what seemed like the ground rumbling beneath me. By now, I was accustomed to the night sounds of the forest but this was different. It ended quickly though and I fell back off to sleep again.

At dawn's early light I was forced to rise and go relieve myself a short distance away. Upon returning to camp, I looked over at the line and both horses stood near their halters, dozing side by side! They had returned for whatever reason. I hooked them back up to the line, fed them, then took them to the meadow to nibble on this and that. The episode never repeated itself.

From the very beginning of the Horse Trek, the Calling tested my resolve in dealing with what I thought were threats to my well-being by wildlife — and humans. I recall two encounters that I wish to share in this bayou camp —

the first of many I would endure along the entire course of the Horse Trek.

The first encounter would give anyone a knee-jerk reaction. I had fashioned a small canvas bag with two straps I had made so that I could secure it to a small tree or sapling. The bag held a ration of oats for the horses. One day I untied the straps to refill the bag and right where my hands brushed against the tree bark was the largest Black Widow spider I had ever seen up until then and ever since. I didn't even know they lived in tree bark.

Yet, she was there. More important she never moved to bite me when she could have easily, as they can move with lightning speed, and because my hand nearly or actually brushed lightly against her. Had she, given her size and the amount of venom she undoubtedly carried in her fang sacs, it could have been the end of me then and there.

I can imagine the number of people who would have seized the opportunity to kill her. I thought otherwise and simply stared at her in wonder. Part of me is embarrassed to say, but I felt a strange connection with her, and I sensed the Calling wanted this from both of us. She was my first lesson in shedding my fears of wildlife during the Horse Trek.

My second threat — as I then saw it — had occurred just several days after the spider incident. I was creating a makeshift bed of pine boughs near the horses. No sooner than I fashioned the bed together when I noticed, not several feet away, a colony of large red "fire ants" emerging from a small hill they had engineered, and it was clear they were going to challenge my presence so close to them. I hurriedly stepped back 20 paces to get out of their way, only to run straight into a second colony. For whatever shortcoming of mine, I hadn't noticed either of their "nests" until now.

The Calling came upon me immediately with a solution. One I would use more than once during the Horse Trek.

"Gather rocks and make a ring of them near your bedding," the Calling instructed me. "Build a fire and then smudge it [to create smoke - JJ]. Leave and return before dark."

I did this, and upon my return both colonies had completely vacated the area. With some trepidation, I slept over the boughs that night. Come morning the ants were still gone. They never returned for the duration of my campsite there. Once more, the Calling's instruction was to "do no harm" but make your presence known in the right way.

So, it was a simple message conveyed to the ants using fire and smoke: "The smoke is to allow me to sleep near the horses, not to destroy your nests, which you will be able to return to when we are gone."

I don't wish to leave the reader with the impression that my campsites were makeshifts for a shiftless layabout. Like "retirement," idleness has never been an acceptable word — or practice — in my lexicon or lifestyle. So a word about my industry in Nature that brought me enough income to help finance my Horse Trek is in order.

Some years earlier, I came into contact with what you would call an Indian Trader — someone who buys things of Native Americana from Indians and others to sell to non-Indians. I had acquired many skills that trace to traditional Indian crafts, including natural hide tanning and porcupine quill embroidery, among other things. The Indian Trader and I had struck a deal that he would buy just about anything I tanned or embroidered in the Indian way. So this was how I would support myself during the Vision Quest, at least for those times that I needed money during the Horse Trek. Otherwise, I foraged from the land and fished in the Deep South's ubiquitous waterways.

And so it was that in this first camp in bayou country I began tanning deer skins for him. I would write him to provide my location and he would send them "salt dried" in boxes to me at the nearest post office, "General Delivery." I'm not sure that this manner of shipping is even permitted any longer. But this is where I would pick them up, and then ship them out when they were done. He paid me by check, usually a cashier's check so it would be easier to cash. I used the money for supplies. I can't remember if it was the Horse Trader or a visitor who helped me transport the first batch of hides to my campsite to tan. Most of the time it was the Horse Trader, who possessed a keen interest in my Native crafts. Anyway, it all just worked out, and I'm sure the Calling had a role in it too in the most mysterious of ways.

My tanning set-ups were quite the sight, and I'll describe them here briefly because my survival income during the Horse Trek depended most of all on them. I would soak the hides in the bayou to soften them, then stretch them on frames I fashioned from Pine saplings I gathered in the forest. Each hide was saturated with animal fats and brains that the Horse Trader would get from local stores or butcher shops. I told him what I needed, and he brought it all to me. I believe his avowed interest in what I was doing, is what fueled his willingness to help. But he also knew my survival depended in part on this work, because I had no other source of income. I always declined to take a dime from him or others.

I would have three or four hides stretched and worked to softness at a time. It would take me a month to get everything done before I broke camp and moved along. Some people came to watch, which I encouraged because it was a way to teach leather making that uses no harmful chemicals. And because I was passing along first hand knowledge about an ancient craft that deserves not to be forgotten.

When the tanning was done, I would ship them back whole, or as was the case during longer stays in one place, cut into pieces and turned into quilled garments and other items that the Indian Trader wanted. I sometimes kept hides for myself, and eventually I made my own buckskin shirt out of deer hides, and some gloves, and even a rifle scabbard.

The scabbard was necessary when the Horse Trader brought me a rifle towards one of his last visits, with a word of warning, "You may need this to hunt and protect yourself with."

I custom-fitted the scabbard from fire-hardened rawhide I made, and kept it with me from then on. And he was right, on more than once occasion I needed it. The rifle was enough of a deterrence to save my life from a serial killer. And later, two punks threatening to run us off a bridge. I will get to those happenings later in my story.

I am one given to solitude and contemplation, I suppose my own brand of meditation. But also because it is a fertile ground for connecting with universal information that seems to flow through one's soul into the mind. Yet, I do enjoy being with people who are introspective, and are open to guidance that comes with such information. Said more simply, people who provoke thinking beyond milking cows or the brainwashing shit that flows from TVs. In fact, I didn't have TVs then, and I don't have one now.

But things were such in my encampments as to welcome contemplation and facilitate my solitary ways. There was something almost magical about my Spartan lifestyle in them, what with the hewn tanning frames around me, the Pinto and Ap nearby, the sound of moving water, the wind in the forests, the birds all the time singing or squawking away (very irritating), and things unseen rustling about in the forests around me.

So here in this first encampment, such a life comforted

my soul and helped calm the uncertainty dwelling within me. Especially when I began to think about the undisclosed purpose of the Horse Trek that would soon send me and my equine entourage forward. In spite of the words within me that kept nagging away, I thought, "Man, this is all really weird. What the hell have you got yourself into? You don't even know where you're going!"

Journey to the Sea

I began thinking about the Gulf ocean waters not too far away. I already missed my canoeing adventures, and also the Pacific Ocean, which I was born along — many years before there were freeways and millions of people and cars and their incessant noise. The idea of going to the Gulf with the horses was attractive. I waited for the Horse Trader to visit me, and I would ask him to keep the Ap while the Pinto and I headed to the sea. That day came soon, and he obliged me. In fact, he trailered us there to a fairly remote stretch of beach along the Florida Panhandle, and left saying he'd be back in two days to return me to the forest campsite.

I brought along a few supplies for me (jerky I made at the camp) and the horse (half a bale of hay the Horse Trader supplied). The first thing I wanted to do was get out into the water, and with the horse. She must have been no stranger to the ocean because she kept pulling on me towards the water. I had removed the saddle so it wouldn't get wet. I got on her bareback.

Out we went, and it seemed like the water never really got much deeper, so we kept going out further and further. And to the extent it began to worry me.

"Don't oceans just get deeper and deeper before long?" thinking about my many west coast forays into the sea near where I was born and later grew into adulthood.

I turned around to see just how far we had gone. I was stunned. I could have sworn we had come a mile or more. Whatever it was, I got the feeling we'd better turn back. And we did. Better that we skirt the shoreline instead!

It wasn't long before the Pinto began to "kneel" or whatever you want to call it. It was a cue for me to get off. And as I did, she began immediately to roll around in the water, then getting up and splashing it with her hooves, appearing to have a great time at it from what I could see. I stripped down to bare skin and joined in, and it felt great, especially in the warm sun.

As she got up, she began to shake the water off like a rain storm. I then got this feeling she wanted me back on her back. And no sooner than I grabbed her mane to swing myself aboard, she tore off, with me on her back. There was no stopping her. At first I was more than nervous, to say the least. But that quickly turned into feeling amazed by the sheer strength and power of her movements and speed. I think you call that a "rush."

Some distance down the beach, without a soul in sight, she came to an abrupt halt amid a whole lot of panting and catching of breath. I slid off her back, reminding her that it was her doing, but thanked her for the thrill of a lifetime. I then suggested, with a point of my finger, that we walk back side-by-side. She took my offer and we headed back with no halter or lead line.

I had brought along an old Army poncho I had picked up at an Army-Navy surplus store. It converts into a small tent, that I knew all about in my Army days in boot camp. That would be my home for the night, in case it rained. The mare would rest and sleep nearby. I had made a lariat fashioned from rawhide taken from my supply of deer hides. I secured this to her head stall and the other end to a metal corkscrew with a swivel people use to tie out their dogs. I think it was the Horse Trader who gave this device to me. In fact, it would work well for us during the remainder of the Horse Trek. To both of us, the corkscrew meant it's time to rest, eat, and sleep. All of which we both relished by day's end, typically wherever we were.

Chelators

The sun began to go down and then darkness fell upon us on the beach. The Pinto was now tethered nearby and I took to looking at the spectacular canopy of stars above us. I decided against a fire, and to simply lay on my back and gaze upwards at the myriad of constellations and galaxies that seemed infinite and endless, like eternity. I thought about what that word meant, *eternity*. What it meant for me in that moment, and then for all living things on our planet. I think most civilized people don't look up at the night sky much anymore, what with all the roofs and city lights dimming the stars into pale parodies of what Nature has given us to enjoy and ponder in the darkness of the night.

The canopy of stars were joined by a chorus of sounds coming from the wind and nearby sea lapping at the shore. All comforting to the soul, like the sounds in my forest camp in the bayou. Shooting stars soon began to dart across the heavens. And as I lie there waiting for the next one to streak across the heavens, I fell off into a deep sleep.

Sometime later, maybe several hours after midnight, the Pinto began to stir about, anxiously so it seemed to me. I got up to check on her, but looking about in the dark, I couldn't see or hear anything unusual and returned to my makeshift tent.

It wasn't long before she started in again, this time vocalizing her nervousness in the way horses do.

Up I went, this time with my small flashlight I carried with me throughout most of the Horse Trek. Again nothing. I tried to comfort her with a few rubs and pats and words of assurance. I hoped the tone of my voice would quell her fears and anxiety.

As I laid back down again, I noticed that a new moon was now rising fast, taking its place among the stars, themselves starting to fade behind its beaming light.

Maybe a few minutes later I began dozing off again. But before falling into sleep, the Pinto began to stir again nervously. But this time I began to hear an ominous sound of "click-clack-click-clack" or something like that — if you can try to imagine — somewhere outside the tent.

I spoke aloud, "What the heck?" The Pinto responded with a frantic whinny.

It then grew louder and seemed to be getting closer. Now I flew out of the tent and shined the light outward. Everywhere before me, several yards away, and seemingly forever off into the distance were hordes of large crabs. They were swarming and bunching together, their bodily armor and claws "click-clacking" in a bizarre chorus! I'd never seen so many flailing claws, spiny legs, and protruding eyes congregating in one place in my life. No crab hunter, and having no desire to get swarmed by them, and not knowing their intentions, I figured I'd better take action quick.

I drew the horse in close to my tent. What to do? Right or wrong, crazy or foolish, I began to dig a trench around the tent, the horse, and myself. They would fall into the trench, I reasoned, or better yet, stay back so as not to fall in if they had a lick of brains I was counting on.

As I began to dig like mad, I took notice from the corner of my eye that the whole lot of them had approached closer to my perimeter, but had become silent. In fact, they were just staring at me. What were they thinking? Probably that I looked like a damned fool!

Whatever the case, I dug, and dug, and dug, and they watched the show. The horse watched too, and I swear she began to paw at the sand too. Not to be deterred, I finished the trench. As quickly the crabs came to its very edge and stopped again. The horse was now quiet too. I waited to see what would happen. So did the crabs. So did the horse. One big giant stare down!

What happened next speaks to a phenomenon in nature I didn't know anything about at the time of this encounter. It was a bit different than the ones with the Black Widow and the fire ants. Yet, in another sense, not really different at all. The crabs simply turned and left. I speculated they were females coming ashore to lay their eggs or for some purpose unknown to me. But by drawing a simple line in the sand (the trench) around the horse and me, I had entered into a law of nature that many, maybe all, species respect – like a universal language – in one way or another. I had inadvertently signaled to them that this was my space, that I meant them no harm, and that neither the horse nor I would interfere with whatever they needed to do. Biologists call this the "sphere of intolerance."

I began to sense the same thing had happened with my

anachronistic encounter with the Viet Cong squads. I had told their leader I meant no harm, that this was their land not mine, that I had arrived with no expectation or plan to stay, but that it was my second time in their country. My purpose now was to explore the meaning of an earlier visit, one that had spiritual meaning to me. Probably a dumb-ass thing to say to Marxist guerrillas out to kill the "American invaders." While they hauled me off to that cage, a very serious discussion occurred among them about my very presence. They clearly sensed a mystical dimension to my presence and, whatever it was that came over them, a decision was made to set me free. I had entered their sphere of intolerance, but as with the spider, the ants, and now the crabs, all of which could have done harm to me, the universal knowledge, the voice of an unseen and omniscient power, spoke otherwise.

I drifted off to sleep with the clicking and clacking fading off in the distance. Come morning there was no sign of these ladies of the sea anywhere. They had retreated back into the vast coastal waters of the Gulf of Mexico.

UFO

The Horse Trader arrived at sunrise, a day early, asking for my help. A Mardi Gras parade was to take place that night and he had been contracted to supply horses along the route for various riders. These horsemen were to accompany floats that were loaded with visibly drunken men pitching candy or something to the throngs of cheering people lining the streets.

Seeing that my "horsemanship" skills had developed considerably since I took possession of the Pinto, he asked if I would hold a half dozen horses or so in hand for him until I was relieved, one by one, by these guys (also drunk or high) in glittery outfits who showed up out of nowhere to ride the parade. Unwittingly, I agreed.

I sensed that the horses had put up with this kind of BS before, as they seemed to take it in stride as the riders literally spurred them into the noisy parade ruckus. I also took it in stride, angry with myself as I vowed to never again aid in such abuse of an animal — because that's what spurring is by any other name.

An hour or so into all of this, with two or three horses yet to pass off, the strangest thing happened that further challenged my belief system about our universe. I and about 20 or so spectators were situated in a short cul-de-sac that intersected the parade route at one end, and dead-ended with the Gulf ocean not a hundred meters away at the other. It was pitch black out to sea, and our area was slightly lit by an old lamp post where we all stood around underneath.

There were some young kids in the group. Some of them were fascinated by the horses, and they all wanted to pet them, which I obliged seeing that the remaining three horses I hadn't passed off yet were actually liking the attention. Amid all of this, one of the horses (a gelding, yet another new word for me) looked upwards toward the dark sky. A flickering of light was seemingly bouncing off of him. I looked up too, shocked by what I saw. Others nearby also took notice and soon everyone in our group was looking up. Not a hundred feet above us was what looked like one of those flying saucers you see in old UFO movies.

A man spoke out loudly to a friend, "Hey [so and so] there's a flying saucer you've been hoping to see."

I thought it was a joke some prankster was playing on all of us. At this point, all eyes were now focused on this thing hovering above us and no one was paying attention any longer to the parade.

It didn't seem to be that big, maybe 15 feet across underneath. A ring of flashing flights illuminated the bottom of this craft. Maybe they were different colors, but I'm color blind just enough not to declare exactly what they were. It teetered slightly from side to side and I swear I heard a slight humming sound coming from it. It then began to move very slowly towards the sea, and this began to freak out some of the adults, and even a few of the kids, one of whom started crying. The horses also took notice.

All I could think of was, "This can't be what I'm thinking, can it?"

In less than a minute, it was just beyond us over the sandy beach at water's edge and stopped once again. What happened next confirmed my belief in extraterrestrial spacecrafts, and I could speak for the others in our group of witnesses, too. In what seemed like a split second, the craft disappeared in a flash of light trailing out over the ocean.

My opinion: There is no such airborne technology that's been created by humans on this planet, the likes of which our group of spectators had just witnessed. And no one could convince me otherwise. We are not alone in our vast, infinite universe.

Second Camp — Bison

The Horse Trader and I retrieved all the horses at the end of the parade and headed back to his ranch. It was late, so I stayed in his barn loft for the night. The next morning, we gathered up the Pinto and Ap and returned to my campsite.

Winter was now passing and the Indian Trader up north sent me two huge Bison ("buffalo") bull hides to process. These were the *largest* and *heaviest* hides I'd ever handled. Luckily he didn't want them tanned, just de-fleshed, cleaned and rendered into *parfleche*. That's a term coined by early 18th Century French traders who bartered with Plains Indians for a hide that's had its hair (or fur) removed and dried into untanned rawhide. But that's only a generic understanding of preparing rawhide.

These two hides were going to be further processed into replications of Plains Indian "war shields." This is done by what is called "fire hardening," meaning the rawhide is cut into a circular or other shape, laced on a small frame of wood and slowly subjected to the heat of a fire. The rawhide shrinks a bit, thickens, hardens, and becomes slightly translucent. It may be painted or scrimshawed and painted with designs. Such shields were said to "turn an enemy's arrow," and so the French called it *parflèche* (*parer* to ward off + *flèche* arrow). But there's more to this Bison hide story to tell.

Alligators

Preparing the bison hides meant building larger frames than the smaller ones I made for the deer hides. This meant going back into the bayou Pine groves to find longer, stouter poles. As they were quite heavy, I used one of the horses to pull them out of the forest. Once in my camp I set about to peel any loose bark off with my hunting knife. The finished frame would be 18 by 20 feet to secure one hide. So I would only do one hide at a time. I also needed lengths of heavy rope, which the Horse Trader came up with.

As the hides were delivered to me — also by the Horse Trader — dried and salted, I first had to soak them in the bayou (river) I was now camped along. This was necessary so they would soften and be flexible enough to work. I did this by using rocks to hold them under the water, but tying the neck end of the hide to a rope to secure it to the river bank. So immersed they were ready to work in just a few hours.

But now the hides, with the fur still in tact and saturated with water, were so heavy I once again needed help from one of the horses to drag them out of the river using the attached rope. That done, I laid them out flat on the ground, hair side down, and laced them to the frame.

Growing right along the edge of the water was a great hardwood tree bearing enormous branches that spread outward. One paralleled the water's edge, and for that reason I

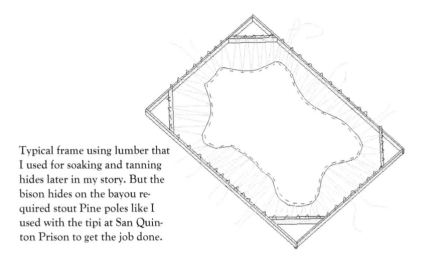

Typical frame using lumber that I used for soaking and tanning hides later in my story. But the bison hides on the bayou required stout Pine poles like I used with the tipi at San Quinton Prison to get the job done.

picked this spot to do these enormous hides.

The first task was to drag the frame and laced hide back into the water. I did this with the help of the Pinto. I couldn't have done it alone, and for sure what came next.

I let the hide soak in the river for several hours more to re-soften. I will add that bayous are waterways rich in minerals, debris from the forest, and other things you can imagine living and dying in the forest. Tannin leached from the many oak trees whose bark, acorns, and leaves added to the healthy biology of the river, is also known as a tanning agent.

The time had now come to raise the frame out of the water. For this, I needed both horses to help.

With the lower edge of the frame positioned directly below the overhead branch, and braced against the river-bank, I secured two ropes at the far corners of the frame, and tossed the loose ends over the branch. I then tied those dangling ropes to the riding and pack saddles on the horses. Next, I urged the horses forward, slowly raising the frame out of the water, which poured off of the hide like a great waterfall. The ropes squealed as they tightened and strained over the branch. The horses grunted as they pulled. I imagined that the sound of the water gushing nearly 20 feet down into the water, made for a uniquely loud and eerie roar probably never heard before in this forest!

Finally, the frame reached the branch, and one by one, I secured the ropes back onto the frame, thereby locking it to the tree. To the uninitiated person unfamiliar with Plains Indian style tanning, the framed hide might easily be mistaken for a giant canvas awaiting the painter!

As I looked over the hide, directly on the other side near the bottom of the frame, was the snout of a large alligator. I jumped back with a racing heart, startled. That was the closest I had ever come to one of them. But he wasn't alone.

Apparently drawn by the commotion of the rising frame and the turbulence of the water below, many others also laid still in the water with barely protruding snouts and a rim of exposed body armor. My movement caused the one at the frame to slide quietly back into the water, joining his fellow giant bayou lizards.

In that moment I reflected on the mass of crabs that

had visited me the night before. Now alligators?

"What next?" I half-assed joked to myself, "A herd of God-zillas?" And why not, I mean if there are flying saucers?

The alligators simply floated motionless in place, staring at the frame, me, and the horses. But there was no hint of aggres-sion coming from any of them. I deduced that they were simply curious, like the crabs.

As had become my way with the horses, I decided to speak out to these water lizards, loudly so in concert with arm and body theatrics, simply to say "by tone" that I'm here to work temporarily, would cause them no harm, and would soon be leaving their hunting ground. A peace pact had been made in my mind, and the frame became the di-viding line, my personal sphere of intolerance.

From that day forward, they came daily to watch me work, here and there nudging the frame as it returned to the water to soak — like horses that sample everything new with their lips and teeth. But never a threatening gesture towards me or the nearby horses. It was clear that food prey was abundant in their bayou home, and their attentions to me were nothing more than curiosity, and always from an acceptable distance. Or so I thought!

The next day I fashioned a makeshift scaffold from ex-

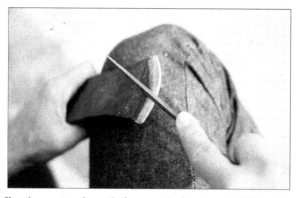

I'm sharpening the end of an auto leaf spring, which I used to deflesh the bison hides.

tra poles taken from dismantled deer frames. This elevated me half way up the bison hide. That put half the hide below me, as I worked the upper half. The alligators had arrived early to watch. I set to work defleshing the hide using a scraper I had the Horse Trader fashion for me from a length of automobile leaf spring. The droppings fell directly below me, some, but not all, into the bayou, where a gentle current brought them within reach of the alligators.

Too busy to notice, several of the alligators maneuvered to the sides of the frame to get at the other droppings. As I scraped fats and other fleshy substances off the hide, they readily snapped it all up. I looked down into gaping mouths waiting for a morsel — like chicks with open beaks in a nest being fed by their mothers! While all this made sense, I didn't relish the job of being a gator mother. I decided to just finish the work.

Soon all the flesh was removed, and the rest of the job

was just scraping off the many fine fibers that naturally cling to the hide's inner surface. 20 minutes or more passed by and I glanced down to see they had retreated back into the water. As the day was coming to an end, the entire congregation departed, probably to hunt.

🐎

Years later, I saw a film documentary about wildlife biologists who had entered a feeding ground full of Alaskan Brown Bears in order to observe them. And I had seen other naturalists who would enter rattlesnake dens to observe them during winter. And divers who would mingle with deadly sharks.

I had asked myself, "What social threshold had we all crossed to enter their worlds unharmed? Where curiosity equates to acceptance and tolerance without fear?"

Clearly, the Calling was introducing me to something with these back-to-back experiences in the bayou. But more was to come.

West by Northwest

Winter had passed, quickly it seemed, and spring was now fully on, and before long, that would be turning into summer. Meaning, time is moving along with the seasons while I'm still camped in a bayou. I was beginning to get restless. The Calling was moving within me: "The time to leave is approaching."

The Horse Trader visited me for what turned out to be the last time. I told him that I would have to return the Ap to him, that it was not part of the Vision, and the Calling had reminded me of that. He understood and took the horse back. I thanked him for everything and he left. I never saw him again.

Years later I heard that he had been murdered. I sensed that, ironically, it might have brought him relief from a troubled life, which I had learned from him was painful for many reasons. But our encounters were good ones, with simple problems that he seemed fitted and eager to help solve. The Vision had a role for him in it, and he knew it. And so he took it and ran with it for the time he had it. Rest in peace fellow traveler, knowing that you were, in fact, part of my journey in the Vision Quest.

🐎

The time to leave finally arrived. I returned my tanning poles deep in the forest where I had found them, where they would begin their return to the earth.

The alligators were there to watch me dismantle everything. I had this urge to say something to them, which may seem foolish, but I did, loudly so. And this became my custom when living briefly, although closely, with wild life during the Horse Trek.

It seems that when we leave a place where significant things happened, we feel that a part of us is left behind. So I clamored a "farewell" to these powerful reptilians of the bayou. I was in their wilderness, and if nothing else, we found ourselves mutually interesting. And, once again, I sensed that the Calling was probably mediating my connection to these predators that delighted in my hide scrapings.

To cross into the State of Mississippi, I plotted a northwesterly course through forest land, avoiding every back country village and paved road possible. The Pinto and I would make good time traveling alone without the Ap. Precise destinations along the way were never well-defined in advance because I never knew what the Calling had in store for us along the way. Which is to say not until we were in the middle of it. But this is something I had to learn the hard way. My first planned overnight was such an example.

Ku Klux Klan

I had planned to get a full day's ride in once I left the bayou. I figured we could do 20 or so miles, before setting camp to rest and sleep. But finding my way out of the west side of the bayou was no easy feat. There was quicksand to skirt around, brush so thick nothing could get through, and at times not even knowing where I was exactly. But I had been well-trained in the Army to find my way out of anything and to establish my bearing. The bigger problem was that darkness was coming upon us much earlier than planned, and it would be necessary to find someplace secure to hold up.

Then, to my surprise, the forest biome of the bayou opened up suddenly onto a gravel road with open pastureland on the other side. This was my cue to follow the gravel road northwesterly until I reached Forest Service land, where I would stay for the night. It was now approaching twilight and I would need to move quickly to find my way into the government forest.

I hadn't gone ten minutes, when I came upon a rolling hill that appeared to be afire. But there were pickup trucks and other vehicles everywhere, and soon I ran into a road block of men carrying rifles. It was a Klan rally, the Ku Klux Klan, and I could see there were thousands attending, seven or eight thousand as I learned later.

The fire was a composite of thousands of torches held by hooded men, and women too. I was stunned. I only

knew what I had read about them, or had seen in old news-reels. This was in the 70s, and it was clear now that the 60's Civil Rights Movement wasn't over with yet by a long shot. At least not here.

The road guards stopped me as I approached them. With my long braids (which is how I wore my long hair during most of the Trek for practical reasons), black hair, dark skin, buckskin shirt, rifle, and Pinto, they didn't know what to make of me. But I had learned that across the Deep South many white men identified closely with Native Americans, often claiming blood relations to the Cherokee, Creek, and other tribes that had been moved to the Okla-homa territory generations earlier.

I thought, "Perhaps my appearance would instill in them this sort of connection."

"Where you headin'?" One asked, circling me and the horse, I think amazed by what he saw. They could see the wear and tear of nature's elements on my face from living out doors night and day for months.

"Towards the west." I responded quietly. "We need to make camp soon before nightfall. The Pinto and I are tired. And we have a long journey ahead of us."

"You tan that leather?" Came another voice.

"Yes, it is buckskin from deer hides," I answered straight away, "tanned the Indian way with brains, livers, and smoke." Which was true.

The interrogation continued. "You make that scabbard, and what kind of rifle you got in there, son?"

"Yes," I responded, "it's made from parfleche, fire-hardened rawhide I made from deerskin. That's a 30-30 caliber rifle inside. Feel free to take a look."

"Where'd you learn to use this?" he countered, sliding it a bit out of the scabbard to check it out.

"Haven't used it yet." I explained. "I used other rifles in the Army."

"You're a vet?" He shot back.

"Yes. I got out just a few years ago. I was a medical corpsman, but not a CO [Conscientious Objector]. So they also put me through infantry training."

Still another spoke up, I thought maybe their head guy, "We heard about an Indian camping back in the bayou. I see that was you."

To which I reluctantly nodded, but countering, "Really, I'm just a human being."

He frowned a bit, I think puzzled by my comment, and then continued, "You are free to go through, son, and be safely on your way to wherever you are going."

The Pinto and I walked slowly through their opening, as a line of men stood in silence on both sides just staring. Creaking leather and clip-clopping hooves against the road bed were the only sounds to be heard.

I was to survive and see another day.

Gas Station Nigger

We found our way to nearby public forest lands, made our camp, arose early at dawn the next day, and continued westward. It seemed the Pinto was taken by the stream of new experiences, and looked forward to the new adventures we would face together. There was never a tug, twist, or turn to head back. I didn't know all the details of her past life, but she had been taken care of by her previous owners. I had seen the victims of neglect that the Horse Trader had picked up and took upon himself to feed until better owners would claim them.

Still, the Pinto had a mind of her own, and she did not hesitate to let me know when something wasn't working for her, whatever that might be. I learned to pay attention to her protests or hesitancies, to make adjustments at any time or place. A rapport of mutual understanding was evolving, something we would rely upon heavily as the Horse Trek advanced and placed us both in alternating gratifying, uncertain, and even life-threatening circumstances.

🐎

A map given to me by the Horse Trader showed a small village ahead. We would go there for supplies with which to take along on the next leg of our journey. It was mid-morning when we arrived. There was a small, old time gas station at the edge of the town, which wasn't more than a short city block long. I stopped there and the owner came out, a white guy maybe in his late 40s or 50s.

"Can I help ya?" he asked, literally staring us down from head-to-tail, with some kind of oily rag in his hands like he'd been working on a tractor or something.

"Do you know where I can buy a flake of hay for my horse, and maybe a small coffee can's worth of oats?" I answered back. "I also need a few dry goods for myself."

"I got hay out back for the horse, and some oats inside," he explained.

Apparently he was selling a little of this and that to the locals with livestock until they could get to a bigger supplier elsewhere to stock up.

"I'm interested," I interjected.

But before I could add another word, he called out to someone inside his roadside store, "Nigger, get out here and help this man and his horse."

Out came a young black man, maybe in his early to mid twenties, a bit younger than me I thought. The owner pointed him to me, repeating himself with a bit more tone in his voice, "Get this man and horse what they need."

I had never heard this kind of talk coming from a white person, ever, and I mean right in a black person's face. Behind a person's back, but not straight away like this. It rolled out of his mouth as though it was the standard language of the day. In fact, I was shocked. I couldn't help but notice the look of resignation, humiliation, and fear blended into the young man's face. Again, I was reminded of where I was, and at what point in U.S. history. I guess a culture of fear and violent reprisals lingering among black folks living in those times in the Deep South explains their reluctance to confront their oppressors. Like a battered woman in a bad relationship, scared to death to speak out or leave for what might happen at the hands of her abusive man.

"I need a flake of hay and some oats for the horse." I told young man. "I'll take it over there in the clearing at the side of the building, where I'm going to stake her out so she can eat." I added, "Do you have a bathroom here I can use?"

He pointed towards the store, "There's one for white folks around the side of the building. It's open."

I must have headed in the wrong direction because he quickly halted me to say, "That's for colored folks, you want to go to the other side."

I had thought that Jim Crow laws providing for segregated bathrooms had ended a decade or more earlier, but apparently not everywhere.

I got a few things I needed, paid the owner, and retreated to the side of the building where I had staked out the Pinto. The horse ate her hay which I had poured the oats into, while I chewed on my jerky and finished off a jar of green beans.

The owner also had a gas pump, and up pulled a pickup truck for fuel. The back of the truck was full of new tires. I guess the owner was going to sell them out of his store.

I heard owner shout out at the young man again, "Nigger, get these tires out of the truck and put 'em inside."

Part of me wanted to throw up, or worse. But I held my tongue. We finished our meals, saddled up, and headed on our way.

To this day, I still wonder if all that racialism has changed down in that part of the country. I almost can't believe I witnessed it, but I did as sure as the sun will set in the west tonight. Had I stepped into a time warp? Was it all an illusion? Anything was possible, I concluded. All I had to do was think back from the day this Horse Trek began. Flying saucers? Alligator congregations? The KKK? And gas station "nigger." Give me a break.

Biker Gang

And so it was that the Pinto and I now traveled north-westwardly through back country. The days were now much warmer, even hot, and always sticky humid. The effect was to slow us down, down to a walk, in fact. But this enabled us to get in shape together for the journey ahead. By the time we had reached the far end of the state, we were in such athletic shape that we cantered (1-2-3 gait) nearly sixty miles in one stretch without a stop, ten of it atop a levee paralleling the Mississippi River. That last stretch figures further in my story, so I will return to it later.

The hot weather made me strip to my levis, which in a day or so darkened my already dark skin to a near black. I imagined the store keeper several days back asking me, "You an Indian or a nigger, boy?"

But we ran into no one for days, maybe a week, because our path was through woodlands without paved roads. Back then, things were a lot less developed and populated than today, reminding me of the Cabrillo Highway running north and south along the California coastline just after WWII. Before the war, there were no freeways running up and down the state. Where once there were farms that I played in as a child, by the 60's they were gone. A giant carpet of humanity, bustling shopping centers, incessant noise, housing developments, and freeways had been laid from San Diego to Los Angeles, and beyond. My father once pointed to the LAX airport, telling me, "That was a bean field not long ago." Imagine that.

As was my practice, I sought out campsites that had running water and streams nearby. A lot of backwoods campgrounds were built across the South and elsewhere during the Great Depression of the 1930s. This included wayside parks along gravel roads where people could stop and rest when traveling across the state. They are seldom used in the present because the roads leading to them have been bypassed with freeways and other major paved highways. So I would access these wayside parks now and then, when other less conspicuous options weren't available to me. I needed solitude because that's when the Calling "spoke" to me. I was still trying to figure out what this Horse Trek was really all about. In fact, the entire meaning of the Vision Quest still remained a mystery to me.

But my preference was to seek out state or national forests that had "primitive" campsites. Here I could camp for days or even weeks on end, like people who would go to them to "get away" from the cities they lived in. But campsites "off the grid" with streams were best because the horse and I would go into them to bathe. And she would quench her thirst in them, and me too — but only if it was part of a clean riparian. Fortunately, not all streams were toxic then. Agribusiness, while trying to expand its corporate and polluting footprint on rural American lands, was often held in check by a new generation of litigious environmentalists. So, public lands were still — to some extent back then — kind of a paradise I could retreat into. One might think I was living in one extended vacation. But I wasn't. How can you be on a vacation when you don't really know where you're going? Or how long you'll be staying?

I avoided major highways at all costs. And paved roads too of any type, except for short stretches, if necessary, mainly to cross over them to get to the other side. This kept us in the company of wild life and forested lands most of the time, with minimal human contact. But along one stretch of border that Alabama shares with Mississippi, fate would have it that it became necessary to travel a brief time along a paved two lane highway, although one well off the beaten track as it seemed to have little traffic.

It was late in the day along a curved stretch of this road that I intersected a group of motorcycles coming from the opposite direction. Like the men back at the KKK event, they stopped in front of me, intending to block my path. To look at them, they were the likes of one of those biker gangs you see in the movies: lean, tough, fearsome to the timid, and faces contorted in bitter scowls. Each biker had a woman behind him. If there's a female counterpart to the biker's looks, these women were quite the opposite: weathered a bit, but well beyond attractive.

Just like the KKK guy who encircled the Pinto and me, one of the bikers and his "bitch" (that's how they referred to their women) rode out and then encircled me and the Pinto, stopping in front of us, and bringing us to an abrupt halt. While eyeballing me, he set the kickstand, got off his noisy machine, and came over to me, real close, I mean right next to me.

Lean and stringy muscular, he wore the scarred fascia of a street fighter, with a slightly disfigured face, forged I thought, by a lifetime of fist-fights. He had a long knife coupled to his belt, and I wondered if he had taken scalps with it in battle with rival biker gangs. But I was equally muscular and tough, and also wore a long knife, and my rifle was equally on display.

No one offered a smile or word from either side. It was a silent encounter checking each other out. Like the KKK bunch, they didn't know what to make of me. What was clear to them, I was as wild looking as any of them, the look of one who is untamed and who fits in nowhere — except in strange encounters like the one we were all in.

I had had enough of the standoff and, well-trained in the Army to kill, I was ready to go hand-to-hand with the skinny one at my side if he dared a violent challenge.

A nod from my heels to the Pinto's sides brought her suddenly into attention, which startled everyone. I'm talking about the power of a "collected horse" with rider now fully on display. Where this impulse came from within me, I'll never know, probably the work of the Calling.

I had taken notice that everyone, myself included, was travel weary. So I spoke out in a firm tone, "Where do we make camp?"

The ice was broken, and both sides acquiesced. We headed off into the nearby woods like animal predators to make our peace for the night, maybe to enter into a capricious brotherhood, if only transient. We all needed to sleep, including their machines and the Pinto.

They watched me make fire for a smudge from leather and sticks: "To keep mosquitoes at bay," I explained. I offered some of my jerky, which was declined.

After some chatter amongst themselves, the skinny one, who I feared the most, and didn't know if anyone could trust, came over and loud enough for everyone to hear, "You got a bitch to fuck, Indian?"

"No," while asking myself, surely he can see that, can't he?

"Fuck my bitch, then," he blurted nearly in my face in a demanding voice.

He was offering an important part of himself, I thought. Unthinkable in a civilized world. But none of us felt really civilized. I knew I had to show him gratitude and respect in some way, but still decline.

"I see that you are offering me your companion, and I see that you two have a strong bond. And that she is very beautiful." Staggeringly so, I thought.

"Please don't be offended, but I can't," I said without an explanation for why, "but I appreciate what you are offering to share with me."

Well, like I said, she was beautiful, and at another point in my life, I would have taken her as a mate. But these two worlds we came from were in collision. It would have been a mistake. And I felt inside that the Calling still wanted me celibate anyway.

He frowned, and said nothing. More important, he didn't knife me. So I figured that I said and did the right thing.

By now the others were under their blankets and sleeping. I let the fire and smudge die down and I too fell off to sleep. I was too tired to fight off the nightmare that if they knifed me where I lay, what the hell could I do about it anyway?

An hour or so must have passed, when I felt a sharp stinging prick to my throat. A second later I found myself staring into the eyes of the skinny one.

"You fuck my bitch, or you're a dead man," came the command wrapped in the weirdest threat of my life. His woman kneeled at his side, naked from head to toe, staring at me with the slightest hint of a smile. I wasn't her first, for sure.

So I did, from behind, hard like a stallion I imagined taking his mare in heat, while she moaned. When it was over, they retreated to their blanket, and I to my saddle, which served as my pillow. The others never stirred, but I thought I heard her moaning again — but with her man this time.

I was just grateful he didn't slit my throat after defiling my celibacy in the eyes of the Calling. What was I supposed to do? And how would he know about such a thing anyway? And would it have made any difference to him?

Come morning, before dawn, I came out of a deep sleep to hear the feint sound of their machines leaving down the highway. Next to me, hanging conspicuously on a stick pushed into the earth, hung his woman's stained panties. I suppose a "gift of life not taken" for me to contemplate with wilderness gratitude.

Supper Table

For the next week, the Pinto and I retreated to a stream fed by a spring tucked away well into a nearby National Forest, and set camp. There was ample forage for her, and for me an opportunity to complement my jerky with fresh fish.

🐎

I tried not to reflect too much on what had just happened with the bikers. I was no virgin, and my sex life has never been barren of women giving and taking as freely as me. A person given to a victim mentality might say it was a rape. He saw it as a gift. I took her as a willing partner. The rest of them seemed indifferent, or maybe not, maybe indulging themselves to the breathing of the biker's woman and me. A distant part of me might have put a bullet in him, let the others go, and taken her with me. And I sensed she'd have gone with me, because we were all outlaws in one way or another. And in such a jungle of edge-city humanity, where there are few laws, we do as we please. You take it, you keep it, because you want it and because you can do it. But, secretively, unknown to the bikers, my way was different. I was trying to unfold a Vision because it seemed my destiny and the right thing to do. But in the outlying jungle, we suck it up. We all do what we need or have to do. If we are to survive.

🐎

After a week, we were both ready to move on, so I

broke camp and headed westerly again. Before long — we were still within the forest on one of its maze of dirt roads and paths — I was approached by a young woman also on horseback. She was as curious about me as the crocodiles were back in the bayou. I was met with a flurry of questions before I could open my mouth. I simply told her the truth as I knew it — I was on a Vision Quest.

That was enough for her to ask me to come to her place to meet her parents and siblings. And also for supper, the mid-day meal of the old rural America, transposed to "dinner" in the new urbanized American vernacular. While my preference was to move on, the Pinto was clearly enjoying the attentions of the other horse. So, what the heck, I submitted in thought waves to the Pinto, "Let's go!"

"We'll be there in ten minutes," she pressed me, "So please come, they'll all want to meet you and hear your story."

I gave her a guarded, "Okay," in a lightly broken voice, doubting the wisdom of my decision.

"This might not be such a good idea after all," I thought to myself. I mean me, an unknown man, riding horseback out of the woods with their young daughter? What would mom and dad think? And how about trying to explain myself? Like the Vision? And what I was doing exactly in the nearby woods? And how about what I was doing with their daughter in the woods? And how about starting off with the biker girl affair? The Calling was turning me into a liar from prudence, because if I brought that incident up, I'm sure dad would level his shotgun on me. But before I could turn the Pinto to make my escape, we were there.

I forgot to say that the daughter and I were probably the same age, she maybe a few years younger. But this was no love affair in the making. I decided I would take and ask questions, enjoy the food, and be gone in a hour, maybe.

Mom was very gracious, and invited me right in. The kids, quite a few of them as I recall, ranged from very young to my short order riding companion. Father seemed friendly enough, but rightfully guarded with me. The kids were naturally curious. I decided to take questions in hopes that none would be asked, a coward's way out. I don't care.

As it turned out, supper was about to be served. It seemed early in the day for the main meal. Maybe it was Sunday? Don't Christians eat right after church? And then it dawned on me that I had no idea what day it was or if they were Christians. In fact, I didn't really know anything about Christianity or any religion for that matter. Months into all of this, and living in the bayou, my days were now defined by when the sun rose and set. I don't recall if I even had a watch.

Everyone but mom was seated at this long table, which seemed to go on forever across the dining room. Dad sat at one end, I was positioned at the opposite. My riding companion was seated next to me on my right, like she was my sweetheart, fiancé, or wife, or something. It was all orchestrated by mom. The food was brought in on a wheeled cart and, dish by dish, passed one-at-a-time: First to dad, who, not serving himself, sent everything down the table on his right side, eventually reaching him again on his left. I saw immediately that this was a family ritual.

To the right of dad was an empty chair, mom's. Dad served mom's plate, then his, and mom put the food dishes back on the cart, which was kept close at hand. Mom then retreated to the kitchen to remove her apron, as I recall. I noticed that everyone sat quietly at the table, waiting, like the start of a race. No one was eating anything. Mom returned to the table.

"Mother, are you ready?" asked Dad.

"I am," came the reply with a nod as she took her seat. Dad then led the family and guest (me) in a Christian prayer, giving thanks for the food, doing good in the world, and several worthy admonitions about not being naughty in the world as he looked me in the eye amid bowed heads.

"Amen," came a family chorus when his sermon was ended. And at which point precisely the mood lightened and a soft din of chatter enveloped the room as everyone began to eat. But it didn't take long before the din was quieted by Dad, who targeted me with the first question.

"What were you doing out there in them woods?" he boomed across the room, *the* family's voice of unquestioned authority.

"Was he a preacher and the dining table his pulpit, the local sheriff, the county judge, all of the above?" I pondered in silence. Didn't matter, but the Calling took over before I could stutter a lie to protect myself.

"Contemplating life," I answered, as though a traveling philosopher on horseback.

"Be more specific!" he demanded.

We were now in the people's court as far as I was concerned, and I needed to mount my defense — like making for the door and getting the hell out of there before his verdict came down with a gavel. But what blurted out of me next came as a complete surprise, a reckless surprise to be sure.

"Why is it that white folks around here still call black people 'nigger' to their face. Why are the schools still segregated. I find it very troubling. And how do all of you here feel about that?"

I had learned long before my Vision that "freedom-of-choice desegregation" was still status quo in many parts of Mississippi. And no doubt elsewhere across the Deep South, and even across the U.S. where white folks could get away with it. All of this, I could clearly see, amounted to *de facto* resistance to the Civil Rights Act of 1964. And here I was seeing it first hand.

I thought he was going to choke on his potatoes when he reached for his cloth napkin to cover his mouth. It was a declaration of war, and now I was ready to head for the door and then back into the woods with the Pinto at a gallop. I was pretty certain we could out run him. But before I could rise from my seat, an "Angel from Above" arrived to save my dumb ass.

"You're right, it's wrong, and I don't believe that people should behave that way!" Everyone was shocked to their core, including me — but it was not Dad, but his young daughter who brought me out of the woods.

I was sure she was thinking her hero on horseback (me) would rally to her side to continue the cause. But it was the Calling that was the true hero, not the coward sitting next to her now fumbling like Dad for words.

"Well, we do need love and peace in the world," I meekly offered as an olive branch. But that wasn't enough for the Calling.

Turning to the daughter, I asked her, "How did you personally feel not being allowed to attend an integrated school?"

I had become a spokesman for a *bona fide* remote troublemaker, unable to hold my own tongue. "Remote" because I tell you it was the Calling speaking through me "remote control." I wanted nothing to do with any of it. I just wanted out — like out the door.

She made it clear she didn't like it at all. Like being left out of something that was historical, important, and good to do. It was also clear that this was probably the first time she spoke out about it before the family. So, maybe that was the purpose of me coming here, to unlock a prison door, to go public on the right side of history.

Dad wasn't happy about any of this, but he didn't stand in the way of further discussion. She and I talked a little bit more about such barriers in society, but basically not drawing others into the dialogue. That felt okay with me. I wondered how hard it had to be for young white kids who detested racialism from instinct to grow up in communities where such hatred and traditions prevailed. Here, in this household, I learned it was not easy for everyone.

185

Opinions and beliefs varied. Some secreted.

I then tried to explain that I had this Vision of being on a Pinto horse, just like the one tied outside. And that we were riding up a ridge and seeing this "worldly" transformation of bad to good in ways that I couldn't really explain.

I then gambled angering the Calling to say, "The Vision had a Voice that guided me from within, and, right or wrong, foolish or otherwise, I felt compelled to go with it." They all just listened.

I then told mom that I really enjoyed and appreciated her food, and that I would probably think of it often, especially during leaner days on the trail. I then rose and announced I had to go.

The daughter exited with me and asked if she could accompany me for a short distance. That would be nice I told her. And so she did. And after a short distance, it dawned on both of us that the time to part had arrived. I felt a bit sad inside, and I sensed she did too. In but an hour's time, we had connected and established a special bond for life, whether or not we would ever see each other again. Which we didn't. I wished her well in life, which she reciprocated.

I've thought about her many times over the years, but nothing more came of it. The Calling had other plans for me in the unforeseeable future, including being alone like a monk in a monastery or in the bamboo cage of the Viet Cong.

I had only a few hours left of light and decided to lope

off to quickly get to where I thought I needed to get to before dark. Of course, I had no real idea of where that
would be, nor what I would find once I arrived there.

Feed Store Incident

It seemed that another week or two had passed by as I found myself trekking more and more towards the north than to the west. We were slowly trudging along the winding eastern edge of the same massive National Forest near where I had met the young lady on horseback. Not two months had passed since I vacated the bayou, and already I was feeling weary of the whole ordeal.

I was worn down more by the specter of the unknown cast upon me by the Calling, than the hours upon hours of trail riding in a beautiful country setting. Many people, I thought, would love the opportunity to live closely in the company of a horse like the Pinto "out in nature." But I wasn't one of them. I was waiting for the damned ridge in the Vision to show up, and the sooner the better. That Vision was now in competition with my longing for a comfortable bed with a real pillow, "set meals," and a beautiful woman — any woman at this point. This grinding clash constantly wore away at my self-determination. I needed inspiration, and I needed it soon.

I was now approaching the northern edge of the National Forest. I decided to head west through the last stretch of forest to minimize contact with civilization. There would be enough of that later, I sensed.

On the morning of the second day in the forest, I came upon another of those older, less used paved roads. I presumed it linked private forest land owned by lumber companies, with government land I had just passed through. I decided to go north alongside the road and stay out of the private forests.

It was early in the morning with no traffic coming or going. In less than an hour I came upon a large clearing. At the far end was a huge grist or grain mill that also served as a rural farm supply, augmented with a large graveled parking lot to one side. No one was there, but a sign promised it would be open in another hour. Who would have thought that in the middle of nowhere I would come across a feed store? I was, in fact, on the lookout for oats for the Pinto, so it was perfect timing. I staked the horse out on the near side of the clearing — opposite the store — and propped myself up against a tree to doze before it opened.

I was awakened to my senses by a pick-up truck. It was the merchant, who also ran the mill, arriving to open the store. I wasn't sure he even noticed the Pinto and me. Leaving her staked out, I walked over and went inside. Not seeing or hearing a vehicle pull in, he was startled by my presence.

"Can I help you, sir?" came the words of an apparent gentleman. A welcome contrast from the previous merchant with the young black fellow he employed and felt privileged to demean.

"My horse down there," pointing to the far end of the parking lot through a window, "needs some oats. I would like enough to fill this small saddle bag, if possible. I'm willing to pay for a full bag, and maybe you could give the rest to one of your customers."

"That won't be necessary, sir. There's some in the back that hasn't been bagged yet. One minute, and I'll fill that bag for you." He left for the rear of the store.

Hanging out in a feed store was new to me, and I was amazed by all the hardware utensils and equipment, veterinary supplies, all kinds of feeds and supplements, and some clothes and boots. The boots were pretty sturdy, but more than I could afford, so I just admired them. Riding most of the way so far, mine were yet the worst for wear.

He emerged from the back with the filled bag (the same one I mentioned earlier in the Black Widow incident) and a round plastic tub filled with oats.

He handed me the bag. "Why don't you take this tub over there and let your horse eat these, and you can keep the bag for later."

Before I could thank him, he asked, "Where you headin'?" And noticing that I was a bit on the lean side, he continued, "Do you need something to eat?"

"First," I said, "thank you for the oats, but I insist on paying you for them. I do appreciate your generosity, though. I've got some jerky I made tied to my saddle over there. That will do me for now. I've been doing some fishing in the forest streams, and I may need to hunt at some point too." I pulled out a few dollars from my pocket and put it on the counter.

He promptly pushed it back towards me, "No please, you just take them. Where'd you say your headin' to?"

"I've been traveling and camping with my horse over there since last fall. I'm on a Vision Quest, maybe you've heard, like the way Indians do, seeking to understand something that's been given to you that's important, but you have to figure it out. It's a 'Calling' meant for me. I'm still trying to figure it out."

He listened attentively, then declared. "Why you've been on this path for half a year."

"Yes, I guess it has been that long. Maybe longer. I've sort of lost track of time. I don't even know what day it is."

I put the money in his hand, "Please take this."

The smell of smoke in my buckskin shirt caught his attention. "You make that buckskin shirt, son?"

"Yes," I explained, "I tanned some deer skins, an elk hide, and two buffalo hides in a bayou back in Alabama. It took me four deer hides to make this shirt."

I continued, "I did the work for an Indian Trader up on a Sioux reservation in the Dakotas. He sends the hides to me and then pays me to tan them for him because I do it the traditional Indian way. That's how I make my way to get supplies along the way."

"Do you mind if I go meet your horse?" he asked.

"No, I don't mind," I said. "Please come over and I'll introduce you to her."

It suddenly crossed my mind, and I told him, "You're the first human being I've seen in nearly two weeks."

We reached the Pinto. He then checked her over closely, nodding in some kind of approval. He then noticed the rifle in the leather scabbard I made. "You know how to use that?"

"Yes," I replied, "I learned all about weapons in the

191

Army."

"You're a vet?" he asked.

"Yes, I was drafted during the late '60s. I got out after two years, an honorable discharge. I wasn't a CO, but after infantry training they decided to make me into a medical corpsman. We helped save lives. It also taught me to hate wars and violence.."

"Is that why you're on this Vision Quest? he asked.

"I don't know," I explained, "I mean probably not because there was this horse — that looked like the Pinto here — in the Vision."

Just then, other pick-up trucks began to arrive, and he headed back over to the store. Soon there was a dozen trucks, at least. The men driving them all looked like ranchers. Maybe because we blended into the forest backdrop that they didn't take notice of us. Just as well, we both needed to rest for the ride ahead. The Pinto was already fed and now resting. So I leaned back against the tree again, hopefully to snooze awhile before taking off.

That wasn't to last 10 minutes when the ranchers came out of the building and headed our way. As they neared, I stood up.

One spoke up, "He just told us about you and what you're doing. Some of us would love to do what you're doing, but we can't what with our families, our work with livestock and other things. But we'd like to help you."

And with that, they began pulling out their wallets and putting cash into my hands. I was dumbfounded.

"I can't take . . ." but was overrun as my arms were

now full of paper money. I had no idea how much there was. A ton.

Wishing me the best, and ignoring my protests, they turned to get in their trucks, and left. The graveled parking lot was now empty again. Thinking about what had just happened, I saddled the Pinto and led her over to the store front. I went inside and there was the merchant standing behind the counter, like he was waiting for me.

"The Calling has spoken to me." I revealed to him. "I can't take this money from them, none of it. I can tell from looking at them, they've worked their hands to the bone to earn it. I'm also having to face hardships, so, like them, I'll work for whatever I need – no hand outs, no gifts, please."

I placed all of it on the counter in front of him. "Please do something for them with all this money. And please explain to them that I appreciated their generosity, but that I just can't take any of it."

Before he could say a word, I turned quickly, got on the Pinto and headed out. I decided to retreat back into the woods to prevent anyone from following or finding me. All I knew is that this is the way it had to be.

And so it was.

Jerky, Pemmican, and Watermelon

The Pinto and I continued northerly and ever so slowly under a sun bearing down on us like you wouldn't believe. This meant temporarily leaving the bounties of the National Forest behind, meaning, having no access to streams, fresh water springs, campsites, and fish to eat. All that was virtually off the table until I reached the next stretch of forested government lands further to the north and west.

So, it now became necessary to take gravel roads through very rural, but still forested, back country — and privately owned, which always made me nervous. Fortunately, contact with people was still minimal as we skirted well around what few small towns we ran into. The few souls I did come upon were typically curious and friendly, eager to talk, and not infrequently offering food, which I usually declined. Numerous small "ma and pa" country stores now became my food sources. Feed stores like the earlier one I passed through, served the Pinto well. It all seemed to work out.

I began to notice that local populations living in the back country were usually segregated by race. I'm not sure if it's still that way today, but I imagine so even if it gets diluted generationally. Still, people are people, and I have to say that the back country folk of Mississippi I encountered, black and white alike, were among the friendliest I'd ever met, and even given to helping "outsiders" like myself.

Some insisted to the point of irritation that I take a meal with them before moving on. More than a few offered their barns and corrals as bunkhouses for me and the Pinto. But, with few exceptions, I stayed reclusive and apart as this is the way of the Vision Quest. So it was that Mississippi began to feel like a home to me, even though the Calling would deny me settling there.

It seemed that summer was now full bore upon us in the worst of ways. I decided to lay low in the coolest spot we could find during the day, and then travel by night. This opened a whole new world to me. When there are no city lights, the sky bursts with beauty as a trillion stars flicker away and shooting stars are in dazzling full display. Moonlit nights made navigating the back country as easy as by daylight. The extent to which nature has adapted our eyes to see in the darkness of night surprised me — a welcome surprise, in my case. But the cooler nighttime air was the greatest reward for weary travelers like the Pinto and me seeking their way through the unknown.

Here and there I was compelled to stop, make camp, and prepare certain things for my survival. Most important was food that I could take with me, when sources like the country stores were otherwise too far and few in between to count on.

Twenty or more years earlier my father had taken me to different Indian reservations. Back then, many "old timers" born in the 1800s were still alive and so were their ancient crafts, including making jerky. Seeing this inspired me to make my own, creating my own recipes, and now adapting them to Horse Trek life. Hunters of many ethnic backgrounds also made jerky, even made from smoked fish! Many people used fruit as well as flesh. So they all influenced me too.

My favorite was to mix chopped bell peppers, honey, soy sauce, and salt with ground beef — a variation of what is known as pemmican (from Cree pimihka·n). I made this if the local feed store sold any kind of metal screens — basement screens being best — which they always seemed to have, and which served as my drying frames.

I would form the mixture into small discs, like miniature hamburgers, pressed flat with my knife or a suitable stone. The discs were laid on the screen and allowed to dry out over a day or more. The screens were set up on a makeshift platform I would construct from saplings or other natural materials available to me in the forests. These were fashioned high enough to deter 4-legged visitors. I also laid a swath of mosquito netting to keep birds out during the drying phase. Flies were never a problem, though you'd think they would be. But I suppose it was my constant presence in the camp that kept animal opportunists at bay! In the end, what I got was some great tasting and nutritious jerky, perfect for my current nomadic life on horseback.

Sometimes the Pinto and I became food opportunists ourselves. And it was along this northerly stretch of the back country that one of the most memorable and "satisfying" of such opportunistic experiences occurred in the course of the Horse Trek.

Coming out of a forest we had been traveling through, we entered upon a huge watermelon patch. This was strange because it was out in the middle of nowhere. And only a dirt road in the worst of shape led to and from it. But it was clear from the moment we arrived, we were going to get some.

I grabbed two and split them open with my knife. One went to the Pinto, the other was mine. It was hot and the melons were the perfect antidote for dehydration and lack of energy. The Pinto dove right in and the two of us, side by side, made for the most slurping sounds I've ever heard. We were like two wild animals feeding on a carcass we'd just hunted and taken down. It was a messy affair too, to say the least. But it was good, and I actually was given to thought that those melons might have saved our lives.

In gratitude to the grower, I began to figure out a way to leave a thank you note and some cash. Looking around for some rocks or something to secure them, I noticed a small wooden box at the edge of the melon field, and went over to check it out. There was a slot on the top.

"Ah!" I realized, "The grower served locals, who would come by and drop money in his box."

I put the cash in — as good as a note of thanks.

After a brief rest, we departed.

Predator

Once again, I plotted our path across more government forest lands. Our trail then darkened and we were cooled by the shade of the forest's dense evergreen foliage. With that relief, we switched back to movement by day, camping at night. A clean waterway we came upon made for an extended stay of a week. I relished these private moments in nature, giving me time to explore intuitive thoughts, and also rest the Pinto whom I actually walked alongside much of this leg of the journey due to the heat. We often came upon and observed wildlife around us, and readily took in the sounds and smells of the forest. But it was the refreshing cool waters of the stream that we both relished the most.

The Calling had been quiet, maybe patient with me is a more accurate way to put it. I checked my compass settings and plotted my path ahead. Events, I learned, would dictate my heading, and gradually I began to trust them. Endure them is more like it. But for now, this camp enabled me to sense time and space in new ways. It is hard to listen to the mysterious voices that emanate from the natural world, when one's mind is constantly barraged with artificial manmade noises.

The Calling certainly was one voice, but nature has many others, which form their own communication network from one wilderness species to another. One either learns to listen to them, or one hears only oneself. Never given more clarity than in my camp was the clash between such voices and the insistent voice of "having to make a living" born of civilization.

Obsession with money and possessions, I came to see, was a yoke around humanity's neck, maybe even a mental disease. A manner of thinking that would take any wilderness and reduce it to a possession, to exploit it for gain or pleasure. This pressure on nature, squeezing it to near death, or even to death, becomes its own Calling — a warning — one we can hear when we pass from what we have molded apart from nature, to that which is still wild, or nearly so. A simple tree represents a life form, with its own voice, versus its conversion to lumber to be processed and nailed together as boards smothered in paint or injected with toxic petroleum products to keep them from biodegrading. From this dichotomy comes the concept for "progress," and only the natural world stands in its way.

In my camps, I was visited by many creatures curious of my presence. Like the alligators in the bayou. These forests, the least touched by humans, made these encounters exploratory rather than predatory. But I would learn shortly, the worst intrusions by troubled humans could turn explorers into prey. Yet the Calling prepared me for such outcomes, even in my unwitting innocence. The purpose of the Horse Trek would not be usurped and denied.

The time had come to leave our encampment. For a short distance ahead we would move down a less traveled gravel road within the forest. On the second day, we came upon one of those New Deal wayside parks I mentioned earlier. There being water available — even a lone picnic table! — and darkness now falling upon us, I decided to set camp. Actually, only a temporary bivouac, and back in a ways from a road that led to and away from the park. We would then leave early the next morning.

"Camp" was nothing more than a cord strung between two close-by trees that would fit me stretched out between them, my head on the saddle as usual for a pillow, my rifle, and mosquito netting draped over the cord to give me some protection from these vampires should they come in the night. None did as it turned out, possibly in some measure due to my smoked buckskin shirt. But I decided on a small smudge fire anyway just in case to keep them at bay.

I staked out the Pinto nearby within my view in a small meadow that opened up to a starry sky. We were both a bit bushed, and before long she finished foraging and was asleep on her side. Not long after, I passed out myself.

Several hours or so passed, when I was awakened by an eerie sense of uneasiness. The moon, now full, was overhead, with tufts of clouds drifting by. Moonlight shined down upon the Pinto, who was now standing and looking straight at the nearby wayside park, ears on full alert. This was a warning sign that something was wrong.

Turning my attentions to the Wayside park, it was too dark beneath the understory to see anything. So I listened. And then came what I hoped not for . . . a crunch in the forest debris on the ground. Then silence. Then another crunch and more silence.

The Pinto, it was clear, was a beacon for whatever was lurking towards us. Whatever, or whoever, was coming was still on the move. The movements were those of stealth, possibly curiosity, but I would take no chances.

In a few more minutes, the intruder proved to be — gauging by a silhouette — a large man. He was now standing over me to one side. He had entered my space, unannounced and unwelcome. Not one to be prey ever, I prepared myself with rifle in hand: If he starts to come down, I will go up.

He made his move.

In a second I sprung to my feet. In so doing, the netting draped over my head. In my right hand was my rifle loaded and finger on the trigger, in my left hand was my small flashlight which in advertently shined upwards into my shrouded face, no doubt casting a ghoulish caricature, because I was met by a terrifying scream.

Taken by surprise, he was now the prey, I the predator. I pushed him back. He retreated, turned and stumbled, sobbing and babbling like a baby. I continued to push, rather than pull the trigger. This continued until we reached the Wayside park, when he suddenly got up and ran to his car, which was not visible from where I stood. He stormed off down the road, tires squealing.

I rushed back to my camp, saddled the Pinto, and retreated deeper into the forest. I wasn't sure if he was just a traveler stopping for a break in the night, then becoming curious by what he saw in the moonlight – a horse! Or that he was a night stalker looking for victims and I simply crossed his path. Whatever the case, I wasn't waiting around to find out. I would hold up for the night in the forest, and come out in broad daylight to face the music straight on, whatever might happen.

The next day, we were back on the gravel road again. Not two minutes later came a sheriff's patrol car racing towards me. Throwing on his brakes, he got out and confronted me.

"We're looking for a man whose been back in these parts last night." He described him, then inquired, "Have you seen anyone who fits this description?"

I explained my situation only to the extent I had a visitor in the Wayside park, but leaving out any details. His description was a perfect match though. Without revealing anything more he advised that I keep my rifle handy if I were going to be camping anywhere in the forested area.

It wasn't until some time later on the other side of the state that I learned he had murdered an entire family also camping in a Wayside park. Possibly others too. Should I have pulled the trigger? Put a bullet in him, as others wished I had later? My actions and narrative will have to speak for themselves. But I've wondered what drives people to murder others. A mental defect from birth? Raised in violence? Feeling wronged, and violent retribution is justified? Frustration? Take your pick.

The Gate

Moving northward again, I began to encounter more law enforcement along the way. Mainly sheriffs checking me out. Typically, "Let's see some I.D. People have heard about you, a stranger. Some are nervous the way you're traveling about on that horse with that rifle."

It always seemed to satisfy them when I said I'm just moving through, and mean no harm to anyone. But not everyone was nervous. Along this northerly route I also met two young women, one of whom visited me in my cabin years later and briefly became a lover of mine. She later married, moved east, and had two daughters. I heard from her for the last time in a letter just a couple of years ago, a sad one it seemed, thanking me for the friendship we had amid some other personal matters. It rung of despair and finality. I wrote her back but she never responded.

♞

It was time to turn directly west, and we would travel through more government land. I chanced a remote forest service road, thinking we would reach a spring for water before dark. It was still terribly hot, but if we moved along without problems we could make it in time and not die of thirst. Not a pleasant thought, but a real concern as my story is about to relate.

It seemed that we were well more than half way there when we ran into a metal panel gate, like you see on ranches to contain livestock. For whatever reason, the Forest Service wanted no vehicles back in there. I dismounted to open it, only to find it had been locked. My heart sunk with a bitter dry mouth. I was beyond just being thirsty, and the Pinto wasn't doing much better. I checked the fence line, which was secured with four strands of barbed wire as far as I could see. There was no way around the gate. And I had no way to cut or untwist the wires to get us through.

Panic began to set in because in no way did we have the time, energy, or water to hydrate ourselves in the intense heat to retrace our steps. Gathering my senses, I contemplated my options. I could turn the Pinto loose in hopes that she could make it back out to civilization, then climb over the gate in hopes I had enough in me to make it to the spring. But we were partners in this, and separating seemed wrong. So no way. I ruled out trying to jump the fence with her, risking an entanglement in the wire if we missed, or breaking my neck in the fall. And I ruled out putting a bullet in her head to spare her the agony of dying of thirst.

My mind began to wander almost incoherently in despair, for I had run out of solutions that made any sense. I now felt the extreme heat and thirst draining me of my life force. Could it be that I would die here, taking my equine partner with me? All in the name of following a strange Vision that increasingly made no sense? It was here in this moment of crisis that the first miracle during the Horse Trek took place.

It was the Calling. And the command rang loud and clear: "Jaime, crawl under the gate."

But this made no sense, when I could simply climb over it. Putting my faith once again in the crazy unknown, I got down and slithered under the gate on my belly like a snake. There was just enough room for me to fit through. I got up and turned around. The Pinto and I stared at, or maybe into, each other as though information was passing between us. In the next moment, her legs folded beneath her, then stretched forward and behind her, and she then began crawling on her belly towards the gate. Just like I had done. That she would mimic me was miracle enough. But more was to come.

I jumped the fence and released the saddle from her back. I suddenly was filled with renewed energy and vitality and hope. She crawled on and on. How could she fit under the gate? There wasn't enough room. It's hard to explain what happened next in a rational way, so I won't even try. I will simply say that "a camel can fit through the eye of a needle" when one is on a spiritual journey.

We made water well before the day ended.

A Night in Jail

We continued northwestward away from government lands, but not entirely so. As fate would have it in our favor, more privately held forest land lie ahead, with a sprinkling of open farm land here and there surrounded by public lands. Supplies were now easier to come by, making movement through surrounding forest lands easier for both of us. As before, I was met along the way with county law enforcement checking me out. But this time, there would be an entirely different outcome.

Having ventured unwittingly too close to one community, a squad car was sent out for what was to be a kind of lower level "meet and greet." Meaning, to allay locals of any fear of my nearby presence, and I to avoid those who might want to make trouble for me.

The officers requested that I spend the night in their jail. While they were genuinely cordial and inviting, truth is, I really had no choice. Also in my favor was that one of the officer's family owned land right where I was at. He said the Pinto could stay with his family who would look after her during my bogus incarceration.

I was whisked away into town, and taken straight to the jail. Once there, I was introduced to other officers, all of whom were friendly and curious. My rifle, of course, was secured with theirs in a locked room. A bit of discussion followed and I told them what I could about the Horse Trek, not mentioning anything about the encounter at the wayside park. They seemed reassured by the fact that I had been in the Army and that I appreciated their own service. But facing busy schedules out and about town, all but two officers manning the station cleared out.

To my surprise, they had ordered a dinner for me from a local diner. It had been well over a month since I sat at a table to eat like a normal human being. I had become accustomed to eating with my hands, my hunting knife being my only "utensil" — which had also been taken and secured with the rifle. I'm not sure what they thought as I ate the meal with the butter knife and my hands.

When I was done eating, they escorted me to a jail cell, one with an unlocked door that remained open to the office area. A neatly made bed with a blanket awaited me. They pointed to a bathroom nearby, and said I was free to leave the cell to use it at any time. So, for the first time in my life, I spent the night in a jail cell with an open door.

I did sleep well, not having to worry about intruders, psychopaths, and the uncertainties that come with being a nomad. I awakened as the early morning shift arrived for duty. The officer on call briefed them. A breakfast was offered, but I declined. Within minutes, my belongings were brought out and I was taken back across town to find the Pinto waiting for me. They waited while I saddled her, and then handed me the rifle to secure in the scabbard. I tucked the knife in there too, which they appreciated.

Before I could say anything, one of the officers spoke up. "We know now which way you're going, and word of mouth has let country folk in your path know you're okay.

No one will bother you."

I thanked them, mounted the Pinto, and rode off. It all felt like a good omen for the remaining Horse Trek.

Typical of the Vision Quest, I couldn't have been more wrong.

Wetiko
"evil spirits in the forest"

I decided to navigate to the north once more before heading west again. This took me to the edge of a great forested area dotted with swamps that invited much wildlife. I learned later from descendents of slaves who once toiled these lands — and whom we will visit in the next chapter — that it was at one time part of a vast slave plantation. I learned that terrible things happened here to their forbears — both before the Civil War (1861-1865), and long after their fragile liberation in the wake of that great and devastating battle of good versus evil.

I was somewhat familiar with the brutality of slavery in the South from my schooling, but couldn't began to imagine the terror and fear for one's life with its uncertainties in the wake of their purported emancipation, and thence into the era of Jim Crow. Earlier in this story, I have shared its living vestiges in the Klan rally and the verbally assaulted young man at the gas station. Others may wish to disagree, but it was clear to me that the Horse Trek carried me through a still struggling civil rights era. Racial hatred was still active and vocal, and these descendents of slaves were not spared.

A savannah, of sorts, lie adjacent to the forest, stretching as far as the eye could see towards the west. It too once formed part of the plantation, and I wondered what they grew there. Cotton I'm certain and probably other things

to feed generations of owners, overseers, slaves, and livestock. But no mansion or outbuildings survived here into
the present. At least I saw none. The population in this
area seemed scant, as well. In fact, no person inhabited the
forest nor the visible lands across the open fields to the
west. I had wondered why.

Almost as quick as we arrived, my own animal instincts
began to alert me that something was not good about this
place. As though something evil came to inhabit it, to lurk
within it. The instinct to be on guard now prevailed within
me. I began to dread the night ahead in the forest, which
seemed so different than the government lands I had
passed through recently that didn't know human slavery. In
this moment, to me slavery's dreaded legacy somehow felt
palpable in the forest. "A curse," I thought, "if ever there
was one."

It is said that long ago among the Plains Indians, the
Indians of the Great Lakes, and the coastal Algonquian
tribes of the northeastern forests of the U.S. and southeastern Canada, dwelled an evil forest spirit. It went by different but similar names, I recall the Metis saying Wetiko and
Wendigo. As the sun sets in the west, it would emerge in-
carnating as a terrifying creature with humanoid and fierce
animal features, embodying and unleashing the worst elements of human avarice, predation, and even cannibalism.
The Metis and I had talked often about this spirit and how
we believed it manifested itself in any place where human
barbarism and depravity may have reigned. I began to sense
that the Calling brought me into this forest for a reason, to

endure yet another ominous challenge. So, before continuing with my story, I want to stop here to say I don't believe in werewolves, Frankenstein's monster, and all that Hollywood bullshit. But what happened next to me and the Pinto is something else, and whatever it was that came upon us, I wouldn't wish on anyone. So I'm forewarning my reader, *if you are given to nightmares from things that deal with fiendish evil spirits, you might wish to forego the rest of this chapter and move on to the next.*

Dusk was now upon us as I sought out a meadow within the forest for the Pinto to graze. As was my custom by now, I moved deep enough into the forest to be beyond the reach of humans who might wander nearby and spot us.

"But who would want to come into this creepy place?" I countered myself.

A hazy mist descended upon the forest. I attributed this to the humidity of the regional climate in summer fused with the fumes and dankness of nearby swamps that pervaded the forest and now clogged my nostrils. Given the sense of dread upon me, I marveled at the mental fortitude of the Pinto who went forth readily, if not eagerly, in this strange and eerie place. The Calling remained silent, offering no comfort or warning to vacate. So I assumed that we were meant to be here, as everywhere we had gone before, for a reason.

We then came upon an opening, a glade just discernable in the dim light that would suit the Pinto's needs and

provide us both with a secure place to rest and sleep, so I hoped, in peace.

What I thought might work was interrupted in that very moment by what seemed like a shadow, or something akin to that, fleeting around us in haste off to one side. This drew the Pinto — with me still in the saddle — into high alert, followed by a quick turn in its direction. No sooner than we made the turn, then it or another of whatever it was, circled around the woods behind us.

This time I could hear it, the dead debris of the forest floor being trampled beneath its feet or paws or whatever it was.

Before the Pinto could turn again, it rushed by in front of us. All I could see in the dim light was that it moved upright like a human, sort of, but moved more like an animal covered with fur or hair given to standing on its hind legs. Seconds later, another shot past us, brushing the hindquarters of the Pinto, which struck terror into her. Its silhouette now played against the mist revealing to me that it was not human. It was a large animal hybrid of our human species, with fangs and claws, and eyes more revealing of a werewolf or demon than a known animal. Nor was it the elusive Sasquatch, of which I will talk about later. It was not alone either, but maybe it was. I thought, "It is Wetiko."

The Pinto was now moving quickly in place and in fear, waiting for me to take command and do something. We were encircled by it or them, rushing in and out of the forest curtain at will, threatening us but not yet attacking. My head began to spin, threatening disorientation. Panicking, I moved to draw the rifle from its home, when what seemed like a superhuman grip, stilled my hand.

From within came the Calling: "Do not use the weapon. Turn the reins loose that the Pinto may take you from here safely."

I released the reins, and, as though on command, she tore through the woods like it was familiar ground she was born onto. I had by now learned to ride without hands attached to the reins or the horse's mane for that matter. We were locked together in flight. As I understood it then, but otherwise later, we were running for our very lives.

To either side there were shadows keeping pace, then slowly falling behind. In what seemed like less than a minute, we escaped the forest and entered onto open land. Whatever it or they were, they retreated into the forest and were gone. I took up the reins again, and the Pinto descended into a trot, then a quick walk, her deep breaths heaving and nostrils flaring like I had never seen before. I was in a similar state, human style! We came to a halt.

There was still dim light on the western horizon, as the sun had not long vanished below it. I turned to look back at the forest we had just escaped, trying to fathom what had just taken place. Ironically, I no longer felt fear, for whatever these tortured entities were, now invoked pity in me.

What were they? Perhaps this was an education, albeit a surreal and terrifying one, the Calling invented. A trial to test my resolve. Or, like Sasquatch, real when properly understood and approached in the right way. It would take the next leg of the journey to get an answer to what they were and why they were there. For now, I settled on spirits, evil spirits in the forest, embodied as Wetiko.

We traveled a bit further and set camp for the night. Side by side, we were comforted by each others' presence and mutual trust. We both fell off to sleep, guarded, I was certain, by the Calling. But with my rifle loaded and in hand . . . just in case.

Plantation Village

We now traveled westward across a great level plain of mixed farmland, swamps, and small islands of forest. It was a diverse landscape that loomed as far as the eye could see. Depending on the lay of the land, I hoped to reach another National Forest in a full day's ride.

By now, the Pinto had developed into a great athlete, and together we could lope along 20 or more miles at a stretch, rest and continue on for many more miles. I mentioned the near sixty-mile jaunt earlier, that's about to happen now in the story. But most of our time was spent on spontaneous forays off my loosely planned route, visiting historic spots, talking with back country folks, and other excursions that I will, with a few exceptions, spare the reader any mention of. Such detours, I began to realize, extended the Horse Trek into many additional months of travel time than I had figured on — should our purpose have been to make a beeline straight to our destination. But this was all fantasy, because I never knew exactly what route the Calling had prepared in advance, and when we'd be on it. A general message of "westward ho" was about all I had to go on. And time had become relative anyways. The cliché, "being along for the ride," perfectly applied to me.

The many swamps and waterways proved more of an obstacle to swiftness than I had hoped for. Several hours of skirting and going around them meant I would have little time to explore the government forest land for a secure campsite come nightfall.

So, it was that an hour before sunset, with at least ten more miles of riding still ahead of us, that we came upon a small village of black people. Only black people. From what I can see today, the village no longer exists — or does not exist as it once was — as the location and surrounding area is so transformed I am barely able to recognize any of it in the present.

Back then, their homes lined up in two rows, one row on either side of an old, single-lane and barely used paved road that badly needed repaving. Actually, I'm not sure it was actually paved, or at least completely so, as so many years have passed by to challenge my memory. Starting at the southern end of the village, we commenced to walk slowly across its length, which was as long as two American football fields.

Almost immediately, people, mainly children, began to come outdoors and follow behind us. As we continued on, more children and now adults joined the entourage!

By the time we reached the far end of "main street" and the end of the village, where it turned abruptly to the left and headed off to the west as a state highway, I think every able-bodied soul in the village had joined in and were at our heels. I could distill from the din of their voices that they were trying to figure out what I was. Nothing new.

But the Pinto and I also had our own chorus of sounds: clip-clopping hooves, the string of jerky hanging from the saddle horn twirling and rattling with each hoof beat, and the creaking sound of moving saddle leather beneath me. Everything about us was drenched in the smell of smoke from my many campfires. We kept going, now thinking it best to hurry along in hopes of reaching the forest and leaving the horde behind us "in the dust."

I then noticed that our audience had stopped behind us and divided to either side of the narrow road. An old convertible of a car with top down came through driven by a young black woman. She stopped in the middle of the road directly in front of me — reminiscent of the biker gang bringing us to a halt — and got out. I didn't know what to think.

She came right up to the Pinto and held her face with both of her hands, like they were pals for years, then kissed her on the nose. The Pinto accepted it without a wince, and I had to smile.

She then looked up at me and asked the usual, "What is you?"

At this point in the Horse Trek, I had already stripped to my jeans, revealing my chest and back, both blackened by the sun. So, "what I was" could be seen as debatable.

But by then my much rehearsed response, given more than a hundred times across the middle section of Mississippi, had settled into a benign, "A human being."

That drew a laugh from her, but she pressed me further, "You some kinda Indian, or are you black, where you going?"

The string of questions invited more dialogue, so I

stated my predicament first in one long breath, "I am traveling to the west, I'm on a Vision Quest, and I need to make camp before dark in the forest ahead, so I must hurry along."

In the background, people were still there and had drawn closer, the kids wanting to touch the beautiful Pinto. I told them they could, and the Pinto accepted it all in clear delight, offering no resistance.

The black woman, my interrogator, appeared to be a voice in the community, and she wasn't done with me. It struck me also that I now found myself equally curious about this place, it's people, and her, in particular, because she was so vocal, disarming, and engaging.

She continued, "You come back and spend some time with us. You can stay with me and my family."

I started on one miniature protest, "But . . . ."

And that was the end of that because she had ignored me, taken the reins, and I was now being led back to her place, which, as it turned out, was the last house in the village, not five minutes away. Once there, she told me to dismount (I did) and stay put (I did) while she walked over to her car and brought it home.

I'm using the word village because it was more than just a town. It was like an extended family that shared the same values, experiences — and curiosity, to say the least. So, I just went with the flow. And what else could I do? This woman was in full control!

She told me that the others would return a little later. Because what was going to be was a party-like gathering with me as the special guest. Meaning they could poke, touch, jab, and ask me anything they wished just to figure out what I was. She said that I would spend the night with her bunch. She had a daughter. I told her that I couldn't be separated from the Pinto.

I was immediately chastised in a tone, "I know that, you think I'm dumb?"

Her house was old and tiny, maybe one, possibly two bedrooms. She led me and the Pinto into the backyard, beyond which was lightly forested land, possibly crop fields further back. The yard reflected her poverty, an old time clothesline propped up with forked branches, several broken down cars stripped of anything salvageable from what I could see. There was a small garden and a nearby hand-dug well for water, apparently still in use. As an aside — a few years later I was a guest of a Muskogee Indian family in Oklahoma, and their well sat in the middle of their frame home built a century earlier by their ancestors when it was still Indian territory. Here, too, I sensed I was walking into history.

She next related to me, "The mosquitoes are bad here at night, so I'm going to fix your bed in that car there."

That was a jalopy which had no wheels or doors or seats, just the frame. In a minute she had a bed made for me with a small mattress she brought out from the house, a blanket, and a pillow. I then produced my mosquito netting, and she said, "I figured you had that, or you would not come this far alive." She was right.

She now pointed to the horse, "You can tie your lady

horse friend to your rope, and she be near you all night. No one will bother you here. That okay with you?"

I said nothing but, risking a slap in the face, I gave her a spontaneous and an admittedly affectionate hug. Her frame felt small, delicate and movie starlet slender.

I had also hit a "shy bone" with a mixed twinge of embarrassment and a faint smile in her come back, "Time you and me go into the house *now*."

And away we went, rather away I was led. And to be presentable and appropriate, she required that I wear my buckskin shirt. I did as I was told, and the way she held my hand, I got the feeling she wasn't wanting to share her muscled bare-chested guest with any "untaken" lady friends that might be coming to the party.

The town arrived within minutes of our entering the house, as though some circadian clock went off in everyone simultaneously. There was barely anywhere to stand, and what few chairs that were there were taken in the first 60 seconds. Mostly older ladies and children came. Those not given to shyness, came with questions, which I tried to answer with civility by saying as little as possible. I think my host's guests were coming and leaving the entire time. Maybe this was just a daily custom: To come visit, share greetings, exchange gossip, and then leave.

Soon, everyone was talking, and I begin to drift into the background in silence. I could barely understand their English dialect. I thought it was possibly influenced by their ancestral African languages, several hundred years of plantation slavery, followed by share cropping, Jim Crow, segregated schools, and denied opportunities right into the present. And amid the worst imaginable racial discrimination our American society could muster. The Klan rally I witnessed, eight to ten thousand strong, told it all.

Within minutes, my host approached me with her young daughter, maybe eight or nine years of age, and as preciously cute as her lovely mother.

My host then said, "My girl would like to show you something she wrote for school."

I offered a smile, "I would like to see your work."

She handed me a small tablet with sheets of paper scored with lines. She was learning to print and had written a little story a paragraph or so long.

"I wrote this," she told me.

"I would like to read it, so give me a minute," I replied softly. It was a cute little tale involving little animals.

"Well," I said as she waited with anticipation, as though I were her school teacher ready to grade it, "this is a very nice story, and you know something, your writing is so nice, so easy to read. Thank you for sharing this with me."

I handed it back to her, and this broke her into a shy smile, no doubt inherited from her mother, who had taken off to circulate and gossip with the others.

As I gleaned the room of guests looking for her mom, it became apparent that she did not have a man, as in husband or boy friend. Or so I thought. After I found her, I told her that I would like some time to talk with her in private.

"We can do that soon," she said, "after these people

leave."

At this point, it was clear to me by her tone and in her eyes, that she was feeling the same "spark" that I was for her. And her female glow it seemed would surely attract the jealous attention of any male suitor in the village who might be coming.

And come he did, and he was right on me within minutes. He was fairly well-dressed, like a college professor or something, and wore no friendly smile like the others.

I could hear the Calling warning me to head to my bed outside as soon as possible, like before he could cross the room to get his hands on me. Or, better yet, get the Pinto saddled pronto and ride the hell out of there and never look back. After all, the purpose of the Horse Trek, so far as I understood it, was not about incurring dangerous love affairs like a backwoods lothario or seeking a mate around the next bend. Although it was beginning to feel a bit like that.

Before I could escape out the back door, he snagged me, demanding, "Who are you, and what are you doing here?"

He might as well have hit me with a club. But the chill of his voice was enough to deliver the message.

I offered my name, which he ignored, and then offered him a very neutered explanation, "I'm riding horseback across the United States to see all the wonderful sights."

I almost puked, aghast by my cornball lie. I must have sounded like an ass to him. Unimpressed, he took another shot.

"How do you support yourself?" he demanded.

Came another lie, and the very worst imaginable my thoughtless brain could have given him. "I am independently wealthy."

He returned a look of perfectly blended outrage and disgust, and he was right. It was a very disgusting thing to say. Worse, it was another lie. I had nothing and owned nothing, not even a bank account.

The Calling couldn't take it any longer and came to my rescue — I then knew what to say, "I mean to say, I own nothing, live off the land as I go, and have a trade that I take with me for work so that I can buy what little I need. My wealth is neither in money nor material."

He shook his head and walked off. I imagined him thinking, "This wacko itinerant isn't worth my time or energy."

But this angered me. If he couldn't accept something so contrite and harmless in intent, what kind of a person was he? He could go to hell as far as I was concerned, and if he wanted to make bones with me, measuring by his chunky little pot belly, he would be an easy take down.

"No you won't," came the Calling.

Instead, I did the unthinkable and raised my voice above the din, like a roar, causing him and everyone else, to turn their heads, maybe with a hint of fright.

I belted out: "Gather around, I want to show you all something very interesting. But I need your help."

This voice of manliness brought my hostess right to my side, delighted that I had a backbone and could hold an audience. The Calling would go with it, thank God.

"I need a chair — that one right over there." It was brought to me. "Now I need a victim, er, a volunteer," I chuckled, "to sit in the chair."

My hostess took it immediately, as I stared the male intruder down, which made him feel a bit uneasy. I was of no mind to take any more of his bull.

I continued, "Now. I need three more volunteers."

At this point, I just picked them out of the crowd one by one. There was now an air of excitement in the room.

"Perfect!" I announced. I then positioned one at the shoulder and one at each knee.

"Now, without touching anyone, including our 'victim,' put your hands above her head, first your left, then your right, but alternating with each other — starting with you," as I pointed to the lady at her left shoulder — I stood at my host's right shoulder.

Naturally, they screwed this sequence up to start, as everyone does who has done this with me. But my hostess squirmed and squealed with nervous delight. This was going to be fun.

Four times I had them practice the sequence, going slowly, until they got it down pat. Women are better at this then men, who tend to be devoid of intuition and patterned behavior in the way that the female naturally excels. Grumpy, therefore, still hanging around, and now curious, would not be invited to participate. His penance, as I thought of it. Tribal shunning.

They were nearly prepared for what was to come next.

Sounding like an obnoxious circus bitch-barker full of hype, I presented the purpose of our group's efforts, "We are going to levitate this lovely lady right out of her chair. She will be lighter than a feather, and she will zoom up off the chair like a rocket aiming for the ceiling."

It was a "fake lie." She would be levitated, but only with the Calling's intervention, or cooperation as I wanted to think of it as.

I continued my rant, "We will turn Einstein's Body Mass into Potential Energy. And, er, that kind of energy into Flo-thru Kinetic Energy."

No one understood a word of my pseudoscience rhetoric, not did they care. Nor did I. At least it sounded impressive. But I wasn't done yet. First, I decided to deflect Cupid's arrow from my host's wishful thinking suitor to me.

I let my imagination flow, "This fair damsel will fly so high that I will be forced to catch her in my arms, and hold her closely, and lay her gently down on the sofa and comfort her if she is distressed by the experience. I may ask you all to leave at that time so that I may tend to her privately."

That was it for him. His black skin was turning red with jealous rage. But before he could break through the crowd to grab me by the neck, I moved quickly for the levitation.

I then told my hostess to hold her arms out straight to the side, I commanded, "Like a soaring eagle in flight."

She got it, as I figured she would. We were like "one" at that point.

"Now, I want you to put your two index fingers, side

by side, underneath her arm," pointing to the lady on the left shoulder again. I then had the other two ladies do the same at the knees.

"Very good, now lift her out of the chair." I commanded.

Try as they all may, she could not be budged. Came the expected chorus: "You want us to break our fingers? Did you glue her to that chair? I think she too heavy." Etc.

"Next, I want you to do the same thing, but don't actually make contact with her body." They nodded, waiting for the command, "Okay, ready, lift!"

Of course, still nothing happened.

My hostess's suitor was now totally convinced that I was not only a fruitcake, but a *bona fide* traveling charlatan.

There was now a sense of disappointment in the air. Exactly what I had planned for.

"You are not quite ready yet. We have one more thing to do to get you all ready."

With anticipation, and maybe a little leery too, they were still all back with me in spirit. "Now, I want you to bring your hands back over her head, as before, except this time, do not touch her head or each other's hands. But this time we must go very, very fast!"

I continued my outlandish rant, "We are generating the eagle's flight energy. Okay? Are you ready?"

They all shouted, "Yes!" in a single loud voice.

"Let us practice to get it right," I commanded. "Ready, get set, Go!"

This speedup was new, so a bit of fumbling and touching happened as expected. Not waiting for whining or grumbling, I marched on to the next practice round, then another, and still another.

"Do not touch hands! We cannot make contact or the harmony will be lost and the 'Magic Eagle Energy' will not happen!" I declared, forgetting that Einstein got replaced with a bird.

This was more than the suitor could take, and he was ready to head out the door.

"Does anyone deny that we will levitate this beautiful woman without making contact with her?" I shouted out across the room.

He had had enough. "You're full of it buddy and are misleading these trusting people," he declared aloud.

He was as articulate as a university professor, too, and the kind of skeptic I hungered for.

I baited and taunted him, "If you doubt me sir, I challenge you to put your money where your mouth is. A simple twenty dollar bill will do, I wouldn't want to break you." I figured he probably had some expendable cash, as well-dressed as he was.

Insulted, he begrudgingly coughed up the money, and everyone roared with delight. We were on!

My hostess was now really squirming and squealing in her seat.

Now I wound-up the show a bit more with additional theatrics.

"The beautiful lady must stop her squirming, sit still, and stretch out her most lovely arms as before." It was hard for her, but she did it.

"Now!" I addressed my unwitting, dedicated collaborators with as much bravado as I could muster, "We are going to repeat everything from the top. Then, when I say 'Go to your positions!' in a loud voice, you are as quick as you can to put your two finger beneath her arms and knees as before, and yell 'Rise!'"

Came the "oohs and ahs" from bystanders waiting in anticipation. The room was now electrified.

I added one more layer of excitement in the most affected voice I could muster, "I will catch the beautiful lady in my arms as she flies into the air, so that she does not fall and injure her sweet loveliness!" This brought a round of applause from all the swooning ladies, and dagger eyes from the suitor.

"Now, the time has come. Ready yourselves!" I ordered.

Everyone leaned forward in the audience to watch.

"On three, we go!" I reminded them.

Came my final command: "One, two, three, Go!"

The hands moved perfectly in unison, and when the last hand fell into place, I bellowed, "Go to your positions!" they following my lead.

Everyone fell perfectly into their assigned positions, when we then all roared in one loud voice, "Rise!"

Came the screams and laughter and amazed faces as my hostess rose into the air. At my arm's level, I reached across and grabbed her in my arms, returning her to her feet — after a quick kiss to her cheek.

It was done.

At this point, everyone in the room wanted in on it.

I waved and crossed my hands, "No, no that's all I can do now."

This didn't satisfy anyone, but they had to accept it, as they closely examined the chair for evidence of chicanery.

I held out my hand, before her suitor. Nothing. "Forget it," I told him, "I don't need your money, and this wasn't a sideshow for you either."

With a wave of my hostess's hand, the house was cleared of her guests, including dagger eyes. I waved them goodnight. This left her and me alone, as her daughter and a girlfriend retreated to the bedroom.

"Let's go outside," I suggested. And out we went.

☙

Once outside, I told her I would be leaving early, probably before sunrise. The mosquitoes would be coming out soon, so I knew this encounter would end quicker than I wanted.

"Can you tell me a little about the people living here — you all seem very close?" I asked her.

"We all come from folks who were slaves here many years ago. This land here was part of the plantation where they lived."

I then asked her, "Do you know how big this planta-tion was. "

"All around here. Even that way [she indicated towards the east] where's that big swamp forest."

I decided to tell her that I had been in that forest to

the east.

"You don't want to go in there," she insisted. "It ain't safe. There be evil spirits in that forest. We think they come from the dead plantation masters."

I decided not to pursue the evil spirit stuff with her.

She continued, "After the plantation slavery days, our people stayed on to work the crops so we would have food. They created a little store a long time ago, where we could buy supplies from them."

I asked her where they go now.

"That store is still here. It's not far from here. Some of the people walk there." She said.

At that point I pretty much got the picture of what was going on. Just then, the first mosquitoes began to arrive, which signaled the end of our discussion.

I thanked her for everything and made my way to the car. She followed, but then went ahead of me. She opened the mosquito netting and fiddled with the bedding a bit.

"Okay, you can go in there now. It's ready for you." In I went. As I laid down, she reached across and pulled the blanket up, fussing with it. "That right for you?"

"Perfect." I told her.

She then pulled the netting down. "Good night, you be safe on your journey."

As she walked off, she added, "I'm gonna put some stuff on your horse to keep them off of her too."

The mosquitoes soon began to descend all around me. Whatever she put on the horse, kept them away from her too. Soon they left for easier prey, or so I figured.

I actually slept well that night, comforted by the genuine warmth and loving kindness of a fellow human being I hadn't known but a few hours and would never see again. Yet, I felt my life touched and enriched in the best of ways by her, her daughter, and all her neighbors. I suppose even dagger-eyes, too.

☙

As I began to doze off, I couldn't help but think of the supreme irony of my situation. Here, I lay secure in the skeleton of this old, broken down jalopy, a rusty makeshift shelter provided by a woman, a descendent of slaves who never left the old plantation grounds, who owned little to nothing material. When not a day and a half's ride away, fearful white people who knew nothing of me, who never once inquired of my purpose or needs, who very possibly were the descendants of slave owners, had me incarcerated. But there was also kindness. I was fed a meal, given a nice bed to sleep in, and engaged in friendly conversation by my jailers, who also provided the Pinto with a safe place to be with forage and oats.

Here in the shell of a jalopy, I was the guest of a simple black woman with tremendous heart who promised me safety for the night; yet in the jail, I was also a guest, and made to understand in no uncertain terms I would be equally safe for the night.

In a final fleeting moment as I drifted into sleep, I remembered that even the Klansmen near the bayou had wished me safe travels on this most strange and increasingly mystical journey.

Horse Trainer

My plan was to reach a suitable campsite from which I could make my way across the Mississippi River. Locals had mentioned a town about 60 miles to the west that would be my best bet. It was now full sunrise since leaving the village in the early morning dark, and I figured we had come ten miles already. If we could get to the crossing by nightfall, I would set camp, and get over into Arkansas the next morning.

Of course, I had no idea what I was going to run into once I arrived at river's edge. I'd never faced this great river by horseback, and I didn't even know if it was feasible to get across on a horse. There had to be a way, or the Calling wouldn't be full-force upon me now to get there. I had learned to trust this inner Voice, no matter how harrowing a challenge I might be faced with.

Fully rested, the Pinto was as eager as me to set out. With little prodding, she broke into a lope and took the lead. With the sun rising on our backs, and a warm breeze in our faces, we loped ten miles westward before turning north and then west again for another forty miles.

This was perhaps the strangest leg of the Horse Trek in my recollection. It was seemingly effortless and we never stopped, not once, to rest. In one respect, it was like it never happened. I mean we were just suddenly at the river as though we were in a time warp. *Very strange.* But then, most of the Vision's Horse Trek was strange by any accounting or reckoning.

The river was bound on both sides by enormous banks of earth — levees — bull-dozed into place by what must have been an army of tractors many decades before my arrival. The slope of the embankment that intersected my route was very gradual and I decided to course north upon it, paralleling the winding path of the river. So elevated, I caught glimpses of the river to the west and the open, but sparsely populated farm and ranch lands to the east from which we had traveled the day before.

The Spanish Conquistador and explorer Hernando de Soto had crossed this river, so historians believe, not far to the north of where I planned to make my own crossing. Months later in Arkansas, I would camp where de Soto and his men had also camped over 400 years before me. At one such campsite, the Calling visited me to explain what happened there in a major battle between de Soto's army and local Indians living there. I'll discuss that later in my story.

This leg of the journey would add another ten miles, which I planned to complete before nightfall. But fate would alter this destination, undoing nearly all that the Pinto and I had gained before sunset.

At some point along the levee I passed a ranch off to my right. I noticed a man who was apparently training a horse in a large corral. The horse appeared to be another Pinto or some breed with similar markings, but very stout. Perhaps a stallion?

We were in the usual lope, so we soon passed him by.

Just ahead of us, the levee seemed to steepen. So we moved nearer the top where the levee was more level. We then continued on.

Half an hour or so later, I sensed we were being followed. I turned about in the saddle as the Pinto sustained her gait and took view of what appeared to be the same man and his horse trying to keep up with us, but still quite a ways back. I had no idea what it was all about, but with nightfall less than an hour away, we had to keep going forward.

Finally, we reached a small country store, probably built in the 1930s, maybe earlier. We put in there, and I went inside to get a few supplies and permission to use the outside water hose for the Pinto and me, which was granted. I asked also if we might camp back behind his store in a wooded area that encroached upon the levee and he agreed to that too. He then closed his shop and drove off. There were no nearby businesses or houses as far as I could see. This would work well for us, and the river crossing would somehow be solved tomorrow, or so I hoped.

When I returned outside, the horseman and his Pinto — a "registered Paint" he later corrected me — were waiting for me. Actually, here at trail's end, I was tired and not wanting any company. Even the Pinto was ready to turn in and showed little interest in the Paint, who, as it turned out, was a young stallion! Like human females, equine females are equally picky about who they want to share personal space with.

The horse trainer introduced himself and explained

that he was impressed by the "harmony" in which the Pinto and I moved together. And that we had "cantered" (as he called it) nearly ten miles without stopping, and without showing any "wind," as his Paint was still showing and blowing. He then, like many others before him, began to ask questions about me and what I was doing. As far as he was concerned, I was an "Indian" arising out of the past, a real mystery, out of place, out of time — an embodied anachronism.

I sat down against a tree — sylvan "chairs" as I by now thought of them — having staked out the Pinto to graze the dry, summer grasses all about.

"I'm on a Vision Quest." I offered.

This piqued his interest to such a great extent that he asked nothing, but begged me to return to his ranch to meet his wife and two very young daughters, I recall babies still or toddlers any way.

"We've come sixty miles today. We're tired and need to rest. We have to cross the river, and we plan to camp back there in the woods tonight."

He pressed me, "You can stay at our place, eat with us, rest for as long as you like, the Pinto can be with my other mares, and . . ." before I could counter him to decline, "I can get you trailered across the river."

The Calling had clearly spoken, and I accepted.

♘

We rode back side by side, part of the ride in the dark. Very little was said along the way. We finally reached his ranch, where the Pinto was introduced to and put in with several mares, much to all their delight. Extra hay was thrown in. We headed to his house, which was a modest double-wide mobile home.

Dinner was waiting for us, as though she knew for sure he would be dragging the "Indian" home with him. They were a loving couple, and very religious Christians. The kids, both daughters, were put to bed early, as it was an "early rise" household with all hands on deck for breakfast.

We talked for some time, mainly me answering questions about the Vision, which they considered an important spiritual journey. The uncertainty of my ultimate destination or what would be revealed to me at some point as the Vision's purpose, did not trouble them nor detract from their interest, warmth, and sincerity as my hosts.

Nor were they deterred by what had become my way to retreat from conversation and to enter into contemplative thought beckoned by the Calling. Instead, they mustered patience as they awaited "my return." Likewise, my smoky buckskins and minimalist possessions suggesting regress to a more primitive era, was welcomed as genuine, necessary, and serious.

"I struggle within myself to listen to the Calling, as it directs me amid the uncertainty of the Vision," I offered. "It seems that facing hardships, even danger, is part of the journey. That's all I know."

I then half-joked, speculating further about the risks and its potential consequences in such a journey, "You know, I am not married and have no children. Not the sort of thing to do if that's what you want — or want to keep!"

Thinking that everyone must be getting weary after such a long day, I offered, with genuine concern, "I must be keeping you from your sleep. And, you know, I don't even know what day of the week it is — if you need to head off to work some place else in the early morning, so forgive me."

The Horse Trainer came to my side, and it was agreed to call it a day.

To this day I can't remember if I left to sleep under the stars that night, or on their couch, or on their floor — which one grows accustomed to after sleeping on the ground for months, and then years. In fact, for months after the Horse Trek, I always slept on the floor or outside on the ground, even if I had a bed. And, to be honest, I can't recall even having had a bed back then.

The next morning over breakfast, there was a bit of conversation about their religious beliefs. They were dedicated to Christ and Christ's teachings — no easy feat, as I have come to think of such commitments in the politicized and polarized world of religions today. I don't recall that they belonged to any church. But it was clear that Christ was front and center in their lives and daily conversations.

The Horse Trainer was very vocal about his Christian beliefs, insisting that his goal in life was to be so "filled with Christ" as to become a decent human being in their Creator's image. I admired this in him, and contrasted it with my own failings as an adult dedicated to what could easily be defined as a "wild goose chase" — not to mention my indifference to organized religion altogether. But the fact was at the time, I knew nothing about Christianity or Christ. From the brief conversation I had with him, it wasn't clear to me that Christ was a male, female, or neither. I would spare them nearly every detail of what I had encountered and participated in up to that point in the Horse Trek.

He then told me a bit more about himself, "I'm a professional horse trainer. I work right here with all those horses outside. I am also a part-time horseshoer."

His wife added, "And I keep the house, take care of the girls, but we usually accompany him on his shoeing route. We go all over this part of the state."

Of course, I didn't know anything about horseshoeing and less about training horses. I had run into several shoers along the way, and they always wanted to be part of what I was doing by shoeing the Pinto. They never charged me for it. They just repeated the same old story, "Wish I could do what you're doing."

The Horse Trainer pointed out to his wife that he was really impressed by the way I rode. He then asked me, "Who taught you to ride?"

I point blank confessed, "The Pinto was my teacher."

I didn't confess that the Calling was also involved in it, letting me know to pay attention to the Pinto's behavior and movements. So that's what I did.

The Horse Trainer noted, "I see you don't wear spurs, use a whip, or put a bit in your horse's mouth."

"Why would I do that?" I asked.

All of this invited more conversation, but instead he

said, "I've got several horses to shoe today. Why don't you come along with me and I can teach you some of it?"

I thought to myself, this seems like a smart thing to do, sensing that dealing with the Pinto's hooves was something I should probably start thinking about doing myself at some point in time.

So, off we went that morning, and I got a good look at how it's done. He was entirely hand's-on with his teaching, and not inclined to venture into any science that might be associated with horseshoeing.

At day's end he suggested, "Why don't you stay on here with us, work with me with the horses and learn to do the shoeing?"

It was clear he liked me and wanted my company. He felt a spiritual bond had been laid between us, and we could learn from each other.

I told him, "You know, I've really enjoyed being with you and your family, but . . ." and, interrupting me, he completed my thought, "You've got to fulfill your Vision."

I nodded, "Yes."

I learned that night over dinner that he was estranged from his father, who owned one of the state's largest farming operations, and who wanted his son to follow in his footsteps. But his son's destiny was with Christ, trying in his own way to fulfill that in the same way I was trying to do with my own Vision. So, we shared that ambition. We had to follow our own paths, wherever they led. So be it.

"What I would like to do," I offered, "is come back when I've completed this journey and we'll pick up right where we've left off." To this, he eagerly accepted, and then made arrangements with another horseman to get me across the Mississippi River and into Arkansas the next day.

So that you know, I did return later — and before the Horse Trek was over. The Calling saw to that, which I'll return to later in my story.

Vampires in the Night

The next day, the Horse Trainer arranged with a rancher buddy for a stock trailer to get us across the river. I thanked him again for his hospitality and interesting conversations. We said our good-byes on the east side of the river and a few minutes later the rancher let us off on the west side in what seemed like the middle of nowhere. I thanked him also and headed southward along the river. It would be dark in a few hours so I decided to set camp next to what looked like a lake, or maybe a cove or an inlet of the river, at any rate a large body of water that seemed like miles across.

Next to the water's edge was a small open area surrounded by trees, which made it very private. I learned later that no one lived in this area — and with good reason, as you'll see why in a moment. I also learned that my campsite was almost precisely where de Soto and his Conquistadors stayed near the end of their legendary explorations. So the story goes, de Soto had been mortally wounded in a defensive battle with Caddo Indians further to the west. His men, it is thought by some researchers, buried him here or nearby, possibly in the river, weighted down by rocks. This would not be the only time that I crossed paths with de Soto's historic trail.

A pleasant breeze came across the water, and I thought to myself what a great spot. My own lakeside "hideaway" to enjoy! I staked out the Pinto to nibble on the dry bunch grasses that sprouted here and there in the meadow. I looked about for firewood in the woods as I was anxious to have a campfire again. The Horse Trainer's wife had prepared me a small stash of food that would make for my evening meal. In less than an hour, nightfall would be upon us. So I set about quickly to make camp with my mosquito netting rigged between two small trees at the edge of the meadow. My saddle "pillow" and my loaded rifle were tucked underneath the netting. The firewood and my fire making tools were now readied too. I cleared a spot at the center of the meadow and kindled a small fire.

I decided to take the Pinto over to the water's edge to quench her thirst. I don't know how I overlooked mentioning this so far, but I used an old Army canteen for my own water. I tied the canteen to paired straps below the saddle cantle on one side. Normally, I attentively rationed my water, and targeted my rides from one destination to the next accordingly. But I failed miserably on the "Gate" leg of the Horse Trek.

The Pinto pawed the water to let me know she wanted back on the grass. I staked her out again and returned to the water's edge where a large rock made for a perfect seat with a view out over the lake. And there I sat waiting for the sun to edge slowly down below the horizon on the far side of the lake. The wait was worth it.

The sunset made for a fiery blast of yellow and what I imagined to be crimson — diminished color vision being a life-long scourge I've had to endure — as the last bundles of clouds disintegrated into near darkness. Nearby chirping birds grew steadily more quiet as they retreated into their nests in anticipation of the night. Moments like this made the hardships of the Trek worth enduring.

As I gazed over the water, I drifted into the same thoughts I faced at the end of every day: What will happen next? What will it mean relative to the Vision? Will I even survive this Quest?

The temptation to return to some modicum of civilized life and find another way to survive continued to tug at me. The Vision, with the Calling its Director of Operations, and I its soldier and collaborator, had reduced me to a bizarre survivalist. Normal people, I reasoned, simply don't do this sort of thing. This was not comforting. And on this point, as it happened every night, came the same steady stream of self-awareness that opened the door to *despair*. I turned to the natural world around me for the only source of solace. I would see it through no matter what.

My gaze was awakened by what appeared to be a dark cloud rising above the water in what was now a fading twilight. Whatever it was, it was new to me. Otherwise, all was quiet over and about the lake. I stared at it, trying to deduce what it was. It seemed to be moving across the lake towards me. I roughly calculated it to be maybe a quarter mile (400 meters) away. But now, it was clearly a black moving cloud. I quickly rose to my feet and listened. There was a faint hum, which began to grow louder. The Pinto had also taken notice and began to move about nervously on her tether.

Within seconds, nature revealed itself as the first scouts of a vast cloud of mosquitoes arrived at my camp. I instinctively retreated to my netting. But no sooner than I took shelter, the forward edge of the cloud arrived at land's edge and strangely stopped. I could barely hear myself over the hum. More scouts then arrived, penetrating the edges of the netting. The Pinto now whinnied, a distress signal for me to take protective action.

The Calling signaled within, "Horseshoe!"

"Horseshoe?" I questioned aloud.

What did that mean?

The Calling again, "Create a smudge in the shape of the hoof."

This I understood and I took action pronto.

The cloud was seemingly held at bay — perhaps the work of the Calling? But it was also clear the scouts were signaling to the cloud that prey would soon be safe to take. More scouts arrived. It was an emergency, one like I had never faced before.

The meadow was covered with dry grasses, much of it nearly dead, but still holding some moisture in the stems. I gathered as much as I could and laid a curved wall of it midway between the cloud and the fire.

The cloud, like a single organism, sensed that I was creating a defensive network. This signaled an attack, and the cloud moved to the edge of my grass perimeter and stopped again. Like the crabs surrounding my trench on the gulf coast, they seemed aware that the grass arrangement was different and intentional.

I grabbed one of the sticks in the fire and lit the grass. Immediately, a smudge was created. The cloud retreated a meter, then divided to pursue our flanks. I was struck by their herd intelligence. They knew exactly what they were doing. I ran for more grass and laid it to the sides, and then realized that I was forming the shape of a horseshoe. The smudge caught fire quickly and followed the path of the newly laid grass. The divided cloud held back on each flank.

I brought the Pinto within the hoof-shaped enclosure, which silenced her whinnies and calmed her. Fewer and fewer scouts dared to enter the rising plumes of smoke — apparently, the swarm's mortal enemy. I laid more fallen tree branches to keep the flames of the fire alive and to build the coal bed. With the Pinto within the wall of smoke, I ran to gather more grasses outside the hoof, as I had depleted what little was still within. I was struck by the cloud's hesitancy to completely surround the horseshoe, but to keep to its flanks and hold there. This enabled me to make several foraging runs to our advantage.

By now the sun had long settled below the horizon. Darkness prevailed across the sky, and now blended with the blackness of the cloud, which formed a frustrated wall of vampires around us. An uncanny *déjà vu* flashed across in a single thought: This horseshoe shaped smoke screen was yet another "sphere of intolerance."

Soon, the hum noticeably began to fade. And then all became quiet again. I stepped out from behind the curtain of smoke to confirm that this terrible menace had retreated or left altogether to seek out other, easier prey. They were gone, and not a single scout was left in their wake.

The smudge fire, an ancient defensive tool given by Nature, had saved our lives. Many years later I learned that such giant swarms of mosquitoes had systematically hunted, attacked and killed many livestock and deer populations across the bayou states. In some regions, mosquito abatement programs were developed to control their burgeoning populations.

I gathered more grass, sustaining the smudge for another hour, and kept a pile close by should they return to swarm us again. The Pinto, exhausted more by the ordeal than what little traveling we did that day, laid down to sleep. I laid down near the fire and the grass pile, and held vigilance until sunrise, when all vampires must retreat to their darkened lairs.

Third Camp (Buckskin, Quill & Bead)

If the Mississippi River delta meant having to endure mosquito swarms, we wasted no time getting out of the area. I charted a course northwest. I had learned from locals the Ouachita mountains and a National Forest of that namesake lie in that direction. The Ouachitas, they said, had the state's highest mountains, most scenic rivers and lakes, and, I deduced — mistakenly so as it turned out — cooler temperatures than where we now stood. In fact, the entire South from Georgia to West Texas was one big humid blast furnace from June 'til November, October if you were lucky, and no one could convince me otherwise. But, looking back in time, we did escape the mosquito menace of the bayou and delta lowlands. That much was good.

To reach the Ouachita mountains and forests we first had to traverse an area known as the Arkansas Timberlands that rose out of the delta country several miles inland from the Mississippi River. This is a vast hilly area that comprised the state's portion of the Piney Woods, an ancient coniferous forest that once extended all the way to East Texas, Oklahoma, and down through parts of Louisiana.

In departing the delta lowlands I was reminded that I was also leaving what was in the previous century an extension of the same slavery culture I had left behind across the Mississippi River. I had unknowingly camped the night before in the outskirts of the old Lakeport Plantation. Several hundred slaves toiled the soils there during the lucrative cotton trade. Their lives of forced labor ended only with the threat of Union troops and Lincoln's Emancipation Proclamation. Maybe the black cloud that menaced my campsite on its very grounds was a gut reminder of that evil. Like the plantation across the river with its evil spirits embodied as Wetiko. Meaning the Calling would afford me no tranquility on such grounds in my Vision Quest. So be it, I would hold no ground but move on.

Not necessarily related to evil spirits, locals I would run into not far ahead warned me about the so called "Boggy Creek Monster," a purported large Bigfoot type creature inhabiting the far southwestern reaches of the Ouachitas. Many sightings are still common in recent years. Real or imagined, whatever it might be lie further west of my planned route, and I gave it no further thought.

But other concerns were pressing upon me to move along. Fall would be arriving soon and I needed to establish one more buckskin tanning camp while I still had summer heat to work with. The Indian Trader up north wanted me to do some bead and porcupine quill embroidery during the upcoming winter months, so I needed several smoked deerskins just for this work. It would take me a month to get the raw hides and complete the tanning. So I needed to be on the outlook for a suitable place to do this work.

I will add here that locals also warned me that winters could be severe anywhere in the state, particularly in the mountains to the far north. They said winters anywhere in the state would be harsher than what I faced in the bayou country where my Horse Trek began. Looking ahead, this meant that following this tanning camp, I would have to move on quickly to find suitable winter quarters either in the Ouachita Mountains to the west, or trek still further north to the Boston Mountains of the Ozarks I had heard about (see my nearby sketched map). From either of those

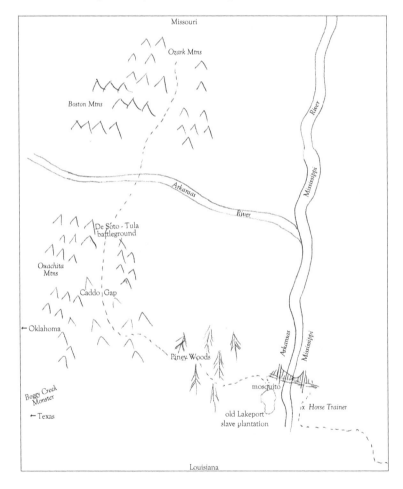

mountains ranges, I planned to go straight westward across the Great Plains and eventually set camp somewhere in the Rocky Mountains for the following winter. There, I assumed, my Horse Trek would conclude on one of its great mountain peaks, just like in the Vision. Of course, that was only a guess because, truth be told, I still had no idea where it would end. The Calling would decide that, not me.

On the first day leaving the Lakeport Plantation area on my way to the Timberlands, we traveled on raised gravel roads moving past swamps to avoid alligators, if they were present. Like much of the American South, alligators are also native to Arkansas, living in swamps and rivers from the Arkansas River to Louisiana. I hadn't seen any since crossing the Mississippi River. Possibly they had been hunted out to make way for agriculture and deforestation in the delta region I was passing through?

Sticking to these gravel roads, on that first day I stumbled on a huge smokestack in the middle of a field, which I couldn't figure out why it was there. A day or two later I was told by locals it was a remnant of a laundry facility in a Japanese internment camp, called the Jerome Relocation Center, during WWII. It also housed German war prisoners after the Japanese were sent elsewhere. Thousands of Americans of Japanese descent had been rounded up by our government and taken here and other centers across the U.S. I had no idea such a thing had ever happened, until I reminded myself of the mass removals of American Indians from tribal lands to reservations a century earlier.

Third Camp (Buckskin, Quill & Bead)

Jerome Relocation Center during WWII.

Horse Trek, I came to realize, was also a history lesson in the making. Things that were never talked about in my elementary education.

🐎

Several days into the hilly Timberlands I came upon a small community. Very small. There was a gas station with a supply store inside – practically a mirror image of the one in Mississippi. But there was no street lined with houses. Tucked in surrounding woods were the houses, scattered about here and there with no rhyme nor reason. It was a mixed ethnic community of whites and blacks. As I learned over time, the whites were descendents of poor pioneers that came here in the 1800s; the blacks were ancestors of freed slaves from the delta plantations dotting the edge of the Mississippi River.

The brands of racism I witnessed in Alabama and Mississippi gave way to a bizarre, rather than mean-spirited, re-lationship between the white and black races, at least in this tiny community. The owner of the store, who was my father's age, was a good example. It was "nigger this, and nigger that" during the day, but come night he spent it semi-clandestinely with his black girlfriend whom he was totally in love with, and vice versa. Crazy.

He owned this old house, passed down to him from his parents, and from their pioneer parents before them. For whatever reason, like the Horse Trader, he took a lik-ing to me and, after I explained enough about what I was up to including the need for a place to do the tanning, of-fered me the use of his property and his house to stay in while I was there. Probably because he was never there at night after running his gas station, being with his girlfriend instead. No one said anything about it in the community, because others were doing the same thing!

I found out about their love affair after going for an evening ride on the Pinto to check out the surrounding countryside. By chance, I stumbled on her place, a small one-room wooden building, what uppity whites denigrated pejoratively as "nigger shacks." But there they were on the front porch with his arm around her, both enjoying the evening air. I quietly retreated into the woods, unseen.

🐎

One day I decided to learn more about him. He re-vealed he had been in WWII, a marine in the Pacific Iwo Jima campaign. I asked him what it had been like during the beach landing, as I was somewhat familiar with it from what others had told me who were there too, and from other accounts I had read about. Of what he said, the following has since stuck in my memory.

"After we landed, we faced mortar and machine gun fire that pinned us down on the beach. So we all laid down broiling in the hot sun unable to move forward, practically dying of thirst. All day we passed our emptied canteens to the rear to be refilled at the landing crafts that were also beached to support the units pinned down, and then sent back out to us. Finally, a colonel, an older man who was among us, stood up with his pistol waving us forward with it, telling us, 'Okay boys, time to get up and go kill these bastards so we can finish up and go home.'"

His story ended there, and history records that thousands of Marines died on the beaches and inland on the island, more so than the Japanese defenders. I did not ask him about the Jerome Relocation Center. I had thought better to let sleeping dogs lie.

There was a pond on his property, which worked perfectly for the tanning. "Mysteriously," two deer hides showed up once word got out that I needed them. Venison was part of the local diet, and I realized they hunted when necessity said to. The store owner also had a pile of old 2x4 boards I could use. I bought some cordage he had in his store, and, I guess it was no surprise, fresh hog brains — as they were also part of the local diet!

The summer sun was still on the hot side so I completed the tanning in no time and shipped them to the Indian Trader, who would send them back to me later during the Horse Trek. He would trim the finished leather to the size and shape he wanted me to work with. He also provided the dyed porcupine quills in the traditional Sioux colors and the design he wanted me to follow.

On my last night at the shopkeeper's house, just before dark, I settled in the bed of his guest room, where I had been staying all along. My plan was to awaken early and get back on the trail leading me to the west before turning north. As I lay there, I began hearing this scratching sound coming from the wall next to the bed.

"What in the hell's that?" I mumbled to myself.

There was still enough light from outside to make out the wall, but I put my little flashlight to it anyway. There was nothing but the wall covered with very aged wallpaper that must have been a hundred years old. I laid back down.

A minute later came more scratching, and I was up again to investigate. This time I ran my hand over the wall paper where I thought I heard the noise coming from. Sliding my hand along, I came upon a slight bulge in the paper. But the bulge was soft and slightly giving. "What the?" And then it moved!

I stood back, noticing that there was a nearby tear in the wall paper. The bulge was moving towards that tear. In less than a minute, the tiny black head of a bat appeared! Seconds later it freed itself and flew out of the room and into the huge hallway that divided the house into two halves. At either end were screen doors, one with a gaping hole. The bat knew where it was going, and in a flash it was gone out the hole for a night of hunting or breeding.

Some time in the pre-dawn morning, it returned and slipped back behind the wall paper. I was still asleep so didn't hear it. But after I arose, I saw the bulge and gently palmed it with my hand, stimulating a slight flutter from the bat's wings.

Before the community arose from its sleep, wherever they were and with whom, the Pinto was saddled and we were gone.

Oat Mountain

Several days later we came upon a large farm. It had a huge barn that housed a giant combine — a grain harvesting machine as big as a house. Outside the barn, there was a mountain of oats. It had to have been 20 or more feet high! Both the Pinto and I eyed it and headed down the gravel drive-way that led to it.

A farmer, an old fellow, came out of his nearby house to greet us. He was friendly and engaging. He told me to turn the Pinto loose and let her graze some of the nearby grass where we were talking. I removed the saddle and let her go. We continued to engage dialogue, me mainly explaining the best I could what the horse and I were up to. I then asked if I could purchase some of his oats for the Pinto.

"Not necessary," he said, "just go over there and get what you want for her."

We both turned in her direction and she was gone.

We both looked about and there she was half way up the mountain of oats! We had a good laugh as I brought her back down. I filled her feed bag with oats, insisted on paying him, which he declined once more.

He invited me in to eat with him and his wife, which I declined amid copious thank-yous. We said our good-byes and the Pinto and I headed west once more.

✝ Christian Camp ✝

Although early fall had by now arrived, so far as the Pinto and I were concerned, it was still a blazing summer. I swear the temperature had to be approaching 120°F midday. I had been in temperatures like that in Arizona once. I thought hell must feel like that, if such a place existed: Enough heat to keep you totally uncomfortable for all eternity, but not quite enough to kill you off and end your misery.

At one point, we stopped to seek relief from the sun under the boughs of a great pine tree. It was so hot I was certain I was going to pass out, and maybe even die. There had been no rain or thunderstorms for months. My throat was as dry and raspy as desert sand. I had taken to wearing my bandana over my face to keep from breathing the dust stirred up by the Pinto's hooves amid an occasional swirl of wind. Such was my state of misery, and I'm certain the Pinto wasn't feeling much better.

I felt sure we were near a river I had plotted on a map earlier in the Horse Trek. But that map had been worn out and tossed away a month earlier. Anyway, we had failed to reach it and I had no idea how much further it lay ahead. If it laid ahead. So, to survive, we once more switched to traveling by the stars at night, and laying low during the days. The lure of cool mountain air in the Ozarks and what that would feel like gave me enough hope to keep pushing us along.

Several small ponds tucked away in the woodlands presented themselves along the way, making the day time camps bearable. Less than a week later we stumbled upon a large stream, actually a small river, cloaked on both sides by dense woods.

I thought, "This must be the river I saw on the map. Hallelujah!"

There was no road that I was aware of nearby, just forest. But who cares? There was only one thing to do: Strip down and head in!

The Pinto required no encouragement and we waded in together up to our necks. It was pure bliss! I carried a small bar of soap I picked up at the gas station store where my last tanning camp occurred. It also served as my shampoo. So I scrubbed myself down from head to toe. After dunking myself in the water for a rinse, I became aware for the first time that my hair, under the weight of the water, had grown down to my ass.

I laughed aloud to the Pinto, "I must look like a wild man — maybe a Sasquatch or something — to a passerby!"

She gave me a very short attentive look, but dismissed me as quickly, unwilling to entertain anything else but the cooling waters of the river.

So, there I stood in the water near the shore, stark naked, while the Pinto stood nearby half-submerged and slowly turning into a freshwater seahorse. It was clear neither of us wanted to leave this forest refuge.

I questioned the Pinto, "Maybe this is where we should ditch the Calling and do our own thing?"

"Talking to a horse now?" You say. Surely I was going mad.

Just then, out of nowhere, came a chorus of giggles. Girl giggles. I looked all around, and I swear out of nowhere was an old bridge just barely down stream, almost overhead! I never noticed it, such was my focus on the cool, healing waters of the river.

Well . . . standing on the bridge, and looking down on us was a flock of older teenage girls, and young ladies, whatever, now breaking into a laugh.

"Who are you?" they pried with one shout. "Are you an Indian?"

I could have passed for an Indian or Hippy, but I'm not sure hippies were in Arkansas back then. I thought they all headed to California, because — recalling the Freak Faire — there sure as hell were thousands of them back there in the Bay Area.

Before I could count to ten, they were off the bridge and heading down to me and the Pinto. I furtively slunk down in the water as my clothes were draped over a rock onshore.

"No, I'm just passing through." I called out. "And what are you all doing here, anyway?"

"Well, in those woods over there," one of the older ones spoke up, while pointing to the west, "is our Church's summer youth retreat."

Not knowing what such a retreat was or what to say, I offered, "Well, that's very nice."

She continued, "That sure is a pretty horse. Does she have a name?"

Like most women — well maybe all women — I learned along the way, horses are a great attraction.

"No, she doesn't have one and she doesn't speak English anyway. I call her Pinto, 'cause that's her color marking."

Came her comeback: "But we heard you talking to her from the bridge. If she doesn't speak English, why were you talking to her? Can Indians really talk with horses?"

I had dug myself into that one.

Feeling corralled, I came up with, "Well, I was just mumbling to myself, wondering where we were going to spend the night before moving on."

"Why don't you come stay with us?" She asked and then answered with a string of good reasons in a single breath, "And then you can eat with us tonight, and we're gonna have a play, and you can camp with the Pinto there too."

"Well, I suppose so." I said, adding a semi-enthusiastic, "Thanks!" At which point they all stood silently staring at me.

"Well then, come on out of the river and let's go," was their unified comeback.

She, they, were already in control ordering me to do this and that. Kajeezzz!

Trying to drop a hint, "Well, I've got to dry off first and get dressed. So I'll find my way over there in a bit. Okay?"

"No," they commanded with the charm of an overbearing schoolmarm, "we'll just wait and show you the way."

I was had. And there was nothing left to do but come out of the water. Sort of like coming out of that OR room, minus the saber-toothed scowl of the Colonel.

"You sure got dark skin and long pretty hair," came a voice, "can we brush it for you?"

"I don't have a brush," I said. "I just tie it in braids, or keep it out of my face with that bandana over there."

I don't know what they did over in that retreat, but my nudity didn't seem to phase this bunch. Maybe it was some kind of New Age Christian nudist camp or something. I would soon find out.

"I've got to dry off a bit on this rock, before I put my clothes on. Maybe you all should just go on ahead, and I'll be right along."

Two of them then left, but the third one stayed put, "I'll just wait here with you until you're ready. I have a brush at our retreat, and I will brush your hair then. Can I hold the horse in the meantime?"

"Sure, here's her halter," I submitted, "just put it on her and bring her over to the sand. She'll want to roll in it and dry off too."

"Good," she exclaimed with delight, "I will brush both of you down."

Once again, I had lost complete control of my life with strong women.

✠

In short time, the hot sun baked me dry, and the Pinto

and I were ready to go with her.

I then offered her, "Would you like to sit in the saddle while we go to your retreat? I'll just walk alongside."

That struck gold with her, and I figured it would set better with the adult chaperons, if there were any.

Ten minutes later, we arrived at the camp.

Alerted by the other girls ahead of us, the camp counselors, all women, were right on me near the retreat's entrance. I assumed they were on the way to the river to rescue the lone girl the others had left behind.

The first thing to go was my rifle, "We'll keep that for you until you've moved along," my Christian overseers decreed as they freed it from its scabbard.

They had a corral for some reason, and pointing to it, "We'll keep your horse for you too, and we've got hay she can eat."

The younger ladies then took over, and off we went to see the place.

There were lots of small buildings with screened windows, which, thinking of mosquitoes again, made sense for a summer gathering. A large fire pit for after-dark gatherings and singing was near the center of the camp. I recall there was also something that resembled a stage, and I figured that's where they were going to have their religious enactment from the Bible. And I guess where their preacher, a young man slightly older than myself, would give his sermons.

I was amazed by the outgoing friendliness of everyone there, maybe fifty girls and the camp counselors. I don't recall seeing any boys, teenaged or otherwise. But at the same time I felt like a fish out of water. After a bit of friendly greetings and well wishes, I decided to retreat to the edge of the woods where the Pinto was in lockup.

I sat down against this big tree, realizing how tired and drained I was. I gazed half awake at the Pinto, "Why don't you lay down and get some sleep too. We're going to leave this place before dawn."

I was ready to fall asleep myself, when the young lady who stayed behind at the river appeared and sat down beside me. She wanted to talk. I sensed the other girls got the hint and stayed behind.

"Can you tell me why you're doing this ride across the country?" she asked.

A fair question, but how to answer her?

"Well, I don't know that it's actually a cross-country ride, because I don't really know when it's supposed to end or where I'm heading exactly." I told her in a soft voice.

She seemed like a gentle soul to me.

"Is Jesus telling you to do this?" she asked.

"I suppose so, if you want to look at it that way," I said. "There's this thing, a voice in my head, that I think of as a spiritual 'Calling.' It directs me. It began after I had this Vision of me being with the Pinto on a mountain. The Vision was about this beautiful change occurring in the world as I saw it."

Maybe thinking I was some kind of lower level prophet serving Jesus, she probed further, "In your Vision, have you seen Jesus?"

Here I potentially entered dangerous territory. I didn't really know anything about this Jesus.

My father had taken me aside when I was young and told me, "I'm not letting your mother send you to any church or religious order. You're going to have to find your own spiritual path in life."

Which I did, but which amounted to nothing really. Except nature and the mysterious universe. I gambled a response . . .

"Well," I fictionalized, "Jesus has long hair and great skin. Jesus is very beautiful."

"How old does he look?" she pressed me.

"Jesus doesn't appear to be a 'he.'" I answered.

"What?" she blurted out loudly with a giant frown on her face.

"From what I could see in the Vision, Jesus is a beautiful woman." I knew right then I was in blasphemous trouble of the worst kind.

Clearly miffed, she retaliated with a tone, "You didn't see Jesus, did you?"

"Well, I thought I did. Maybe he has a sister?"

To tell the truth, I had never read the Bible, although I once tried. I got lost at the very beginning when I began to question where Adam and Eve's boys got their wives? So I never got to the part about Jesus.

Young, pretty, naïve, and trusting, is how she seemed to me. I decided to not draw her into the dark side of the Horse Trek I had experienced up to that point. Or to dwell on the uncertainty and promise of hardships that plagued my role in it.

"Can I bring you something to eat now?" she asked, without a hint of an invitation to eat with the others.

"That would be nice," I said. "I have to leave early in the morning, before sunrise. Maybe you could ask your camp counselor to bring me my stuff in time for me to leave. I would appreciate that."

A little later she brought me a small bag with some food ready to eat, and some things I could take with me. I sensed she wanted to stay, but I told her it's probably best that she return to her friends.

"Please thank them for me, and thank you too for your kindness" I added, and she left, no doubt thinking I was a lost cause or soul. I never saw her, nor the others, again.

As I sat there eating, I had my first encounter with a very strange insect. What I thought was a small twig, maybe 8 inches or so long, that had fallen from the tree and onto my pant leg, started moving up my leg.

"What the heck?!" I blurted out in a knee-jerk response.

I looked closer only to see that it had legs. I learned later it was what locals called a "walking stick," and that's exactly what it looked like to me. Turned out this species could also spray an acidic fluid into the eyes of a predator, including people. But as had been my experience all along, wildlife caused me no harm. I offered my hand and it slowly climbed up my arm, stopping on my shoulder, then across to my chest.

I let it be there, reflecting on what I had been told by

The Ouachita Mountains "walking stick" insect.

the Métis years ago: The rhythm of the heartbeat, applied to the Indian's drumbeat, signaled a unity among all living things." In the still and quiet of the forest, I sensed this wild animal could feel the Ancient Calling in my own heart beat. After some minutes, I could feel the stick animal leaving me and climbing up the tree.

🐴

Darkness was beginning to fall. Just as I started to doze off, I was quietly approached by several counselors with the rifle, my saddle, and other belongings. They laid these down beside me without a word, and left as quickly as they arrived. I decided to get the Pinto out of the corral and

266

stake her out next to me. That was our way, and I saw no need to change the pattern here and now.

Other wildlife let me alone that night, and I was able to sleep deeply and restfully. The Pinto, in short while, lay down on her side too, twitching as she always did in her own deep dream state. Two species, two souls, on a journey together with no known destination.

Ouachita Mountains

The Ouachitas are a mountain range in southwestern Arkansas, rising off the western flanks of the Piney Forest that the Pinto and I were now leaving. "Ouachita" is thought to be a word of the Choctaw peoples, possibly meaning "land of the buffalo" or maybe "hunting ground."

Long ago, buffalo roamed the lower reaches of the Ouachita range along its western edges. But they met the same fate as those millions roaming upon the Great Plains as the forces of Manifest Destiny ravaged their populations for commerce and profits. In the 16th century, 25–30 million bison (also called buffalo) inhabited North America. As a species, they were hunted almost to extinction in the 19th century. Less than 600 remained in the wild by the late 1880s, although some historians think possibly less than 100. Which is to say, "There ain't no buffalo in the Ouachita no more.'"

My attraction to the Ouachita mountains meant higher elevations with the possibility of a cooler, early autumn than in the Timberlands or delta country below. But this wasn't the case at all. It was just as hot, so we returned to night riding as before. I was also aware that most of the range I would be passing through was on U.S. government land. So I could fish, even hunt if need be, and travel more freely without distressing local private land owners . . . or curious Christian ladies.

Weeks passed as we slowly moved up, down and over

The Ouachita Mountains just east of Oklahoma. Here Caney Creek flowed through these rugged ridges and peaks. I contemplated wintering here.

successive fingers of mountain ridges with intermittent streams. The solitude was as welcome and refreshing to my soul as were the protected clean waterways we bathed in between our night rides.

The Calling charted us north by northwest through the great forests of the Ouachita Mountains. Locals told me about the Caney Creek Wilderness Area in the Ouachitas that lie in the Calling's general path to the west. And that the area would serve my nomadic needs for survival. So I set my compass in that direction, but fully expected that the Calling might decide otherwise and turn me towards the north. But I still had to traverse the entire width of the state just to get there. And that alone might take a month or more. As usual, only time would tell.

Rattlesnake Healing

So, here in these mountains were, if not the most memorable experiences of the trek, certainly the strangest. I had learned about a remote Forest Service campground reached only be trails some miles ahead. I was told there was a hand driven water pump, like one of those old time "pitcher pumps" found in rural schools. Counting on that, we would cross through stretches of forest lands where otherwise there was no indication of water.

Locals also said that there was some beautiful views, virgin stands of trees, and rock outcroppings worth seeing. I suspect the Calling had some other purpose in heading me in that direction though. That became clear halfway to our destination atop one of the many spectacular ridges along our path. So I switched back to day riding to take in the views. The sense of being beyond any road, alone in a wilderness setting like in some of those canoe treks, and in a beautiful spot rewarded me for whatever hardships I had to endure during the Horse Trek.

I decided to set camp for the night. Perhaps it was the dense canopy atop this mountain that rendered a cooler evening than in the lower reaches of the Timberlands and delta country, where one baked endlessly in the sun and heat. Even nighttime brought little relief! Whatever the case, as I was preparing camp, to one side I spotted what appeared to be a rattlesnake coiled up.

I inched closer to see and was met by the tell-tale warning of the snake's eponymous rattle. I had been confronted by rattlesnakes in the past, but always made my peace by circling around them to get by, or letting them go first. But the rattling of this snake was distinctively different. It lacked the volume and ferocity of a rattler who was fearful and threatening. To me, it seemed faint, weak even, lacking vitality. Perhaps something was wrong with it.

As it made no indication to leave, I moved closer to investigate. If this was to be our campsite, I needed to know what this rattler was doing here and why it hadn't taken flight.

I got close enough to see that it was injured, part of it's flesh midway down its body was torn open. I thought maybe it was a failed taking by an owl or Eagle, as they were known to live in this area and are predatory towards snakes.

The rattling then mysteriously ceased, and the snake, still coiled, simply lay still with its eyes open and focused on me.

The Calling then moved upon me, "Leave the snake there. You will heal her in your sleep."

It was messaging like this that drove me to wit's end. How does a person heal anything in their sleep? And why this rattler? Aren't we supposed to let nature take its course in the wild?

I had the Pinto staked far enough away to keep her out of trouble. But I wasn't comforted one bit thinking that somehow me and the snake were going to be having some kind of midnight healing rendezvous in my makeshift bed.

I prayed it wasn't somehow going to take place in the flesh: Like her fangs in my flesh.

The time had come to settle in and try to sleep. Nothing more came from the Calling to quiet my nerves. Slowly, but surely, the drain of the day ascending the mountain taxed my well of energy and I began to drift off into sleep.

But this passage towards sleep was also very much in the surrealism of the Vision, and in it I was given to solace and a sense of inner peace. Like other profound or mysterious encounters with other wild animals I faced earlier in the Horse Trek, so it was that the snake entered into this new Vision as a fellow soul in need of help, not a predatory threat.

As the Calling had messaged, the rattler uncoiled and moved quickly in my dream state. I was astonished by its speed, yet I felt no fear. In the next moment she lay stretched out, head to rattle, along my right side. She then began to press tightly against my body. The power of this pressure seemed more real than surreal. I sensed this reptile's pain as she quivered in tiny spasms that traversed her body, from head and tail towards the wounded flesh.

As I lay there, a fleeting memory came to me: One never falls asleep when a snake or other venomous creature is in contact with you. To frighten them with any movement is to welcome an attack. But the thought was drowned out as quickly as it had arrived. Instead, I began to feel comforted by my visitor and even relaxed as the pressure of the snake began to soften. I left the dream state and descended into sleep. Perhaps a part of each of us had been liberated in deep sleep. Even the Pinto lay stretched out, quivering in deep sleep too.

Come morning I awakened to find no sign of the snake anywhere. I got up and searched the area. Nothing. I contemplated what had happened. Perhaps the healing occurred as the Calling had commanded? But what I can share here is that this "visionary sleep state" is a healing one, and that brings me to my next Ouachita Mountains story.

Defying Death — a Healing

Within two days of the apparent reptilian healing we approached the Forest Service campground. To get to it, we somehow had to wind our way down the side of this saddle-back ridge. It was steep, but there was a remnant of what looked like an old Indian or animal trail etched in the side of the mountain. I have wondered if this wasn't used at one time by the Caddo people who once lived and hunted in these mountains before the arrival of De Soto.

I speculated, "Maybe this path would get us down to where we needed to be?"

There was no turning back, so off we went down the side of the mountain, slowly, actually warily, as some parts were outcrops of some kind of shale that seemed almost brittle and possibly unstable.

Along several stretches, I dismounted and led the Pinto on foot as here and there slabs of this rock were actually slippery. Without me on her back, the Pinto could set her hooves to her advantage. I would do the same.

As we got midway down, the hillside began to morph into cliffs here and there and suddenly we found the trail and ourselves literally niched into walls of rock.

Part of me was saying, "Turn back and find another way down." Another inner voice joined in, "This is an animal trail, not for humans." But those inner voices were mine, not the Calling's. We would continue downward.

Not soon enough, our cliff-hanging turned back into a

less daunting descent with the trail leveling into a less precipitous and precarious slope.

The trail was actually a zigzag of sorts, a planned switchback trail as I read it, which unfortunately put us back on new veins of unstable shale. After an hour or so of this meandering, with more mounting and dismounting along the way, the campsite came into full view below, and not too far off.

As we continued down a bit further, immediately below us, maybe several hundred feet, was a graveled Forest Service road. I anticipated that our trail would intersect it at some point soon, and I began to feel a sense of relief. This was a mistake as I then became less vigilant with our footing.

🐎

As was often the case along our way since we started this Horse Trek, I would take notice of nature's beauty all around us. This forested mountainside was no different, offering spectacular glimpses here and there as far as the eye can see of nature's wilderness bounty. As we descended the path, I was mesmerized by the distant rows of herringbone like ridges forged one after another, no doubt during our planet's violent formative youth.

But at the same time, it weighed heavily on me that my life had come to spending less and less time with my fellow humans. My company was now the many voices and presentations of nature, animal sounds of all kinds, gurgling steams, leaves chattering in a howling wind, and the stars and meteor showers I counted in the night as I fell off to sleep. "Had it been already a month since I last heard a human voice and experienced a human presence?" I had no idea.

The Calling had put me at the edge of civilization and its din had increasingly abated in my mind. I began to feel like an alien species, a wilderness animal. Things like getting an education, having a career, planning a family, going to movies and watching television, were now remote abstractions. But, yet, the Horse Trek was not aimless wandering either. It was as directed as it was supernatural, and I learned to listen for the Calling's guidance.

In all of this, the Pinto and I had developed a strange manner of communication, a mere thought and gesture had specific meaning between us. It evolved from survival, I speculated, contrived by nature and its latent mystical forces — not by wishful thinking from my side.

Nor was it a Messianic Calling because I don't believe anyone's coming down from above to save anyone's ass. It was simply a Quest based upon a nascent Vision that promised good. Nothing more than that, though I felt hard pressed into it by the Calling that drummed away within me.

🜚

The trail, now ever closer to the bottom, narrowed into the steepest decline yet. In the very moment I took notice, the shale suddenly gave out beneath us. I imagined it like the trap door of the executioner's hanging scaffold releasing its victim into a terrifying freefall.

Down we went completely out of control. I have no recollection to this day if I was saddled on the Pinto, actively dismounting, or leading her as I peered down the steep mountainside. All I remember is the two of us falling, tumbling, one over the other, again and again and again, totally without any sense of orientation. In my mind's eye, I recall the Pinto sideways going over the top of me, but with little or no pressure, then me lifting and going over the top of her. Gravity had taken over, pulling us ever downward to the destination below.

We had landed hard on the graveled forest service road that looked like it hadn't been used in years. I think one or both of us had been briefly unconscious, because I remember opening my eyes like from a sleep. As I came to my senses, I realized what had just happened. I turned my head and there lay the Pinto next to me. I called out to her.

She gave a groan and began to get up. I tried to do the same, but realized my right leg wasn't right, and was now in great pain. The telltale feeling of broken bone revealed itself — a break in my lower leg.

In a flash, my survival instinct told me to grab the saddle horn as the Pinto began to raise herself. The saddle had not torn loose, and miraculously, it wasn't damaged at all. Soon, I was pulled up and standing on one leg at her side. Before I lifted myself onto the saddle, I noticed that a large flap of skin the size of a saucer plate had ripped loose from her chest. The raw flesh underneath was exposed, but it didn't seem to bother her.

I realized then and there that we were both in what many would call a medical emergency. My leg felt like it, and her chest looked like it too. Before panic could set in, I was greeted once more by the Calling that directed me to go straight to the campground ahead. It was only a short distance away, to our good fortune. I pulled myself up and onto the saddle. Due to the pain in my damaged leg, I forsook the stirrups and let my foot dangle freely, although that didn't help the pain any, really.

It wasn't much of a campsite. There was one sturdy wooden picnic-like table that had to have been put together 45 years earlier in the New Deal by one of those conservation corps battalions. And there was the hand water pump I had counted on, and which was in working order. A small trough lie below the pump's spigot, which I filled with water for the Pinto to drink from.

I staked the Pinto to the table and fate would have it that ample dry forage surrounded us. She immediately took to eating, ignoring her own injury.

But not so ignorable for me. My leg began to swell beneath my leather cowboy style work boot. I lifted my Levi pant leg up enough to reveal small amounts of blood oozing from the top of the boot. The pain was practically unbearable. Removing the boot was an impossible task, as now my back began to throb in pain too, and bending over only added to my misery. What next? Leaving it on, I limped my way to the trough and drenched myself in a splash of cool water. I filled my canteen, now bearing a dent from the fall, from the spigot. From the saddlebag I took out some jerky and pemmican to eat. I sat at the table pondering what would come next.

The weather was still unbearably hot. But I was grateful that we had water, forage for the Pinto, and enough food for me to survive. But for how long? And the pain, not mitigating, grew worse and worse.

I understood pain. I had been a medical corpsman in the Army. I saw men in pain, one with half his side completely blown away, and still he lived. I don't know how long he lived, because I never saw him again. But he was in extraordinary pain. It was frightening to see and hear him cry out. I've thought about him and others wounded in battle many times since then: Surely young men would not want anything to do with guns and war if they really only knew and saw and heard what I witnessed and dealt with. There is no glory for the victim of such violence. Better that people talk things out. As the hippies cried out in the '60s, "Make love, not war." Much better, I believe.

It was midafternoon, and nightfall was still a ways off. I began to think about what I should do next. But the intense pain had its own mind and decided for me: "You aren't going anywhere." It was true. I could barely move and we were many miles from reaching any rural settlement, let alone a medical clinic.

And there was no indication that forest service workers had been here recently. And maybe, I thought, they wouldn't be returning at all for the rest of the season. In fact, it was clear to me that no one had been here for a long time. There wasn't even a trash can, a clue that maybe only hunters came here during the hunting season and packed their garbage out. I accepted my fate: No one was likely to come and rescue me, and I was too disabled to get out of here on my own. Maybe, I hoped, if I rested for several days, I could get the boot off, make a splint, and ride out of here.

Night came and went. I didn't sleep a wink. The pain wouldn't let up. I began to contemplate the possibility of going into shock. Or with daybreak, maybe someone would just show up miraculously and get me to a doctor. No such luck.

The next day dragged on and on, minutes feeling like hours. I began to despair. A foreboding sense of the morbid possibility of dying in the middle of nowhere began to sink into my thoughts. As at the gate incident. The Calling, I now speculated, was nothing more than early senility setting in. Proof that the Vision was nothing more than an illusion infused with delusional thinking. But I was only in my late-twenties, so, delusional maybe, senility no way. I simply had to face reality and take some kind of action. But what?

I now faced another night on the bench with no let up in the pain. Soon, twilight fell upon us.

I spoke to the Pinto, "I'm thinking once again to cut you loose and let you find your way out of here. The pain is just too much and I feel like I'm beginning to lose it."

The heat, the uncertainty, and the pain were truly taking their toll on me, both physically and psychologically. The Pinto's flesh still hung down and I began to feel again the dread and guilt of having brought another living soul into my Vision, only to cause her harm.

The Pinto stood close by. I sensed her half-relaxing and half-waiting for me to direct our course of action, as it had always been. Twilight now descended into darkness and the forest surrounding us became still and quiet. Uncannily so.

The pain now worsened even more. "It is clear," I thought, "I am now going to die."

If only the pain would go away, I would accept this fate unconditionally. Death maybe wasn't such a terrible thing after all. What do all those Indians say in the movies, as I tried to dredge up a smile, "This is a good day to die."

I looked up into the sky with its galaxy of shimmering stars and planets, and the pain began to fade away. As it did, my eyes began to close as I succumbed to my fatality in peace.

Whether I actually died or not, or entered another plane of existence, I'll never know with absolute certainty. But I did enter into a strange dream with no specific details that I can recollect, except a bizarre sense of an impending resurrection. From the dead, who knows? I then fell into a deep sleep with no memory of any other dreams.

At some point, my eyes opened and it was early daylight. The Pinto still stood near, like a faithful friend, or guardian, or healer. Previous experiences I've shared in this Horse Trek are revealing that I had already become a believer in spiritual powers greater than what we are otherwise led to believe and accept from powers invested in modern or alternative medicine — or even religious sacraments contingent upon faith.

I've related earlier in my story that I had never gone to church, nor was I raised in a religious dogma or belief system. Some Biblical stories I had heard about on the street sounded okay, but I could never get past the suggestion of castrated Cherubs and frocked female Angels flying around in Outer Space with wings growing out of their backs. Give me a break, what a turn off! I mentioned earlier in my story, that my father told me I must find my own spiritual path in life. This enabled me to open my eyes and mind to the mysteries and revelations of a spiritual life evoked by nature. Such an outlook is the antithesis of atheism, and a welcome corridor to a genuine spiritual life. Or so it has unfolded to me. And I am one not to have asked for any of it.

🐎

The first thing I noticed upon awakening was that the loose flap of the Pinto's hide was no longer hanging but had fully healed and there was no sign of the injury.

The Calling then abruptly intervened and commanded me, "Get up and leave, now!"

Without a second thought, I did. There was no pain and no visible sign of the injury, except some spotting of blood on my sock above the boot. I walked as normally as I ever had.

The Calling spoke again, directing me to a small settlement at the outskirts of the forest. There, I was told, an event would happen that would explain what had happened to me. But my map had indicated no such nearby community.

Elated, but guarded in thought, that I had actually undergone a healing of some sort, we set out to find whatever village I was supposed to somehow recognize and become enlightened by. In the early morning of the next day, we reached the settlement, where I partook in yet another surreal experience of the Horse Trek, surely the most bizarre.

Medical Clinic

That something was strange about this settlement, which bordered the forest, became apparent the moment we arrived. I thought at the time it must have been a Sunday morning because there was no visible movement in the community. There weren't many homes or business storefronts. Similar to the plantation village back in Mississippi, houses and businesses were strung out along the little traveled two-lane paved country highway, with maybe a few houses scattered here and there in the forested area behind them. It didn't take long before the directive of the Calling made sense.

The first building I came upon was, in fact, a medical clinic. I assumed I was to go in, but from the side of the building there was no evidence that it was open — no cars, no people, nothing, all adding up to the possibility it was all an illusion. That I was dead, and this is what dead people go through. But it wasn't an illusion and I was alive.

I began to hear a slight bustle of people moving about somewhere in the community, though I saw no one. I thought, they're probably on their way to church, because once more it seemed like it was a Sunday morning. But I had no real idea what day it was. Long ago in the early months of the Horse Trek, I never concerned myself with the day of the week, or the date. In retrospect, it didn't seem to really matter then, or now either.

The land immediately next to the clinic was pasture-like, not a conventional parking lot one might expect next to a medical clinic. It was sparse with dry, dormant grasses and brush of some type or another, all withering in an early but still hot and dry "Indian summer." I pulled the saddle off the Pinto and staked her out on the long line, then went around to the front of the building to see if any of this was real.

The front door was not locked, so I let myself in. There sitting at a reception desk was a very old woman (in her late 80s or 90s I thought) dressed in a white colored nurse's uniform, including the traditional white cap they wear. She was all alone. From here on things got really weird, to say the least.

"Hello," she greeted me in a pleasant voice. "We've been expecting you!"

"Well, I'm not sure why," I responded, feeling like an idiot.

Why would a person walk into a doctor's office not knowing exactly why they're supposed to be there? A minor matter, under the circumstances, because how could they be expecting me in the first place? And why are they open at the break of dawn? And on a Sunday, if, in fact, that was the day of the week?

Ignoring my confusion, she said, "That's okay, let me take you to the examination room. The doctor will be in shortly to see you." She was as kind and respectful as her impeccably neat uniform was professional.

So she got up and led me into the examination room, which also had an x-ray machine in it. "He will be here in just a moment," and then she departed to her desk up front.

I had no idea what was going to happen next. It was the Calling's work, and I had learned to trust it with my life. The examination room was similar to other doctors' offices I had been in. The doctor arrived almost as quick as the nurse left.

"Good morning, sir," he greeted me also in a pleasant voice.

He was as old as the nurse, with a shock of white hair neatly groomed, and wearing the traditional doctor's white coat with a stethoscope hanging from his neck. He had in hand what I surmised was my medical chart, which he studied briefly.

Not knowing what to say, or what to expect, I replied in turn, "Good morning, doctor."

Lifting his eyes from the chart, he said, "We'll need to take an x-ray of your leg. But first, I wish to examine it."

He then immediately left the room.

The nurse promptly returned as quick as he left with a gown, which she asked me to put on after removing my Levis and boots. She then left, and I put it on, and the doctor was back like clockwork.

"Okay, young man," he greeted me again. "Come sit here on the table."

I did and he took my pulse and listened to my heart.

"Now, lay down here so I can examine your leg." I did, and he ran his hand over where the leg had been broken.

He said, "I see that there is no bruising or lacerations

to your leg, and the color looks good. Let's take that x-ray now."

The x-ray was taken.

"You can put your clothes back on, and leave the gown on the table." He then left, and I changed back into my clothes. The nurse returned on point to tell me it would be a few minutes before the doctor returned with the x-ray. She then offered me something to drink, which I declined, "No thank you, ma'am."

A short while later, the doctor returned to the examination room. Holding up the x-ray over his light box, he informed me, "I see there was quite the fracture here that has healed very nicely."

I didn't know what to say.

"You can go now, everything looks very good." He turned and left the room, leaving the door open. I walked out into the waiting room, where the nurse had returned to her desk.

"Thank you for coming in," she said.

"And the doctor says you are good to go!" She added in a cheerful voice.

I was starting to ask what I owed when she interrupted me in a surprisingly stern voice, "There is no charge for seeing you today. We believe it is time for you to return to your very important journey."

I thought to myself, "They know more than I do about the purpose of the Vision."

I thanked her again, and headed out the door.

As I saddled the Pinto, I took notice that the settlement still sounded like there was activity. If there were people living there, however, I never actually saw any. But to this very day, I cannot forget this strange encounter with these two very elderly and kind medical professionals.

To the North Country

We retreated back into the forested and mountainous back country. But we now headed due north instead of more westerly towards the Caney Creek Wilderness Area, as I had anticipated. This would be the last and least eventful leg of our Horse Trek journey — in the paranormal sense. But an important one in terms of our destination in the Boston Mountains, and what I would be doing there. In fact, the Calling now revealed to me, that in this north country I would be preparing for the final leg of the Vision Quest — still unknown to me at this point in the Horse Trek.

The plan, as I understood it, was to reach the Buffalo River watershed before the end of fall, find campsites, possibly tan a few more hides, try to survive the winter, and continue to the west again in the early spring. But my stay in the north country of this state — through which the strikingly beautiful Buffalo River meandered through — would last more than a few years.

The Buffalo River is thought by historians to be named after the general region called "Cibola" as recorded in a late 1700 Spanish land grant. It is an Indian word for the iconic American Bison. Whether or not the animals actually foraged in this upper river basin in the days of the Spanish Conquistadors who came through this area is debatable. But it seems unlikely to me given the dense forests and many cliffs that trace its course, none of which would favor a foraging animal given to travel in enormous herds.

The river had only a few years before my arrival been anointed with "National Scenic River" status and government protection. Many locals, allied with the U.S. Army Corp of Engineers, actually wanted it dammed for various reasons. But their local congressman, whom I met many years after the Horse Trek, stood against it, and helped secure its protection. Not everyone was happy about it though. I heard later that he was once fired upon by a recalcitrant local ensconced atop a cliff while the congressman was conducting a tour of the river by canoe.

The river was to be my home "on the move," while trying to avoid park rangers for part of the first winter. It wasn't long though before the Calling soon had me integrate with the local community — probably to keep me from being arrested and jailed! My stay turned out to be a temporary hiatus during which time I created a new career for myself. At the time, however, I didn't realize the relevance of my new profession to the Vision. That connection would have to wait — because the Calling was still not done preparing me for the Vision's revelation. But I digress from my present situation.

The Ouachita mountain ranges, most of which were within State and National Forest government lands, reached to the north where I was now heading. They provided me with refuge from larger local communities that sparsely dotted the state's landscape. Numerous meadows provided forage for the Pinto, and water was plentiful. As in Mississippi, small local settlements provided me with supplies for my own needs. Thinking about it, the extraordinary lands I traveled through provided me with a lifestyle that many would consider a dream vacation — aside from the weekly trials the Calling was putting me through.

I soon reached a gap in one mountain range that coursed northward. Through the gap passed a river bearing the Indian name for the Caddo peoples who once lived in the area. Local legend inscribed on a statue erected by the State's (history) archivists said that a local Caddo band, the Tula, skirmished here in battle with Conquistadors of the Spanish explorer Hernando de Soto, whom I've mentioned previously. This was during his 1541 expedition across what 300 years later would become the Southeastern United States, where my Horse Trek began. Historians are fairly certain that de Soto's army traveled somewhat north of my own route, 430 years earlier in October, by coincidence I think possibly the same month I passed through the gap. I had wondered if I would ever intersect their path. The claim on the monument said this was the spot. But the Calling soon deigned otherwise, of which I'll discuss shortly.

We came through the gap, and then pushed on to the north again, setting camp twice over a two days ride. It was here, during the second night in yet another pass, that the Calling shrouded me once more in an ominous sense of inner darkness with a different Vision.

Here where I camped, de Soto's men, in the hundreds, clashed violently with Tula warriors, who, in the end, were repelled. The Tula may have been related to the Caddo peoples. Much blood was shed, including de Soto's horses. Historians today believe that this encounter weakened the resolve, stamina, and resources of de Soto's soldiers and forced the expedition's retreat back to the Mississippi River. But, according to the Calling, the battle did not take place at Caddo Gap. It occurred two day's ride to the north in my present location — half way to the Arkansas River from the gap.

🐎

Not far from the Tula battle site, I decided to set another camp with a nearby stream born from a jewel of a natural spring I could drink from. Both the Pinto and I were trail worn and we needed a break. My supplies and what I could gather from the stream, coupled to ample dry forage for the Pinto in our private meadow, meant we could stay for awhile.

Here, I felt the first early wisps of welcomed cooler air in the breezes, down from the north. Fall was coming. I had kept a large smoked buckskin I tanned earlier in the Trek under the saddle — a makeshift saddle blanket — and I decided to make myself gloves from part of it. The bulk of it continued under the saddle as before. The gloves were something productive to do while we camped out. But I was always busy making things like this, sometimes from dire need.

Later, in the Buffalo River country, I made myself a new buckskin shirt from deerskins I got from local hunters. I then turned the well-worn remnant I was now using as a

Me and the Pinto in the Ozark Mountains a bit later in my story near an old abandoned homestead. That's the buckskin shirt I made from deer skins I tanned the Indian way along the Little Buffalo River.

saddle blanket over to a woman who made moccasins (that she wore daily) and other items with it. By winter, I had also crafted a full length coat with a hood made of Icelandic Sheepskins with fur nearly a foot long. I got these hides, already tanned, through a trade with a band of gypsies who were traveling through the area in a horse pulled covered wagon fitted with automobile tires! That may seem far fetched, but not that many decades earlier, many rural Americans were still using horses and wagons. But, again, I digress and am ahead of myself. At this point in the Horse Trek, I've still not reached the Arkansas River.

Tipi Village

And so we retreated and sequestered in the heavily forested and mountainous back country of the uppermost
reaches of the Ouachitas. Midway during our stay in the
camp with the fresh water spring, the Pinto and I ventured
out to explore some of the surrounding countryside. On
one of these forays, maybe a mile from our secluded campsite, we stumbled upon a huge encampment of Indian tipis
and old time miners' tents surrounded by a ring of covered
wagons. They were situated in a large meadow.

I couldn't believe my eyes, "What is this?" I spoke
aloud.

But there weren't any Indians in it, nor "settlers" and
"miners" for that matter either, at least that I could see. But
there were many horses and mules, enough to pique the
Pinto's interest too.

I decided to venture closer to see if this was another of
the Calling's doings, or something else. We weren't a
stone's throw away when out of the tents came a pack of
screaming teenagers running towards us. They were a mix
of males and females of high school age.

Soon they warned me in words to the effect, "Do not
enter the 'sacred circle.'" I wondered if this was some kind
of New Age gathering.

Joining them almost immediately were young adults. I
assumed these were camp counselors or guides or something.

The Pinto and I stood motionless, silent, and just stared at the spectacle. Soon they calmed down and shifted their attention to the horse and rider (me), as I said not a word. They continued to stay on their side of their "sphere of intolerance."

Without asking a single question of me, they began to explain what they were about. In short, they were an entourage of young troubled souls who had escaped incarceration by agreeing to endure life "on the trail" with their counselors. It was clear to me, this was to squeeze out their teenage rebelliousness that apparently led many into drug addiction and other anti-social behaviors. So, for them, it was about healing their souls and rejoining the human race in a better way.

I listened in continued self-imposed silence and wondered if they wondered what I was all about. Perhaps I wasn't entertaining enough as they began to retreat back into their village amid much chattering. Without having said a word, I turned the Pinto and we loped away in the direction we came from. I can't recall the exact date, but it seemed to be a year or more later that I ran into them again further north. I heard also that there were other such wagon trains, all of which were to meet up in a great rendezvous somewhere. But after the last encounter, which didn't really differ much from the present one, I never heard of them again.

North to the Ozark Mountains

Fall was beginning to show itself as cooler air was now beginning to stream down from the north almost nightly. I decided to break camp and cross the Arkansas River, a major natural boundary line that divided the state in half from north to south. I had never seen it before. It was powerful with a bold and swift current, though lacking the majesty of the Mississippi.

I reflected on de Soto's expedition which may have camped on its shores right where we stood. It also divided the Ouachita from the Boston Mountains, a stately chain that formed the southernmost stretches of its mother range, called the Ozarks. Our objective was to cross these mountains and reach the Buffalo River, set a winter camp along its banks, and prepare for winter. If the fall turned warm again, I would also seek out more hides to tan before winter shut me down. But for now, I sought out how to cross the river before us.

Like the Mississippi River, the Arkansas, which fed the Mississippi further east, posed a current too strong, water too deep, and a width too great, to swim across like we did in lesser bodies of flowing water in the Ouachitas. To our great fortune, nearby was a fairly low-level constructed bridge hardly above the water line, which provided us with a perfect crossing. In those days, traffic on this bridge was minimal compared to the present — if that bridge even exists today.

A pullover lane existed to one side, which we would take to avoid any traffic. But fate would have it that this would not be enough. And for the second time in the Horse Trek, I felt compelled to draw my rifle from its scabbard.

We were nearly across to the other side when I heard the roar of someone gunning their engine behind us. It was a pickup truck with two young men barreling down behind us in our side lane. It was clear they were intentionally aiming for us, weaponizing their vehicle, or maybe a bad joke. For a split second, I considered jumping the rail with the Pinto to make water and take our chances there. Instinctively, instead, I pulled the rifle and aimed it directly at the driver, finger to the trigger. This was enough to put the fear of God in him once he saw I meant business. He threw on the brakes and they turned around and sped off. I've asked myself a hundred times since, would I have pulled the trigger had they kept on us? Or jumped the rail? One way or the other, a person has the right to defend themself when their life is being threatened by thugs.

🐎

The Boston Mountains, like the Ouachitas, were heavily forested. Unlike the Ouachitas, they were sprinkled everywhere with back country roads — byways that were rarely paved. At least back then. This worked well for us, keeping us off main roads and away from troublemakers roaming about on them like the two punks I'd just scared off.

Nights were now chilly, and on one occasion I decided

to resort to a campfire to keep warm. The area is noted for its many rocks, of which several I heated in the fire. I placed these in a depression in the ground where I would set the rocks covered with dirt, which held the heat, and which I then laid upon. I then gathered leaves and covered me with them in the depression. I slept in great comfort, blessed by nature with the means of doing so.

The mountains were full of "hill people," many of whom had pioneer ancestors who settled here 150 years earlier. But they were a mix of the "old way" and the "new," as the forces of modernization had not escaped them entirely. Droves of "back to the land" escapees from cities had also found their way here during the 1960's and 70's. Although not being one of either, and given to being more elusive and private, I generally got along with most.

One woman, whose cottage I was riding past, stopped me to talk and offered me some apples she had just taken from her orchard. I clamored over how tasty they were, thanking her profusely. She offered me a room for the night, but I declined, accepting instead a place in the open next to her barn. She did bring me blankets and kept me company until my eyelids forced me to sleep. She was only a tad older than me, but attractive and awakened in me a sudden crave to meld my flesh with hers. The Calling held me back though, saying my time would come again soon.

I left before she awakened in her home the next morning. More than once, I thought about returning to see her again . . . and maybe more than a simple visit. I had relished her company, even thinking about settling roots with her if there was mutual interest. But the Calling had other plans for me, and we never met again.

"God Knows No Stranger"

We trekked north, days into nights, nights into days. We had both grown weary as whatever trail led down, meant having to go back up. I decided to take us to the spine of a long ridge that spanned the entire Boston Mountains range from south to north. No sooner done than we came upon a small, quaint, "old timey" church that sat just off the spine's edge on the eastern side. It was made almost entirely of stone and wood. It struck me as being very old — a pioneer church, I surmised, no doubt serving many generations of Christian families down in the valley below it.

Night had just fallen, yet there was singing going on inside, loud enough, I thought, I could pass by undetected. But the sounds of hooves, the smell of smoky leather, and horse and human breathing, drew their Preacher's attention, and out he came like a guard dog!

But I got in the first word, "I apologize, I didn't mean to interrupt your service. I was just crossing over the ridge."

The Preacher came back in a surprisingly stoic voice, "Come in son, you are the image of campfire, dust, and travail. You are welcome to join us. God knows no stranger."

It was hard to decline. The Pinto was staked out front, and in I went.

The congregation was small, less than a dozen old folks. I was at least 50 years younger than the youngest. The majority were sweet older ladies, whose husbands, I guessed, were not present and had probably passed on. The pews were old, but the wood smooth and polished as though lacquered.

The Preacher took the pulpit. I had expected him to rail against the wicked ways of the world and especially the sins of flesh. I slunk down and cringed at my wanton desires of just two nights before, not to mention my OR escapade. The Calling had clearly brought me here to be punished. But I was spared, as the Preacher's attentions were turned entirely to the old folks, preaching Faith and the Light in the impending meeting with their Lord and treasured loved ones who had passed and were deeply missed.

He then addressed me in a friendly tone, likening me to the quintessential pioneer Arkansas Traveler, perhaps seeking a bed, but shown the good road instead. I think he sensed that I wasn't seeking to set my roots though. Afterwards, a few refreshments were set out along with friendly gossip about this and that down in the valley.

Later, I followed the Preacher outside as he closed and locked the doors as the last Believer exited. A smart wind came down upon us, and the old ladies clutched their sweaters close. The entire bevy of Believers loaded onto a small bus, awaiting their Preacher who would take them all home. But first, as I looked on, he took the Pinto to the rear of the church and re-staked her in another small meadow that had been cleared of brush.

"Why don't you stay here tonight?" he implored. "It will be safe and no one will bother you and your horse."

I accepted. Then he and the congregation trailed off down the side of the mountain.

Fate would have it that I would run into the Preacher several years later. He was as kind jewel of a human then as on this night. He was well along in his years, and I surmised he passed on not long after our last encounter, joining his flock in the Heaven above he so eloquently preached.

"No Such Luck!"

We headed out just before dawn, and my plan was to continue north in search of the upper Buffalo River basin. Since there was no trail or gravel road traversing the spine of the ridge, we headed down the eastern flank of the ridge, and took another graveled bypass on the valley bottom. This diversion added another day of riding to the trek going north.

In the distance, I could see that the spine of the ridge ended in an abrupt bend to the east. The valley road took us to the base of the ridge. A cow trail crept up its southern flank and I decided to take it. I also realized we were now on private property. But I decided to take the trail up anyway. It was steep in places, but the footing was solid, unlike the one from which we took the calamitous fall a month or more earlier in the Trek. I didn't want to repeat that, for sure!

We eventually scaled the summit, and found ourselves in a forest. An old, unpaved ranch road, almost a trail itself, lie just ahead. Once on it, I noticed it traversed the narrow spine of the ridge, trailing both westward and eastward, the latter rising upward towards a peak.

I thought, "Could this be the peak in the Vision?"

The Pinto's ear radar, pointing west, suggested otherwise. But I overrode her, hoping to discover the meaning of the Vision going east and put an end to the Vision and the Horse Trek once and for all. In my defense, going east did look promising. For one, there were steep cliffs on either side of the ridge, just as in the Vision. Plus the peak I could see from the valley bottom we had just departed. And not to forget the Pinto with me on her back!

We soon passed what looked like an old pioneer cemetery on the right, tucked away in a small clearing. I got off the Pinto to take a closer look. It was just that — the birth dates on the tombstones, not all of which were legible due to the wear and tear of the ages, dated back into the early 1800s, and maybe the 1700s. The names indicated it was an extended family, possibly two. There was something warm and comforting to my soul about it: Relatives who had pioneered this mountain top, worked the land together, died here, and finally were buried here in the privacy of the forested ridge of their homeland. Part of me thought this is something I would want too. But I had no such homeland, nor even a speck of land anywhere with a home on it I could call my own. I would simply have to move on again.

We followed the old road to the top, which opened into an immense domed pasture with a few cows roaming about. I was quite blown away by the grand view which had to have ranged a hundred or more miles to the north.

Could this be the end of the Vision?" I asked.

As quick as my mind posed the question, a powerful wind rose out of a gentle breeze. As it came upon us, the Pinto's long mane swirled into the air and mingled with my own, which trailed nearly to my waist. Just like in the Vision. There was now hope that the meaning and purpose of the Vision had arrived!

The Pinto stood her ground and to this day it seemed that we had fused into a single entity, like a mythical centaur. The feeling was powerful and even inspirational in a spiritual sense. A deep connection with nature. I savored the moment like none before in the Horse Trek. Surely, this was what the Trek was all about: To awaken me to the very roots of the natural world through my equine companion.

"No such luck!" came the Calling's voice from within. It was simply a pleasant diversion and nothing more. We were to move on.

I decided to spend at least one night on this spectacular promontory. At the lower northern edge of the pasture was a small grove of large pine trees. They bordered a bluff with a vertical drop of a hundred or more feet. So, it was "almost like the Vision," I mused. But that was just me begging for an end to the Horse Trek. I nestled me a spot amid the ambience of trees to hear their enchanting voices in the night — brought on by the incessant winds that swept the pasture like a great invisible broom.

The Pinto was staked out close by. So ensconced, no one would see us and we could rest, and even sleep, in splendid peace for at least one night.

The Buffalo Rivers

We backtracked to the west, and eventually found a
another trail that led off the ridge and down into a northern forested valley that was virtually uninhabited. None of
this, so far as I knew, was government land. Its maze of old
logging roads, most abandoned long ago, made for a winding but generally northerly path towards our winter destination.

But first I would cross the "Little" Buffalo River, which
fed it's mother, the grand and recently federally protected
"Big" Buffalo River. There I would winter, or so the Calling would have me to believe. Beyond that camp, I had absolutely no idea where we were to trek to next. I would
have to wait, "par for the course," I submitted myself to.

As I approached the Little Buffalo, I stumbled upon a
local farmer. I decided to inquire about the area. Seemingly
not put off by my sudden appearance, he pointed up river
and suggested that I could get supplies at a small village, the
only one around he said, with not more than several hundred souls. I thought the better of it and backtracked once
more to another series of graveled back roads and made my
descent into the place.

What I rode into was some kind of county "pioneer
days" celebration or something to that effect. People from
the surrounding mountains and valleys came with their
horses and wagons, dressed up in both western and hillbilly
regalia straight out of Dogpatch USA.

I thought and hoped, "I surely will fit in and not be noticed."

But some of the women were right on me with unbridled curiosity. It was clear to them that I wasn't costumed for any event, but wore the dirt, grime, and smoke of one who lived outdoors in the elements. The questions came at me rapid fire with the usual, "What the heck are you?"

Blackened by the sun, and hair straggling down my back, even my race as a human couldn't be deciphered. I didn't know what to say, other than to thank them for inviting me to visit and eat with them at one of the many booths surrounding the county courthouse, but which I graciously declined. I needed to get supplies and find my way to the Calling's destination on the river, which would take me at least another two days. I told several of them that maybe we would meet up again soon. They seemed satisfied with that, and I rode off.

Come to think of it, I did blend in with the parade of mock cowboys, buckle bunny cowgirls wearing spurs, and corncob hillbillies, until I vacated to one side and headed out of town. This put me across the Little Buffalo, the town being ensconced in one of the river's many bends.

A small feed store at the edge of town got me a few things I needed for the Pinto, and a small grocery market got me what I personally needed. Taking back roads once more, I passed through some of the most beautiful and breathtaking mountain country imaginable. I'm forever indebted to the Calling for positioning me as an integral and organic part of it, if only temporary.

On the second night after leaving the small river town, I entered the official boundaries of the Big Buffalo. I was astonished by its beauty and vast grandeur. It was without a dam, free-flowing, wild, and free.

The river's watershed came under federal protection just a few years before my arrival. I have mentioned earlier that the Army Corps of Engineers wanted to dam it, but environmentalists sought to block them, eventually succeeding. Locals were bitterly divided on what should happen. But outsiders rejoiced in victory for their personal recreational addictions: Mainly fishing, canoeing, and spelunking in the numerous caves pitting the steep bluffs rising hundreds of feet nearly everywhere along the river's banks. On several occasions I took shelter in some of these. But park rangers roamed and combed the park regularly for squatters and illegal hunters, which kept me constantly on the move less they evict or arrest me on both counts.

My curiosity regarding the name of the river remained piqued as we trekked our way through its myriad trails. I learned later that buffalo probably never ranged in these mountains. But their migrational paths and sharp hooves paved broad traces along river valleys to the west and further north, opening trails used by early European explorers. Among these included French trappers and later American pioneers and settlers who arrived several hundred years after the de Soto and Vasquez de Coronado explorations of the early 1500s. In fact, at one point both Spain and France held questionable and contested titles to the area

I entered the official boundaries of the Big Buffalo. I was astonished by its beauty and vast grandeur. It was without a dam, free-flowing, wild, and free.

and lands far beyond. These were later acquired along with Indian lands by the United States in 1803 as part of the Louisiana Purchase. But there is more history relevant and specific to the Buffalo River country I was now ensconced in, and wish to share.

One hundred and fifty years before my arrival, entire nations of Indians from the Southeast were evicted from their lands and militarily escorted to the new "Indian Territory" in what would later become Oklahoma. On at least four occasions, I had intersected their historic routes as I came west from Alabama. Many Indians were harassed by pioneers along the way, and thousands are said to have died from disease during their removal. I have wondered how many of those Indians escaped into these hills, married into pioneer families, and, as such, were absorbed into the new Ozark culture. Survival can take many forms. In fact, I have learned from many locals, descendents of those pioneers who came to Buffalo River country, who have claimed Indian blood from these dispossessed nations.

Winter would be coming soon, and living on the lam with park rangers on my heels, meant I had to find another location outside the boundaries to gather deer skins from local hunters. And a place with a stream or other body of water for tanning. As though on cue, the Calling drummed up just what I needed.

A preacher living along the Little Buffalo offered me the perfect spot, and word spread quickly among local hunters that "the Indian" needed their deerskins. I soon had what I needed as the hunting season began. Some visited to see what I was doing, even bringing me brains, livers, and bone oils in exchange for seeing how I tanned the "Indian way." Several wanted their hides tanned and others wanted me to tan and fashion them clothes similar to my own. As in earlier camps, I was eventually able to ship my finished hides and related Indian crafts at the local post office in town upstream on the Little Buffalo.

The Chief

By the time winter arrived with the first light snow, I was done tanning and headed downstream a ways before crossing over to the Big Buffalo to make winter camp. Because the weather had turned very cold, I was now wearing that sheepskin parka I mentioned earlier in my story.

The Little Buffalo was flowing freely with near freezing waters, but with only minor ice and snow patches here and there along its edges and upon protruding boulders and large debris trapped within the river. Nor was there flooding from fall seasonal rains. It was still navigable by horseback for most of the way, so we traveled in the water in many places before crossing overland to the Big Buffalo.

I wish to note that great lengths of the Little Buffalo rivaled the Big Buffalo in beauty, majesty, and a welcome feeling of remoteness. It was along one isolated stretch as we were slowly moving along, that we came upon a reclusive fellow the locals called "Chief." He was a full-blood Cherokee who loved this area, forsaking tribal lands in Oklahoma to live alone in a shack further upstream and not far from the village on the Little Buffalo. He was seldom seen, so I heard. But here he was, by himself, leaning between two limbs of a tree that were leaning over the river bank, fishing. I nearly missed him as he quietly blended with the forest surrounding him.

Neither one of us said a word as the Pinto slowly trudged past him over a bed of small rocks burnished to a fine finish by the river's swift flow. We had both glanced at each other, but avoided eye contact. In our own ways, we were relishing the solitude of the river, each us respecting that in each other by saying nothing. The rushing of the water over the smooth rocks further silenced us.

I've thought about him over the years. I wondered what he thought of me, covered with fur, riding a Pinto down the middle of a river, also alone. And why he chose to live alone instead of with his fellow tribal members living just over the western border in Oklahoma.

Long after I left the Ozarks, word reached me that he had died of a heart attack. And that tribal leaders came to handle his affairs. But it wasn't clear if they returned him to Oklahoma or laid him to rest in a local cemetery. Part of me laments that I didn't stop long enough to talk with him. His well-known solitary lifestyle comforted me that I had done the right thing. But, you know, I was a bit like him too. So maybe we both were just doing the right thing.

Encounter on the Big Buffalo

It wasn't long before park rangers were on to me, forcing me to move constantly, only daily if I was lucky. But it was inevitable that we would cross paths, and that day finally came.

Out of nowhere a ranger came upon my campsite on foot. I felt like one of those Indians being hunted down by the cavalry! He was polite enough, but gave me a stern warning that living in the park was illegal and they could remove or arrest me if I stayed too long in one place. Hunting and fishing was out of season, he added, so that was also out of the question.

He carried a handgun on his belt, which made it clear he was also federal law enforcement. My rifle may have made him a bit nervous, like my semi-wild appearance. So there was a bit of uneasy tension going on between us. But I didn't say anything to him at all, just nodded my head with an equally stern look to let him know I got his message. Having said his piece, he turned and left.

Not knowing what to do, I broke camp and headed further back into one of the occasional remote forest gulches. At this time of the year, these typically gave passage to streams teeming with clear, clean, cold water that were safe for humans to drink from. They were also dotted with numerous glades of mixed grasses and other forages that fed the Pinto. Although we were fairly sequestered and out of sight, it was only a matter of time before my campfires would draw the rangers to me.

Mindful of my precarious circumstance, I was surprised and relieved when the Calling came forward again with new instructions that baffled me more than the park ranger who surely wondered, "What the hell is this guy all about?" I was to get ready to leave the Buffalo River watershed, as big changes in my favor were coming. For a change, I found myself blessing rather than cursing the abstruse and esoteric Calling within.

Rustic Cabin on the Mountain

I couldn't understand why the Calling would put me in a heavily patrolled "National Scenic River" in the first place. Where I had no peace and was virtually on the run day by day to escape park rangers. And worse, that I was now fully in their radar. But what came next was even a bigger mystery.

"Integrate with the community, because you're going to be here for several years before heading west again."

I would have thrown in the towel right then and there, but I knew it would do no good. I was in too deep to turn back now.

At first, I camped here and there along the Little Buffalo, mingling with some of the ladies I had met the first day I arrived in the town. One thing led to another, and I was invited to camp on a large tract of pasture on the side of a mountain. The owner was absentee, but the caretakers told me I could stay until something more permanent came my way. That didn't take long, as yet another acquaintance told me about a small vacant cabin on 40 acres atop the same ridge near where I had camped in the pine grove.

The cabin's owner, also an absentee, was a 90-plus year old lady well shy of 5 five feet tall and I doubt she weighed 80 pounds. I later decided to go meet her in St. Louis, Missouri, where she lived alone in an ancient, somewhat musty hotel or apartment building that must have been 20 stories high. She had welcomed me to come visit her, but when I arrived, she greeted me at her door with a billy club strapped to her wrist with a thong of leather! Fearful of armed robbers, this was her defense. I didn't stay long but we had a good visit.

She had been a bookkeeper for a small business for most of her life, and never married. The cabin was owned by her brother, or some other family member, but they had all passed away and it was down to her so far as I knew. She wasn't concerned about rent, but just wanted someone to live in it and not let it go to hell. There were 40 acres attached to it.

I insisted on paying something and she said, "How about $50, Jaime?"

"You've got a deal!" I said, adding, "I'll send you $50 the first of every month."

"No, you won't," she countered. "$50 down, and nothing a month. Just look after it for me, Jaime."

I agreed, thanked her for her time and generosity, and then left. It's been so long that I can't recall her name; it wasn't exactly "contemporary" but rhythmic and humorously catchy, resembling "Cleo Cladiddlehopper" or something like that. God forgive me, Cleo!

❧

Now, a few words about my new humble living quarters. The cabin seemed sturdy, and I think the interior walls were all plastered, the exterior facing was stuccoed. The walls were very thick, not like the 2x6 frames homes are walled with today. It had a long living room with a cement floor and a fireplace at one end. A tiny table sat next to a window near the front door. I ate there, enjoying the view into the forest that tapered down the side of the ridge before falling off into a vertical bluff. I shunned a lone light bulb over the adjacent kitchen, eating instead by candle-light, reminiscent of my campfires with the Pinto staked nearby. She, by the way, at first roamed freely around my cabin, often keeping me company at the window. One day, I opened the front door, a screen door, and she came inside! I realized then that she would need "horse company" soon — as much as I longed for people company. It wasn't long before both began to fall into place.

There was a bedroom, but nothing in it, except for more cement floor and several windows. In fact, I seldom went in there except to use the shower and toilet in what I guess you'd call an adjacent bathroom. But it was really an open extension of the bedroom with more cement floor and a drain for the shower.

I wasn't sure where things drained or flushed into un-til one day I discovered down the side of the ridge a small oasis of greenery and lush growth where a pipe opened out into. Nature had claimed the spot, biodegrading everything coming out of the kitchen and bathroom drains. Building codes were obviously scarce when the cabin was put to-gether decades and decades before I took residence.

The kitchen flowed from the living room, meaning there was no separation. It was small but perfect for a bachelor. It had a stove and refrigerator and ample cup-boards for storage. Most of those sat empty my entire stay.

There was another room off the kitchen that housed a water heater and a utility sink for washing anything, including clothes. I did everything by hand, but then I had hardly any clothes to do.

I had no furniture and simply slept on the floor using my saddle for a pillow (as I always did during the Horse Trek) and the sheepskin parka which doubled as a mattress. I mentioned earlier that the coat was made of long-haired Icelandic sheepskins. I had stitched it together with sinew, which the Indian Trader sent to me from the Reservation. I added a large hood to keep my head warm. It was full length down below my knees. I used it during winter months when riding the Pinto here and there. It was quite the sight, and more than one person wanted to see how it was put together. I even let some try it on! It must of weighed 8 or more pounds. And after being in it for a few minutes, your body temperature rose to oven baking levels.

Thinking about that, I used to bathe in both of the Buffalo Rivers, even in early winter when the water approached freezing. I simply threw on the parka afterwards and I was roasting in no time. Eventually my body adapted to the cold, and I would go bare-chested in a snow storm. But that all came to an end with my new cabin life, meaning when I became more "civilized." Sort of.

Overall, the cabin made for a potentially comfortable, although "fixed in place," shelter I had not known but a few times in well over a year, maybe longer come to think of it. As I have described, I had slept on the ground nearly the entire time, except the night in jail, at the Horse

Trainer's, in the Piney Woods "bat house," and once when a woman and her husband I met on the trail early on in the Horse Trek insisted I stay in their extra room for a night. I will add here that they were kind and more than helpful. The woman, to my surprise, took me to her barn the next morning, where she put new horseshoes on the Pinto. Hoof care is something I faced early on, and I will take that discussion up shortly.

Buckskin Tanner

By the time spring arrived, I had made new tanning
frames with 2x4 lumber and many lengths of ropes used for
stretching hides on the frames. There was a pond on the
property, which I would use for soaking hides attached to
the frames. I won't go into any of the details about that,
but at this cabin I tanned hundreds of deer, elk, moose,
and eventually bison. Most of it went to the Indian Trader
on the reservation I mentioned before. But some of it I
kept for myself, and others went to locals. On one occasion, half a dozen of my lady clients who lived in the countryside came to my cabin to learn how to tan. Everyone got

Removing a tanning frame with deerskin attached from the pond at my cabin site. From there, I dragged the frame to a small grove of trees in front of the cabin where I worked it further, using the same natural tanning ingredients I used in my earlier tanning camps during the Horse Trek.

Buckskin Tanner

Finishing a fluffy white deer skin.

their own hide to tan and keep.

At first, and only part time, this is how I earned money to get what I needed to survive and pay my only (electric) utility bill, and later a phone which I had put on the kitchen wall. This was years before digital this and digital that arrived. I also cut firewood off the property to keep from freezing to death during winter, using an old pioneer type wood burning stove I picked up somewhere.

Earlier, I mentioned the lady who shod the Pinto during the Horse Trek. The time has come to talk about horseshoeing because it was something I had to take up and do for myself. And because it was a significant segue — one of several —into understanding the meaning of the Vision, although I didn't know it at the time. I'll return to "cabin life" a little later because other things that happened there also played a role in my reckoning with the Vision.

Horseshoer

I wasn't long into the Horse Trek when I was forced to deal with the Pinto's hooves. She had been delivered to me shod, that is, wearing horseshoes. Horseshoes are literally nailed onto the horse's foot as though it were a piece of wood. Actually, some folks think that's what hooves are made of! From the beginning, the suggestion of hammering a steel nail into the living flesh of the hoof caused me to shudder. I understood that the contents of the hoof included bones, blood, nerves and other things that I knew nothing about. But I was made to understand that shoeing was necessary if horses were to be ridden. Although dubious, I simply went along with it, knowing nothing about shoeing nor the horse's foot.

Fate would have it that all along the way I was greeted by people that knew how to shoe a horse and simply offered to do it for me. Some took pay, most refused.

Towards the end of the Horse Trek here in the Boston Mountains, a rancher said, "Why don't you try it? You can do it."

He offered to supervise, and I put them on. When I was done, I felt like I hadn't learned anything about the foot and whether shoeing it was harmful or not. I only knew how, and in the most rudimentary of ways. As I think back to that time, I really knew just enough to cause damage.

Within weeks of moving into the cabin I was faced

with shoeing the Pinto again. But I realized I didn't have
the tools to do it, nor shoes to nail on. I felt like I was back
to square one. In fact, I was. By sheer coincidence, although I'm convinced it was the Calling's doing, the Horse
Trainer back in Mississippi who rode with me along the
dike and with whom I stayed with briefly, called. I had
promised to keep in touch, and we shared contact information. He said he had just broke one of his forearms, which
was now in a cast, and would I be willing to come back to
his place and help him shoe his horses and clients of his
too.

"This way," he said, "You can also learn the trade."

The timing was perfect — or what I now think of as
spiritual synchronicity, because he and I shared a bit of that
together in our own ways. I can't remember if he came and
got me or how I got there, because I didn't have a car or
truck. Just the Pinto. Maybe I took a bus. One of the
women I knew offered to look after the Pinto while I was
gone, which took about three weeks.

While I was in pretty good shape, the rigors of horseshoeing day-in and day-out really tested my body. The first
night after shoeing all day left me moaning and groaning in
bed and crying out in the night. He and his wife laughed
and called back across their mobile home, "You'll live!"
The second night wasn't much better. In fact the entire
first week defined misery in my mind. But I didn't give up.
In fact, I learned a lot, and after three weeks of doing it, I
returned to the cabin.

The Horse Trainer sent me off with tools, a makeshift

anvil, and some shoes he thought would fit the Pinto. I now knew what to do, and I shod the Pinto immediately. I felt empowered. I could now take care of my own horse and not have to worry about getting her shod by someone else ever again.

One of the Horse Trainer's daughters recently found a copy of my book, *The Natural Horse*, among her parent's possessions. I had sent it years later to her dad. Although very young, she remembered me. I want to share parts of her email because it means a bit to me, and I had lost contact with him and his family:

> I have a recollection as a young girl, of a traveler on horse back passing thru the place we lived (I believe MS) but I remember my dad inviting this fellow in to have dinner and a few more details here and there. I even remember going to this man's place with my family. I don't remember what year we came to see you but I remember the teepee and you tanning a hide. The traveler I believe was you.

I wrote her back to say, "Yes, I am that person, though I'm not sure how you tracked me down! "

She shared that her father had passed away in 2013 and her mother in 2017. For me, I am grateful for her getting in touch with me, for I'm able to close that chapter in my life as part of the Horse Trek.

Within days, my new found skill began to circulate among my lady friends who owned horses. And also other horse owners in the community who I didn't even know.

The whole lot of them either trailered their horses to my cabin, rode them over, or came and got me and took me to their place. It became clear I needed a vehicle — if I wanted to do this work and let it help me make ends financially.

I had by now saved enough to buy a second hand mini-van. So, before long, I was shoeing horses near and far — including other counties than the one I lived in. Most everyone paid in cash, but some by check. This meant I also had to open a bank account!

I began to ask myself, was this ridge with the cabin the one in the Vision? I didn't think so, and sensed that my new profession was going to be temporary. The Calling said "several years," and that's what I expected would happen, which turned out to be the case.

A neighbor living on the same ridge as me called one day to do her horse. It was the first time. She was experienced with horses and saw that I needed more training.

"Jaime," she said in a caring, non-critical voice, "I've been using an older gentleman from up north who has been shoeing professionally his entire life. He was a licensed track farrier in Chicago, before retiring and moving to the Ozarks where he is still shoeing. I think you could benefit from his knowledge and experience. Do you want to meet him?"

Fully aware of my own deficiencies and limited skills, I jumped at the chance. She called him, he agreed and I gave him a call that same evening.

He invited me to come to his place, which was one county away to the west, several hours time-wise to get there across the mountains.

"Be here by 5 am tomorrow morning," he explained, "because that's when I leave my house to go shoe."

My own schedule was open, so I left early the next day. I arrived two minutes after 5, only to discover he was gone. I returned home disappointed that he had forgotten about me. That evening I called him to find out where he was.

He growled, "I left at 5 like I told you. Where were you?"

That was a major lesson in life for me. My Horse Trekking about in a Vision à la "Indian time" simply didn't cut it in his world.

Snarkily he came back, "You wanna' try it again tomorrow?" He then softened his tone, "Or you can come tonight and sleep on my living room floor."

I slept on his floor. And off we went to shoe right at 5 the next morning, and it was still dark outside. He started me out learning how to hold a horse. Then he had me pulling shoes. Then finishing the nails he set in the hoof wall. This stage went on for several months. Satisfied with my progress, he then began teaching me how to shape a shoe for front and hinds.

After several more months, he said "Let's see if you can trim a hoof."

A year went by and we became an effective team. Clients back home — which he sometimes returned with me to check my work — begin to notice the professional results of my training.

During the second year, he began taking me to far off places to see what other farriers were doing. And what horse owners in different equestrian disciplines were doing.

He also began to share a part of himself that I welcomed. "Jaime, you're not going to like what you're going to see. People can be pretty hard on their horses."

I gulped, but went with him and took it all in. Sparing the reader the details, I came to see that equestrians were not beyond being brutal with their horses. A lot of this went under the radar of decent folks, who owned horses they loved and would never subject them to the worst forms of abuse imaginable. I had held my tongue at his urging, but not my memory.

He introduced me to mules, and how to shoe them without getting killed. One day, at a theme park in the next state to the north, he had a dozen draft mules lined up side by side on a rail.

"Jaime," he warned, "Listen close, because anyone of them could kick you to death in a second. You've got to understand them, and let them know you're on to them and their antics."

Starting at both ends, we began pushing them together side-by-side, leaving just enough room for us to squeeze our way in between any two. The mules recognized this and knew they were had. He had a gimmick for each individual mule to get them to cooperate. And they did.

"Because if we didn't do these things," he said, "neither one of us would come out of there alive."

Eventually, it became clear to him that I could hold my own as a shoer anywhere, and he let me go. We kept in touch for years. After I left the Ozarks for good, I learned from former clients here that he had passed away. He was a chain smoker who didn't believe in God — only his work ethic and commitment to his trade. He liked me because I was industrious and unafraid of hard work. He despised lazy people and hippies, defining the latter in a way I've never forgotten.

"A hippy," he declared, "is anyone who won't get out of bed until they're fully rested." He added it applied to anyone, not just San Francisco flower children stoned on LSD.

Many were scared of him because he was gruff and not afraid to go to fists if someone treated him wrongly. Which he did once, and in his 60s at the time. But he felt bad about it afterwards, telling me he wished he hadn't done it.

He learned that I had interest in the guitar, the classical guitar to be specific. To my surprise he told me that during World War II he had shuttled the famous guitarist Andres Segovia by jeep to play for troops in San Francisco. He had served in the Merchant Marines during the war, and was stationed briefly at the famous Embarcadero in the "City by the Bay." That's right, back where the Vision Quest began.

In late 1977, or thereabouts, another client of mine gave me a copy of a newly released book on horseshoeing. The authors emphasized that there was a natural hoof shape, based on wild horses, to model shoeing after. But they were only speculating, because they had never seen such a hoof in the wild. Regardless, the purpose of their new method was to help horses suffering from what they believed was a type of serious hoof lameness, what is called Navicular Syndrome. And for that reason alone I admired the spirit of the book.

But it was the connection to the wild horse they referenced that caught my eye and remained within me. Yet, I knew nothing about them, except the typical derogatory comments one heard about these animals back then. So I continued to put the wild horse in the background of my thinking. The principal author and I became friends not long after, and we shod horses together and pursued many ideas that centered on horseshoeing theories.

I continued on shoeing horses for another five years during my time at the cabin, but at the forefront of my thinking was the plight of many horses with damaged bodies and hooves caused by brutal horsemanship practices and even shoeing itself. Of course, I questioned why the Calling had put me through this too. I had never planned any kind of relationship with horses, and now horseshoeing?

Life on and off the Mountain

My professional life on the mountain had by now expanded to include horseshoeing, training horses for people to ride, and hide tanning for the Indian Trader and others.

The shoeing was almost full time, but not quite. I had to put controls on it to do other things, including evening rides with the Pinto out on the ridge with the great view. We continued campouts there too in that pine grove. The song of the pines soothed my soul and I had my best sleeps among them. I guess they were also reminiscent of the many forests that I had slept in during the Horse Trek.

In fact, part of me longed to get back on the trail and continue westward. But, by now, I fully accepted being under the spell of the Calling which taught me the meaning of patience, fortitude, self-reliance, self-discipline — and especially self-doubt!

Shoeing across the forested mountains on my own schedule was tailored perfect to my psyche and lifestyle at the cabin. And it wasn't always just about shoeing as I went from client to client. Tucked away in these mountains were a sprinkling of quaint Ma & Pa cafes, where I would stop in to eat and drink iced tea by the gallon on hot days.

I also knew where cold water springs and the clearest streams imaginable were located off the graveled byways. On those scorching days, I would strip down to nothing — like I did during the Horse Trek — and lavish myself with these healing waters in the solitude of the surrounding for-

Me and the Pinto taking a break outside my training corrals at the cabin on the mountain.

ests.

At the very end of most shoeing days, I was too worn out to cook and feed myself. Not too far from the cabin along the ridge was a small café perched on the edge of a cliff with a spectacular view. I actually timed my days to get there before closing to enjoy their home-cooked meals while taking in the incredible view. I could relax and enjoy it all at the table of my choice. By then, their daily customers had gone on and the place was usually empty, except me and the staff. Again, eating alone also fell into my pattern of self-imposed solitude.

I suppose life was good, in fact, it was very good. The Calling had also taught me self-sufficiency and independence. Which provided me with much needed time alone. I had become a true bachelor living on his own, but toiling hard to make it all work. However long it was going to last, I reminded myself daily, was still an unknown.

🏠

Word of my tanning skills soon began to spread near and far. People I didn't know found their way to me to see what I was doing and invariably asked me to make things for them of my tanned "buckskin" leather. I made shirts, jackets, vests, gloves, moccasins, and even a buffalo coat!

Fitting them was always easy. I'd tell them, "Bring me a garment that fits you the way you want and I'll use it as a template."

I then warned, "The garment won't be wearable again because I'm going to cut it into parts to lay them over the

Bison robe (coat) I made at the cabin for a fellow whom I met during the horse trek.

leather."

Sometimes I added bead and quillwork I had learned from the Indian Trader and Indian people who did this their traditional way. Everything was very original though as I let my creative spirit flow.

🐎

I wish to share a less than pleasant incident related to my leather crafts that occurred at the local post office down in the village along the Little Buffalo, but that in the end fate would turn it into a positive outcome for me.

Word of my tanning and gradually improving shoeing skills took awhile to establish with locals. Until then, much of the "Indian" craft projects went elsewhere, mainly to the Indian Trader up north. So this meant my going to the local post office down in the village to ship things. It was on one shipping day that I ran into trouble at the post office.

When I first arrived in the village, I stopped in a store to pick up a small box and some wrapping paper to ship a small garment I made with my tanned leather. It had both colorful bead and quill work that was embroidered into a strikingly beautiful mosaic. The Indian Trader had drawn out the design and left it up to me to put it all together. Thinking back, it was an artistic piece I actually hated to see go out the door as I would have saved and gifted it one day to someone truly special in my life — should that person were ever to have arrived. I headed over to the post office.

I had just arrived and started to package the item in my vehicle when I noticed these three old, balding men that looked like they were trying to hide from me off to one side of the post office. I recalled having seen them outside the store I'd just been in. And they had been staring at me. I believe they lived in town somewhere as I'd seen them regularly when in town. I always got the impression they were not happy with my presence in the area. I was convinced they thought I was a druggy or pot grower using the PO to transport my stash to buyers out of town. Others had thought that too, and even suggested as much to my face. I always ignored them. Anyway, so here were the three of them at the post office carrying on with some kind of antics and gestures through a window in the side of the post office.

I continued to ignore them and walked inside. No one

was there but me. I then noticed the three of them looking in that window at me snickering.

"What the?" I thought to myself.

I put the package on the counter and there stood the Postmaster. He was a well known and respected rancher as a side business who owned countless acres at the west end of the county. His family went back generations to the pioneer days.

"Open the package," he ordered me in an unpleasant tone.

"What?" I asked.

"I said, open the package." He repeated. "The USPS has the authority to require customers to let us see the package contents of anything being shipped out of here."

I was stunned. I looked over at the window and the three of them stood there with nasty looks on their faces, implying "Ah ha, we got you now selling your drugs through the post office." I was surprised they hadn't already called the sheriff to make an arrest.

I turned to the Postmaster and said, "Go ahead, you can open it."

He snapped back at me, "No, you open it."

Now I realized what had happened, and the Postmaster was part of it. I felt humiliated and a bit sick inside. Maybe the reader understands the feeling. I had no choice but to open it.

Now opened and the item unwrapped, I slid it back to him to look inside. He was now stunned himself.

"You made this?" he asked with an apologetic tone.

I answered him, "Yes, it is a Native American garment. I tanned the leather and did the embroidery with beads and porcupine quills. It is a traditional Sioux Indian design. It is going to an Indian Trader on the reservation you see on the address label. It will be a Collector's item."

He looked over to the window, and without saying a word, headed out the front door of the PO and around the side of the building. To this day, I don't know exactly what he was saying to them, but he was yelling at them at the top of his lungs, finishing with "Now, get the hell out of here!"

In a minute he was back inside,

"I apologize for all of this," he told me, his composure returned.

I stood there in silence as he insisted on repackaging everything himself, neatly so I will add. He then weighed the box and its contents and attached my shipping label.

"On me, sir." he said.

I told him it wasn't necessary, but he insisted and I accepted his generosity. And then left.

As I said, the Postmaster was widely known and respected across the county with old timers and newcomers alike. I suppose I'm not surprised that there was a sudden interest in locals wanting me to shoe their horses and visiting to see my tanning operation. Even ordering things.

One day I received a call from him midweek not long after the PO incident. "I'd like you to come shoe my old horse. Can you come on Sunday, early afternoon?" I agreed and showed up as planned.

I was surprised to see that he and his wife, both of my

parent's generation, still lived in the old home that earlier generations of his family once inhabited. I finished shoeing the horse and they invited me inside. Payment was waiting for me the moment I stepped through the door.

His wife spoke up, "Jaime, you sit down right here to have supper with us," pointing to a large dining table.

I did, and continued to at the end of each regular shoeing session for the years I remained in the county.

If you get the picture, horses, hides on tanning racks, my garden, even chickens at one point, made for quite the sight. But I felt right at home in the middle of it. One day I received a visitor that to this very moment, I am sure was connected to the Calling.

SORRAT

The visitor, a man, was as strange a human being as ever hit the planet earth. He was part of a group of psychics who dotted the planet earth, but who kept in touch with each other clandestinely. Their "hub," however, lie towards the northeast corner of the state of Missouri. This is where their "sacred circle" had begun. SORRAT is an acronym for their semi-clandestine society of psychics, Society for Research On Rapport and Telekinesis.

He had heard about me and came to extend an invitation to visit their founder's farm, called Sky Rim, and place of gathering. The founder, John Neihardt, had passed away just a few years earlier. As it turns out, he died in the year of my Vision given by the Calling, 1973.

I thanked the visitor who promptly left. While the Calling encouraged me to connect with these psychics, it was a few years later that I actually went to visit the farm to meet other SORRATS who met there regularly. I suspect many, probably most people would be extremely uncomfortable with them and the things that happened at the farm. Let me explain.

As a group, they were what I would call true psychics with the most profound paranormal connections to the spirit world one could imagine. But I also had the same connections brought into my life by the Calling — and the Vision going back to Korea and Vietnam. Somehow, they seemed to know a bit about what I had been up to during

From left, John Neihardt (founder of SORRAT), Black Elk (related to Wallace Black Elk mentioned earlier in Horse Trek) holding his drum, and Standing Bear holding Black Elk's medicine pipe. [c. 1933]

the Horse Trek, hence, the invitation. Possibly someone along the earlier leg of my journey alerted them, or was a part of SORRAT themself.

The SORRAT society was born of Neihardt's own psychic abilities. But also of his decades old friendship with a famous 19th century Native American shaman, Nicholas Black Elk of the Sioux. Their relationship led to Neihardt's book, *Black Elk Speaks*, published in 1932. The book details Black Elk's spiritual beliefs, which in recent times have been contested by academics and even American Indians as unrepresentative of actual traditional Sioux spirituality.

But such critics never spent a day with either man, and, from what I know from the SORRATs, their evaluations are devoid of any reference to the paranormal realm of spirituality that Neihardt and Black Elk shared. The Swiss psychiatrist Carl Jung, whom I understand was in communication with Neihardt, wrote the foreword to the German edition in the early 1950s, after Black Elk's death in 1950. It is clear to me that Neihardt, Black Elk, and Jung all experienced the realm of mysticism much to the chagrin of naysayers who would have all others believe what they want them to believe. But that's too bad, for these three men are entitled to believe and say what they know to be true.

During my first visit to Sky Rim farm, I was sworn to silence due to the many trouble-making "scoffers" whom they had had to deal with who had discovered them one way or another. One in particular who was truly irritating and who made it his personal mission to publicly lambaste the group was the so called "Amazing Randi," the late magician who had dedicated his life it seems to "debunk" all psychics.

While he did attack the SORRATs from a distance, he failed to enter the Circle, even when invited. My opinion was that he was terrified to do so for what would happen, including changing his belief system from an avowed atheist to some kind of believer. The group made me aware of his methods of "debunking" psychics and I was stunned by how superficial, if not dishonest, a human being he actually was. But perhaps it was best for him to believe in "shams" than to muster the personal courage to explore mysticism within its realms of diversity and complexity that truly define it. Its doors simply do not open to the skeptical explorer determined to remain ignorant. So be it. If such a thing as the paranormal serves no good purpose in the mind of the pursuer, my advice to such a person is to distance themself from it altogether. And, as I've come to understand it, it finds you, not the other way around.

I'm not inclined to speak much further about what happened in the SORRAT circle. Except to say that what came upon me — but not others in the circle that night — was a profound transformation of reality that encompassed animal spirits emerging from what I told the other SORRATs was a booming thunder drum, which shook the entire farm house, but that no one but me heard or felt. I recognized that the drum mimicked the beating heart, as explained by my Metis friend earlier in my story.

Twenty years later I returned to visit them again for the last time in their circle. Some of the older members had passed away. I have inquired very recently about those SORRATS I met at the very beginning. Not surprising, given their ages at the time I first entered their circle, they too have all past on, as have Black Elk, Neihardt, and Jung before them. My Metis friend died not long ago at age 90 in 2018, in Skamokawa, WA. Today, I feel I am among the elders who are scattered far and wide, but who once shared time together in the sacred circle.

Phillip Deere

To the extent that I could get news in the pre-Internet days, I continued to follow the efforts of Native American Indians to get their treaty rights honored in this hemisphere. One Indian activist I became aware of lived in Oklahoma. His name was Phillip Deere.

Phillip (with whom I was on a first name basis) was born into the Muskogee (Creek) nation, living in the Okema area of Oklahoma. I went to visit him several times and we became friends. Like Chief and other Indian men I had come to know, Phillip was also of my father's generation. His ancestors, like the Cherokee, had also been removed from their former eastern tribal lands 150 years earlier. He and one of his daughters lived in what was his great Aunt's house on tribal allotment land.

As a person, Phillip was kind, contemplative, and wise. Yet, he could be a powerful orator and an equally powerful presence wherever he went. But, as friends, our conversations were quiet and comforting. Not unlike with Wallace Black Elk who you recall visited my sewing shop. We went to his local town several times to eat and talk. I spoke very little of the Horse Trek and the Vision, but it was clear there was no need to. He possessed shamanic insights and sensed in me that I was on an important journey.

He was also interested in my tanning work, and acknowledged the Lakota (Sioux) and Cheyenne influences in my method that I told him about. I brought him some-

Phillip Deere (1925-1985)

thing I made on one trip, but I can't recall for sure any longer what it was. Maybe a smoked deer hide I had tanned?

There was some talk about him coming with me to my cabin, but I was aware of the many demands on his time by Indian people who needed his presence in their struggles for equality and freedom. He did confide in me things from his own past, but, as with the SORRATS, they are sworn to secrecy and will remain as such until my death. A great person to have known, Phillip died just a few years after we met. I am eternally grateful for having spent time with him. And I will leave it at that.

Coyote Hills Regional Park

Life at the cabin and all the work mentioned earlier continued on for several more years. Then one day an unexpected letter arrived from the Metis in my PO Box down in the village. He had struck up interest about my tanning with a park naturalist back in the San Francisco Bay Area. That fellow was extending me an invitation to stay at the park and teach him and others.

I thought, "Isn't this coming full circle? I mean going right back to where I started from?"

There was no resistance coming from the Calling, so I accepted. Arrangements were made to watch over the cabin while I was gone. I reassured shoeing clients that I would be back. The Pinto went to the old farrier from Chicago who promised to feed and look after her. Other horses were returned to their owners. The tanning frames and equipment stayed put with the cabin, figuring I would need them again when I returned in a month.

"If I return?" I begin to ponder.

I took up residence with some of the rangers who also lived at the park. I was told the park was once the site of a Nike missile base run by the U.S. Army. I also remembered I was told the same thing by the park ranger back on Angel Island, when I had paddled my canoe across the San Fran-

(Overleaf) Coyote Hills Regional Park, once the site of a Nike Missile base, where I lived for a month while I trained park naturalist to tan the "natural way."

347

cisco Bay. I wondered just how many of these Nike missile bases there were. Anyway, I got the feeling we were all living in former Army barracks — nothing new to me!

The naturalists and I worked closely together to create tanning frames, scraping tools, and other things needed for the project. Within a week the tanning began. From experience, I knew they would get what they bargained for and I would be paid and out of there and back at my cabin in no time.

After several weeks at the park I began to miss cabin life and being with the Pinto and the other horses. On one of my day's off at the park, I ventured into one of the canyons leading into the back country of the East Bay. Along the way, I came across a horse rental outfit. I decided to pull in and see what was going on.

The owners, an older couple, came out and asked me if I wanted to rent a horse to ride on one of their trails. I declined, telling them I was working at this park along the East Bay temporarily and missed my horses back in Arkansas. They seemed to understand and the three of us struck up conversation about horses near my truck. Right off, the husband saw my shoeing equipment in the back.

"You're a shoer?" he asked.

I told them I did that pretty much full time plus the tanning.

He continued, "We've got a horse that needs shoes right now. Would you like to shoe him and we'll pay you cash?"

I thought for a moment and said, "Let's do it!"

The horse was brought out and I set to work. They saw immediately that I knew my way around a horse, and when I was done, they praised my work. (I silently thanked the old Chicago farrier, the horse trainer back in Mississippi, and the author of that shoeing book dealing with Navicular Syndrome). What came next really surprised me.

In one voice, the husband and wife said, "Why don't you stay on in the area, we've got 150 horses and you can do all of them on your own schedule."

I was now begging the Calling to come forward with what I should do. I recall stammering, when the husband got out his phone from a belt holster and made a call on the spot to a local husband and wife hay supplier and horse trader operating right along the bay not far from the park where I was staying.

"This Indian guy has showed up out of the clear blue and we're trying to hire him to shoe our horses. He just shod one of ours, and he's a real professional. Do you want in?"

In less than 5 seconds, he came back to me, "Our friend is in and says they've got all the work you could possibly want."

I had no idea what was going on. I couldn't make sense of any of it. "I go out to see some horses," I thought to myself, "And in less than 10 minutes I've got a complete clientele if I want it?"

I offered to go visit their friend, and would make a decision after that. They agreed and I left.

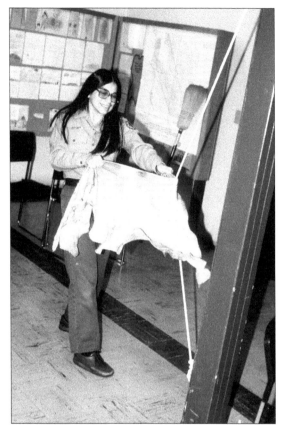

One of the rangers at the park who took an interest in the tanning, softening a deer skin. I later rented a room from her.

Instead, I headed back to the park without a clue of what to do. But no sooner than I got there, one of rangers, an Indian woman, who was also learning to tan, confronted me, "Would you be interested in living at my place? You can rent my spare bedroom for $50/month."

Now I was really flabbergasted. Something inside urged me to ask her, "Well, why don't we go to your place and talk about it?" She agreed, and we headed out.

Once there, she explained she had just ended a messy divorce with a jealous husband who didn't want to accept it. They also had a daughter.

Then came some more news. "I'm about to marry another guy and move in with him. So, you'd be getting the whole place to yourself about the time you're done with the tanning over at the park."

Kajeezzzzz. What the? I didn't need the Calling to come forward to say anything — its unspoken message was loud and clear.

"Okay, I'll take it," I told her.

And I headed back to the park. I needed to take a walk along the edge of the Bay and think about it and try to figure out why all this was happening to me within a couple of hours.

I called the horse rental couple and their hay dealer friends to tell them I accepted their offers. I added that I had to finish my commitment at the park and then time to close down everything in Arkansas. No one objected, and the deal was struck. I wrapped up the tanning operation at the park in less than two weeks and headed back to my cabin. I had a lot to sort through, including my own tanning that had been put on hold, including a buffalo hide.

Westward Again

I lamented that life in the cabin was about to come to an end. An entire lifestyle had been created and sustained there. But the Calling had spoken, and I was to give it all up. To my surprise, I was also to find a new home for the Pinto and leave her behind.

"You will not look back. She has served her purpose in the Vision," came the Calling's words from within.

I then called upon the old shoer to help. He did and the Pinto was put in with a group of retired mares and geldings to live out the rest of her life.

The tanning frames and equipment were let go too.

Clients were not happy that I was leaving, but I offered to train one of the ladies I knew to take over. I made several return trips to that end. But I eventually lost contact with everyone, so I'm not sure how it all ended up. Farriers come and go, a familiar story I had learned by then.

But there is another story that happened here that I wish to share before bringing the current one at the cabin to its final conclusion in this book.

This concerns the tanning of bison hides mentioned in the previous chapter. It was here at my cabin that I figured out how such bovine hides were tanned more than a century earlier by Plains Indian women. The method would have been lost had it not been for the anthropologist James Mooney who convinced a dozen Cheyenne women to tan cowhides and make a tipi from them the "old way." This occurred in 1903 in Indian Territory near Reno, Oklahoma — a little more than an hour away from Phillip Deere's home in Okema.

The Southern Cheyenne had been driven out of their traditional lands in the Great Plains by the U.S. military during the 1860s–70s and forced onto tribe-specific lands set up by the U.S. Government near present day Reno, Oklahoma. Soldiers were garrisoned at nearby Ft. Reno to monitor both the Southern Cheyenne and their allies, the Arapaho, to make sure they remained on their assigned lands and didn't try to escape or make trouble of any kind. Making the tipi would have been making trouble, had it not been for Mooney's shrewd way of dealing with the U.S. Government.

Rath & Wright's buffalo hide yard in Dodge City, Kansas, showing 40,000 stacked bison hides. Destruction of the bison herds spelled doom for the Plains Indian culture.

1892: bison skulls await industrial processing at Michigan Carbon Works in Rogueville (a suburb of Detroit). Bones were processed to be used for glue, fertilizer, dye/tint/ink, or were burned to create "bone char" which was an important component for sugar refining. In the 16th century, North America contained 25–30 million buffalo.

Mooney was assigned by the Bureau of Ethnology to record aspects of the Cheyenne's cultural ways before they were obliterated by reservation life. It was during this time that the tanning took place in order to create an authentic Plains Indian tipi for posterity. In my own research of Indian tanning at the University of Oklahoma (Norman) , I came across an old newspaper clipping about Mooney's project. Eventually I not only discovered detailed notes Mooney compiled about what the Cheyenne women did,

Splitting a bison hide down the center in preparation for making Bison buckskin. Sample below revealing of post-tan soft finish. I used a 100 year old manuscript about Cheyenne Indian tanning for guidance. Bison hides tan out differently than deer.

but located the tipi itself in a museum in Chicago where it had been stored for over 70 years [now nearly 120 years later]. Seeing the tipi and having access to Mooney's notes (which I located in the archives at the Smithsonian Institution) enabled me to tan the buffalo hide seen in the nearby photo taken at my cabin before heading westward again. I consider my findings to have significant ethnographical value. I have written two books about "natural tanning, one that describes the Cheyenne tanning method and its history.

🐎

Continuing back at my cabin . . .

Eventually, everything was done and I left, heading back to where it all started from in the Bay Area. The Calling stayed with me though, saying that resolution of the Vision was imminent. I had no idea of what that meant exactly and it rang of a kind of finality that wasn't exactly comforting.

After a few days of nearly non-stop driving, I arrived back in California. But before heading to my new home, I decided to return to the forest along the Pacific Ocean, where the Calling first imbued my wandering soul with the promise of a Vision that gave direction to my life. Yet, here I was again in the same forest, overwhelmed with a profound sense of loneliness, even doubting the wisdom of my actions up until now. *Nearly a decade had gone by since I set camp here.* I felt like a part of my life had been shredded into oblivion. Maybe I would soldier up and break from the entire ordeal — a direct challenge to the Calling.

358

But then what? So, I abandoned any idea of a mutiny and headed down the coast to the Indian woman's home. As at the cabin back on the mountain, I would work from there until the Calling returned, directing me elsewhere, resolving the Vision as promised. Or so I hoped.

An Unexpected Encounter

I settled into the new lifestyle, even expanding my horseshoeing business up the coast in Redwood forest country. I had an affinity for the area, which provided a respite from the bustle of my working life in the Bay Area. A seaside park was open for camping, and I would often stay there. The roar of the nearby ocean always calmed my soul. So removed from other people, I realized that the Horse Trek was still within me. For now, the Calling held it in abeyance. But that was about to come to an end.

🐴

One day a Bay Area client asked me to look at the hooves of a new horse they had just picked up from the Bureau of Land Management (BLM), the government agency that oversees America's wild horses living in the U.S. Great Basin. The Calling hadn't brought those horses to my attention in a very real, tangible way until this moment. This was the first time I had seen a wild horse hoof.

I was stunned. It didn't resemble anything I had ever seen in my encounters with domesticated horses. And by now, I had faced thousands of such hooves across numerous states. It was the end of the day, and I returned home, completely baffled by such an unexpected encounter.

I sat on my living room sofa, left behind by the Indian woman. It was my only downstairs furniture. In fact, this is where I slept at night, as I was usually too tired to retreat to the two bedrooms upstairs that were basically vacant, except for a small bed in one room that she also left behind for me. Otherwise, both bedrooms were entirely empty. In fact, I don't even recall ever having gone into the second bedroom the whole time I lived there. There was no need to. Very remindful of my Spartan life in the cabin.

As I sat there, the Calling moved over me. "Cancel all your appointments. You are leaving for wild horse country tonight."

U.S. Great Basin

So, I canceled my appointments, loaded up a few belongings — which is all I had, to be clear — and headed out in the middle of the night without any sleep. As I drove east across the state, I thought only of those wild hooves I had just laid eyes on. I still knew nothing about wild horses. The only thing I had heard about them was gossip. They were said to be "scourges" of the high desert, raggedy "broom tails" that nobody wanted because they were broken down animals not fit for anything but eradication from government lands and sold to slaughter. A brutal indictment, to say the least.

But the hooves on that horse told another story, one the Calling clearly wanted me to investigate. They were what I thought of as being unblemished, polished to a sheen, and hard as a rock. Hardly something I would think being attached to a broken down horse. Shape wise, though, they actually didn't make any sense to me as a hoof man. Length, angle, and shape nuances contradicted everything I had known and dealt with as a professional.

"But if what I think they are — hoof care models of perfection," I speculated, "then what?"

I crossed over the Sierra Nevada, the vast mountain range that divides much of California from the Great Basin. As I descended down the eastern flank I suddenly realized I didn't know exactly where I was going. But such uncertainty was nothing new, I'd dealt with it for a decade at the hands of the Calling. If there wild horses to see, I would find them.

I began to worry, asking myself, "How would I get close enough to see them, let alone their hooves?"

Ignoring common sense, I simply continued eastward through the metropolitan area of Reno, Nevada. This town was named after Civil War General Jesse Lee Reno. Among many other tributes, he was also the namesake of Fort Reno back in Oklahoma, the Army garrison charged with overseeing those Cheyenne and Arapaho Indians I mentioned earlier. An eerie coincidence.

I eventually reached beyond the outskirts of Reno on the east side and began to enter sparse high desert rangelands. A little further down the highway I came upon a sign, which read "The Mustang Ranch," or words to that effect. "How convenient," I thought, "I'll just go in there and see them."

So I pulled in and there were these long rows of buildings that looked like some of those barns I had gone into to shoe horses.

"This is strange," I thought. "Why would they put wild horses (mustangs) in barns?" Well, aren't zoos kind of the same thing?

There was a parking lot for visitors and a huge fence with a gate leading into the barns. I parked my rig and went to the gate, which had a buzzer or something to gain entrance. I pressed it, and the gate opened.

I followed the walk way to a door which said "Enter Here." The office, I assumed.

I knocked and a secretary or barn manager or something let me in. "This way," she said and I followed her to a large room full of scantily clad women!

"What the hell's going on in here?" I asked. "I thought this was a mustang ranch, you know for people to see wild horses."

To make a long story short, I made a horse's ass out of myself. I can't believe how naïve I was. Amid a bit of laughing, one of the "ladies" explained it was a house of prostitution, suggesting I might like to stay for awhile. I was shocked. I didn't realize that prostitution was even legal in the U.S. I later found out that legalization came only recently, a year after I got out of the Army.

Making yet a bigger fool out of myself, I said I was looking for real Mustangs and did anyone here know where they were.

One of the other ladies spoke up with a grin, "There's a bunch of them down this hall here, otherwise you've gotta go back into those mountains outside if you want to see horses."

I thanked her and left.

I continued eastward down the highway for what seemed like forever. I began to notice unpaved roads parting off the highway I was on. There weren't any visible signs of human habitation that they appeared to lead to. So, just by chance, I took one off to the right and followed it for some distance. I decided to stop the engine, get out of my truck, and just look around.

As far as I could see, it looked like I was in the "middle of nowhere." My own intuition was that I was now on the right path. I got back in the truck and continued on.

I must have gone ten or more miles into the back country. The area now began to get very rocky. I stopped again and looked about. The landscape was much different than anything I had experienced previously during the Horse Trek. In fact, it was different than anything I had ever seen before period. Land devoid of forests, grass, water, and people. And other than my own breathing and heartbeat, there were no other sounds. Land as soundless as its barren landscape. The stillness was eerie. Part of me just wanted to leave because the land made no sense for horses. In fact, it was a bit spooky.

I asked myself, "I must be in the wrong place. There's nothing for horses to eat here. Not a blade of grass anywhere."

I noticed just ahead a smaller side road, more like a wide trail, or a wash, that led off of this dirt road. I decided to take it. It wound around large boulders, cut banks, and stacks of volcanic rock. Less than a mile in, it came to an abrupt end. I got out again to look around. It was impossible to drive any further.

Before me lay a small field less than a hundred yards long, maybe half that, with walls of more rock on either side. The ground was spotted everywhere with volcanic rocks of many sizes and shapes. At the end of the field was a stand of some kind of stunted, juniper-like trees.

I began to realize I hadn't come prepared with water and other supplies to explore much further. I reasoned that I should return to Reno, gather what supplies I would need to stay for a week and then return back to this spot and move out and about from there.

But before leaving I wanted to see what was on the opposite side of the rocky field. I was hoping it would be horses. I headed out. In between the rocks scattered about was some kind of earth I wasn't familiar with. Maybe a blend of sand, dirt, and volcanic dust? I used that soil to step between the rocks to get to where I was going. This meant I had to keep looking at the ground before me, or trip and fall on my face.

I got half way across the field when I happened to look up. There at the far end, stood a dark brown horse staring me right in the face, actually into my eyes. Maybe into me.

What flashed through my mind in that very moment was, "This is no scrawny, broken down broomtail." Well muscled, I figured it was a he, a stallion. He was a beautiful wild creature that nearly blended into his surroundings. I surmised, "Maybe he was there all along, and this is why I didn't see him until now."

We both just stood looking at each other, neither of us making a sound. Actually, I felt like I was being examined. I began to focus more on him and saw that it was indeed a "he" — large, muscular, stout, and clearly holding his ground. I wasn't sure what to do until he began to move

"I got half way across the field when I happened to look up. There at the far end, several hundred or more feet away stood a dark brown horse staring me right in the face, actually into my eyes."

his head slightly to the left, and then to the right as though to gain a better sense of what or who he thought I was. This made me nervous.

I didn't move a muscle. This was no barn yard gelding. It was clear this was a wild stallion. And here I stood with no way to protect myself, and I was clearly in his domain. With clear intent, he took several steps towards me and stopped.

Nervousness in me then gave way to fear and panic. I was completely vulnerable. There was nothing to do but turn around and make a dash for the truck. Actually, in the moment, I wasn't thinking about the truck at all. Call it cowardice, whatever you want, I don't care, "running for my life" is a bit more accurate.

In what was a sloppy pirouette, I spun, tripped over the first rock ahead of me, and fell flat on my face in what had to be the only patch of "volcanic sand" in the entire field the size of my body. While I was spitting out the debris of whatever it was, I could hear him coming on.

"I'm had," was the message coming out of my own mind. And the Calling was nowhere in my moment of need.

I laid as still as I could, but my heart was pounding so loud I was sure he could hear it. Still he came on.

He was incredibly noisy about it, kicking rocks out of the way with every hoof beat. I then began to hear him breathing — and right over the top of me!

I could think of only one thing, "He's going to kill me right where I lay with one swipe of his hoof. A fitting ending for the Vision," I lamented, "the Calling's grand plan for my execution in a fool's paradise."

Waiting for the fatal blow became an eternity. I listened but there was not a sound to be heard. He had gone totally silent on me. Only my heart beat was now audible and palpable, I was sure, to Mother Earth.

Eternity had turned into nothingness: No blow to my head, no teeth grabbing the nape of my neck, no heavy breathing, no rocks kicked here and there. Just nothing.

There was only one thing to do: Lay there forever or look up and plead for mercy in a "nice doggy" tone of voice. Still laying flat on my stomach, I raised my head just enough that I could see him without being detected, or so I hoped. But he was gone. Nowhere in sight. He left without making a single sound.

I got myself up, brushing off dirt and feeling worse a pitiful fool than back at the Mustang Ranch. It was a bad, bad day for me. I walked back to the truck.

Still shaking, I reflected, "Humility seems to be the way into their world."

I headed back to town to get supplies.

"Tomorrow," I vowed to myself, "I will return and gain their respect."

The Calling in that moment surfaced from its own imposed silence, delivering a cardinal rule I henceforth abided by until my final day in wild horse country four years later: "Return to them as a student."

Epiphany: The Vision

I returned to Reno to get my supplies, but, by now, it was getting too late to find my way back to that volcanic field in the dark. I would need to stay somewhere that night and then head back in the morning. I know what you're thinking reader, but we're not gonna go there. Me maybe, but not you and me.

I headed back to the Ranch and decided to spend the night in the parking lot. Other cars were there now, often coming and going. So I would kind of fit in. I wondered how many of them were married men.

I remember the lady inside asked me from curiosity, "Are you married."

I said "No," and, in fact, I had never been married.

"You are an unusual one," was her comeback.

"That and me thinking this was a stable full of wild mustangs," I sighed to myself.

Earlier that day, I had found an "Army-Navy" store that those militia types often frequent, thinking I could get the kinds of things I would need to rough it in the back country. The Horse Trek — and the Army — had really prepared me for all sorts of eventualities, so going here for supplies turned out to be the right move.

"That small volcanic field," I speculated further, "will be my first 'base camp' in wild horse country. From here I will head out to bivouac with the horses, returning for supplies I'll keep in the truck."

Actually, there was one other gaffe in my planning. I decided to rent one of those small motorbikes, I think it may have been a Honda 50 "cub" and it fit in the back of my truck. My idea was that it could get me around quickly in the back country where my truck couldn't go. Well, it wasn't able to go where my truck was able to go. So, I abandoned that idea within minutes of unloading it. It became clear that to negotiate the back country, I would have to hoof it on foot.

But, at this point in my story, I hadn't found the horses. "I was found" by one stallion who graced me with my life. It was time to go find him, make amends for my pitiful behavior, and hope for the best.

⚞

Here I will return the reader to my mention of hides that I had tanned at my cabin. One in particular was an elk hide. The Calling directed me to paint four symbols upon the hide in red, black, yellow, and white. These were to represent the four sacred directions that are common to many tribal cultures:

⚞ The races of people;

⚞ Mental, spiritual, and physical harmony within oneself;

⚞ The four directions — north, south, east, and west;

⚞ The four winds signifying sacred teachings, and much more.

I would be instructed by the Calling in its use, which was still unrevealed to me at that point following the encounter with the wild stallion.

🐎

I returned to my newfound base camp. I packed water, some things to nibble on, the elk hide, and headed across the field like a soldier. The stallion was not there this time, which was a great relief. He may have simply shrugged me off as a "non threat" and left it at that, or worse, deemed me another "dumb human" fumbling and bumbling in the back country for his amusement. But there was no sign that anyone but me had been out there for who knows how long. And why would anyone bother?

I made my way through the small grove of juniper trees. Emerging from the other side, a narrow ridge leading up to a high peak lie before me.

In that very moment, the Calling came upon me: "Ascend the peak, the Vision awaits you."

So, this was it, my journey's end? The Vision would now unfold itself before my very eyes? I didn't believe a word of it.

"Why now," I asked myself, "after nearly 10 years? And why no Pinto as in the Vision? And why in the middle of nowhere with nothing but volcanic rock, stunted trees, and no water?"

I walked forward and then gradually upwards. In a few minutes I reached the crest, which turned out to be a narrow outcropping forming a level circle only several meters across.

The Calling returned, "Walk to the center and lay

down the elk hide. Align the symbols with the Four Sacred Directions. Remove all your clothes and stand in their center."

It was a strange request, but going naked didn't bother me. I did it throughout the Horse Trek when out of sight, except for the Christian bridge incident. Whatever, there was no one around anywhere to make trouble — like someone reporting a semi-hairless, mini-Sasquatch in the back country. I could imagine myself creating a flood of reporters and Bigfoot hunters. Tabloid stuff.

But I was also aware that going naked was, in fact, done by vision seekers in tribal societies for millennia. So, I stripped down to nothing but the bare and stood at the center of the hide.

The Calling: "Now, turn your head as you did on the Pinto and look behind you but with closed eyes. Then open your eyes and look forward again."

I closed my eyes and turned my head off to my right as far as I could. As I did, I entered into what seemed like a dream, with my eyes still closed. What I saw were thousands of suffering horses such as I had seen over the years in my new profession as a "hoof man." It was a bleak reminder of what I had come to know.

I then turned my head forward again with open eyes. But, unlike in the Vision, there was no change as far as the eye could see across the mountains.

The Calling again: "Step to the edge of the circle and look down into the valley below."

With open eyes, I peered down and there below was

an endless cavalcade of wild horses moving together in one direction like a powerful river. There were so many I couldn't count them all. They were of many colors, and shapes, and sizes, and ages.

"Now, go down among them," the Calling commanded.

Down I went. But now it felt like a dream again. I was ignored entirely by every horse. I could have reached out and touched them, but dared not. All were the most beautiful specimens of horses I had ever seen. Hooves manicured to perfection by Nature, bodies muscled and rippling with soundness and vitality.

I then understood why I was here, the purpose of it all, the Vision. And with that realization, all the horses began to move away and disappear into the gulches, on the alluvial plains, atop the many buttes, and among the volcanic rocks and boulders that are impossible to avoid. In minutes I was all alone again, but empowered by an unforeseen spiritual awakening.

I returned to the peak, dressed, folded up the Elk Hide, and returned to my base camp. Before darkness fell, I had gathered deadwood from the small forest at the edge of the field, and made fire. Mosquitoes began to arrive as the last ray of daylight disappeared over the mountains to the west. But the Calling had prepared me even for this, as the fire and smudge drove them away as it did near the Mississippi River earlier in the Horse Trek.

The mountain air now turned cold, and I draped the elk hide around me. Comforted by hide, smoke, and fire, I entered into a deep state of contemplation, and therein, pondered the future that now awaited me. The next morning I left these mountains and headed home to the Bay Area.

Messenger

The Calling remained with me and had me return to explore other areas of the Great Basin for several more years. I went each time as a student of Nature. And in that way, I was introduced to many wild horses who served as my teachers. What I came to learn represented the essence of their species: Their ancient story, as I thought of it, that was still alive in these mountains. A story I realized that was not evident among their kind living in captivity among humans. The tension between what Nature had intended for their species, and the reality of their lives in civilization increasingly wore heavily upon me.

After another three years of visiting and staying among them, the Calling returned me to the peak once more. As before, the Elk Hide was laid in the circle and I sat down upon it in my nakedness, as is the traditional way of the Vision Quest.

I entered into another dream state: The slopes of the lofty peak shape-shifted into steep walls — like the bluffs in the Boston Mountains framing stretches of the Big and Little Buffalo Rivers. Down below, several family bands of wild horses, antelopes, and other animals trekked along between the walls. As they all passed by, an ominous feeling came over me, transforming into a dark cloud that hovered over my head. I was struck with fear.

Came the Calling: "You are done here. It is time for you to leave and never return. You are a Messenger now.

Go!"

Startled by the tone and intensity of the command, I quickly dressed, gathered up the Elk Hide, and minutes later the truck was loaded. I headed west towards the setting sun.

🐎

I passed through Reno, the name reminding me once again of the ghosts of those Cheyenne women tanners near Ft. Reno, and what I had learned from them. Just as I had learned from the wild ones now behind me.

I reached the summit of the Sierra Nevada and descended into the immense Sacramento Valley. Well before nightfall, I reached the outskirts of the Bay Area. But I decided at the last moment to turn north and make my way again to the ancient Redwood forest where the Calling first arrived to lead and guide me in the Horse Trek.

As I drove north and passed the first Redwood forest, I noticed on a steep hillside that one sector of the forest had been clear-cut. I pulled off the side of the road to get a closer look. Amid the fallen trees stood a lone tree, nearly barren of its branches but had survived the chainsaw slaughter. Perched atop one of the uppermost remaining branches was what I thought was an eagle. It suddenly raised its wings, took flight, and drifted slowly over the carnage below. I wondered if this raptor was a female who lost her nest and now wandered, searching, distressed. Would this also be the fate of the wild horses roaming on government lands I had found? I had by now become aware of the many government gathers depleting wild horses from their homelands.

I soon reached my destination, gathered up the Elk Hide and a few other things and entered the forest. I followed the now familiar trail that led to the bluff overlooking the Pacific Ocean. The sun by now had begun to set and then sink into the ocean, giving way to a darkening sky. A light sea breeze chilled me as it passed by, dissipating into the dank Redwood canopy behind and around me.

I sat down and draped the Elk Hide around me for warmth. The breeze suddenly transformed into a strong wind. My thoughts were momentarily drowned in the welcoming roar of the forest, reminding me of the healing winds passing through the Pine forest on the ridge near my cabin.

I closed my eyes, and once again heard the thunder drum in the SORRAT sacred circle, a sound that mimics the "heart beat" that is shared by all. That also united me with that stallion and his strange invitation to return as a student of nature. And uniting me too with the wind and sea and forest all around me in this moment. With words held silently within, as it always had been, I thanked the Calling for blessing my life with the Vision and its life-changing experiences I came to understand, trust, and appreciate.

40 Years Later

Seeker and the Chosen

Horse Trek's mysticism was rooted in many strange anomalies. Some of these I wish to comment further on before leaving my story. First, I never experienced nor viewed them as things of the Occult. Of the latter, I really know nothing about. Nor did I pursue any of them, like those who have spent lifetimes in search of Bigfoot. Yet Bigfoot, or Sasquatch as they are known among the Salish peoples of old, represents the type of anomaly that sought me out. There is an interesting story to tell here that explains this difference between the "seeker" and the "chosen."

There was this biologist who was determined to find Sasquatch. Indian legends spoke of Sasquatch inhabiting the remote forests of the Pacific Northwest. Logically, he went there to search the forests and find those tribal people who he believed could help him find Bigfoot, as he called the elusive creature.

He prepared himself with camping equipment and other technology to record the encounter he was seeking. All set to go, out he ventured into the remote forests. He hunted and hunted and hunted. Weeks went by, then months, and finally an entire year. But still no Bigfoot.

He thought, "I guess I better go find some Indians to help me find Bigfoot."

After some time asking around, local white people told him to visit the River Indians who lived in the area where there were many Bigfoot sightings. They told him where these Indians could be found, and off he went to get their help.

He drove his jeep many miles up the river to the Indian Reservation. Soon he arrived and found some Indians living along the river.

"I am a biologist," he explained, "who wishes to find Bigfoot and document my encounter with him and prove his existence. White people further down this river told me that you River Indians knew all about Bigfoot and that he lives in these forests. Can you introduce me to one?"

One of the River Indians spoke up, "We Indians living here along this river have heard of this Bigfoot. But he does not live down here near us."

Pointing to a bluff across the river, the Indian continued, "He lives up there in the forests above the river. Up there are the Mountain Indians who can help you find this Bigfoot."

The biologist listened attentively as the Indian provided him with more details.

"But there is no road. You will have to hike up there. There is a place up river where you can cross and find your way up. It is a long way up to those Mountain Indians. It takes us River Indians three days to reach those Indian relatives of ours. So go do that and tell those Mountain Indians up there that we River Indian relatives down here sent you, and that they should help you meet this Bigfoot."

So, the biologist spent three days trekking up to the Mountain Indians. Exhausted, but hopeful, he runs into some of the Mountain Indians up there.

"Excuse me," he tells the Mountain Indians, "The River Indians down below have told me that Bigfoot lives up here and that you can contact him for me so I can verify this creature for science. I'm very tired and dirty. Would you please take me to Bigfoot now and introduce me to him?"

The Mountain Indians looked at each other, then took a few minutes to speak privately in council. "We will be back shortly with an answer to your request."

The biologist waited patiently, now feeling hopeful that at last he would meet the elusive Bigfoot, obtain his evidence, return home to share with the world his remarkable finding, and become a famous biologist.

The Indians returned.

"We have taken your request into our tribal council," one of the Mountain Indians explained. "We regret to tell you that you have been misled by our tribal brothers down on the river. You see, Bigfoot lives down there with those River Indians that live along the river. So, go back down there, and we are sure they can help you find this Bigfoot."

This is actually a true story. And I think it's probably happened more than once. But there is no Bigfoot in the scientific sense or in the realm of our five "earthly" senses. Sasquatch is a spirit, revered long ago by the Salish as the "librarian of our people."

The biologist, of course, was very frustrated and let down by his failure to find the elusive Bigfoot. He wanted to see Bigfoot very badly. But, the truth is, Sasquatch has no time for such antics. In the spirit world, Sasquatch is a "good spirit," a kind soul who remembers and shares the an-

cient history of the people. Sasquatch shares this information through the tribal shamans, who have been chosen by
this ancient spirit and endows them with this Calling on
behalf of the people. So, it is clear, not everyone gets to see
or hear this spirit. It is the Shaman's responsibility to
share this important information with the people as the
Sasquatch's "Messenger."

When the Europeans, and later the Americans, arrived among these Indian peoples hundreds of years ago,
they began to take everything from them that they could.
It was then that Sasquatch retreated behind the invisible
Metaphysical Curtain. This was a signal to the people to
shut down their ancient spiritual teachings less they be
taken and destroyed too. So Sasquatch lies in waiting for
the people and their shamans to return. Of course, there
is plenty of "Indian time" for this to happen. "But not so
good for that biologist seeker," the River and Mountain
Indians would say, "Because he was not chosen."

But not all spirits are so benevolent as Sasquatch.
Many arise from the horrible deeds of humans. *Wetiko*.
These are what I ran into in the Mississippi forest. They
were a reminder of the evils of human slavery and its depravity imposed upon Africans chained to the decks of
ships that brought them here.

The lady who had me sleep in her broken down car
had told me that it was not good or safe for me to go in
that place. I did not tell her that my Calling had protected
me and the Pinto, and guided us to and from the forest in

the right way. That this was part of my preparation as a Messenger. I appreciated her caring for me, and I lament to this day that those evil spirits of that forest would remain lurking there until the wrongs of those days are righted in the present.

The SORRATs are also part of the same discussion. As psychics, they were eccentric if not odd, very guarded and understandably secretive. Together, they were able to open the Metaphysical Curtain to the "other side" through rapport in the most profound of ways. I quickly deduced that this resulted from their individual psychic abilities and shared propensity to come together and put them to use in their circle. But, this requires further clarification because these were not exactly kumbaya get togethers.

As I wrote in their eponymous chapter, what happened and what was a sentient experience shared by all in their circle, was one thing. But what each individual experienced privately within the circle varied from one member to the next. Like me, they were all chosen by their Callings, but their voices held within themselves told different stories.

I understood each SORRAT to be Messengers, reporting back to others as their Callings' decreed. No different than the Salish shamans sharing the sacred knowledge passed to them by Sasquatch, the anomalous "librarian of the people." It was interesting and comforting that each of us in the SORRAT circle could be supportive of each other's Callings and responsibilities without knowing anything specific about what they were or prying for information for gossip. Even in my case, where my Vision had not yet fully revealed itself to me, there was respect. The thunder drum that I heard in our circle (then again for the last time on my last day among the wild ones in the Great Basin), was heard and seen only by me. Even though the drum boomed so loudly, even shaking the room we all shared, that I thought for sure all had to have experienced it. They didn't. The animal spirits that were also unleashed, came to me alone and were also not seen by the others.

But I also shared an equally important connection to a series of older Indian people of my parent's generation. They too possessed psychic — shamanic — powers to be sure. In their unique ways, often as simple as their mere presence in my company with very little said, they influenced me in ways that defy words. Thinking back to them, it was that they embodied an invisible stream of information passing into me from themselves and from those who came before them who faced the white invaders and managed to survive and pass along stories of their peoples. But like the elders of the SORRAT's sacred circle, they too have all passed on across the Metaphysical Curtain.

Then there was the helicopter incident along the DMZ. I was chosen to escort a U.S. Marine I never knew but who bore the same name as me, across the same Metaphysical Curtain. Perhaps it is that we are all escorted thusly when our time has come. As was this Marine who had died so violently moments before Vietnamese soldiers and guerrillas stormed the hill to assess what had happened, but who never saw us. I see it as The Divine extending comfort and meaning during our passing, no matter our sins or good deeds in life, nor the degree of violence or serenity at our life's end.

One psychic I did not mention in the story was a man by the name of Jack Houck. Well-connected among many psychics and non-psychics, Jack was famous for his spoon-bending "PK Parties." He invited me to one, and there must have been a hundred or more people there in on it. Jack had provided spoons for everyone. Where he got them I have no idea, but they were heavier than usual and I mean impossible to bend by ordinary means in one's hand. But no pressure was required anyway to bend them. Spoons were bending on their own everywhere once the person holding the spoon loudly commanded it to bend, according to Jack's instructions. The fellow to my left, unlike the others, said nothing to the spoon but did "massage" the handle and it suddenly wrapped around his finger like a snake coiling around its prey. Mine, in contrast, bent across the bowl in a rapid snap that actually took me by surprise. Jack died in 2013 at age 74 of a serious debilitating disease. I asked a friend who knew him too, "Why was he so obsessed holding those thousands of PK Parties?" His response: "Don't you think he was looking for a Jesus who could heal him?"

I had asked myself many times, "Why did the Calling put all of these people in my path as part of the Vision Quest?"

I eventually came to understand why, and it is really very simple. They provided me with an affirmation that the experiences of my Vision were perfectly natural and not to shun or fear, including death, which is simply a passage of our souls to another realm.

In time, I had come to realize that seeking spirits in the "normal way" that relies on our five earthly senses only creates a barrier to them. Like the impermeable wall that divides the mystic from the skeptic. We can seek all we want, but in the end, it really chooses us or we are left with a desert of disappointment. I feel for those seekers who retreat with disappointment. Perhaps they will rethink things and find solace.

I suspect it is that our variant perceptions of space, time, and matter are also at work in this division. What the skeptic logically perceives as rock solid in their reality, is to me but a massless illusion. In the same way that what the skeptic would declare the delusions of a warped mind, is to me a rock solid alternate existence! And for those who may approach me in skepticism to doubt the very premise of the Vision Quest and its string of anomalies, the only analogy I could muster would be in the purest vein cut by Occam's razor: "Do I care what you think when God speaks to me?"

In any case, the wall dividing the "Messenger" from the "Skeptic" is the same wall that segregates "Believers" from "Atheists." If not a bitter divide, it is one that invites folly and muse from either side. For me? I ignore such quibbling, for it is what it is.

The events described in *Horse Trek: Into the Mystic* took place and ended some four decades ago. I was unable to write the book then because the Calling and discretion compelled me to apply the Vision in life first. I began writing my first book derived from the Vision, *The Natural Horse: Lessons From the Wild*, the year I left wild horse country because those Lessons had begun to formulate into meaningful and applicable principles. I did this without a word of the mysticism that underlies *Horse Trek*. I would have, but *The Natural Horse's* publisher wanted no part of it, striking an entire chapter that opened glimpses into the book's mystical origins.

Today, the Calling is still within me. Still pushing me. Giving me no peace. I hear it now humoring me as this book draws to its own final curtain, "The journey of enlightenment isn't over yet, Jaime." So be it.

I do see now that *Horse Trek* was more than a mystical bridge to *The Natural Horse*, providing whatever legacy of goodness it may bring to the lives of horses living and suffering in human captivity. To me, its spiritual content has broadened the original Vision far beyond the boundaries of wild horse country. Seeing this, I feel destined to explore new realms unharnessed from what I once thought were bound by earthly, physical limits. Those are simply illusions: the mental weight of fear and skepticism.

So liberated, I now see the entire universe as a unified thinking mind and healing force, and we — of the past, present and future — are cognitive expressions of it. And I believe we are all destined to explore it. As I think of it, it is the "Way of the Calling" and our own specie's Great Awakening inviting us *into the mystic*.

Image Credits

Image credits

Front/Back Cover Design. Edyta Jackson

Back Cover Photo. Ruth Rohner-Schlegel

P8. Richards Studio, Tacoma, WA

P29. https://en.wikipedia.org/wiki/Vietnam_War#/media/File:UH-1D_helicopters_in_Vietnam_1966.jpg

P60. Jim Mone/AP file 1973

P63. Ojibwe women in canoe on Leech Lake, Bromley 1896. Public Domain.

P65. https://en.wikipedia.org/wiki/Lake_Pillsbury#/media/File: Lake_Pillsbury.JPG

P69,74. https://en.wikipedia.org/wiki/Angel_Island_(California)#/media/File: Angel _Island _Tiburon_Belvedere_aerial.jpg

P72. https://en.wikipedia.org/wiki/Alcatraz_Island#/media/File: Alcatraz_2021.jpg

P72. https://en.wikipedia.org/wiki/Alcatraz_Island#/media/File: Alcatraz_Island_-_panoramio_(3).jpg

P78. Cheyenne: Stump Horn and family showing Horse Travois: https://catalog.archives.gov/id/523855

P90. https://en.wikipedia.org/wiki/Freedom_Train#/media/File:1976_American_Freedom_Train,_4-8-4_steam_locomotive.jpg

P98. Unknown (c. 1973).

P102. https://commons.wikimedia.

org/wiki/File:Horno_(305406541).jpg

P104. Richmond Independent News (1982)

P105. Laguna Pueblo (1879). Public domain. U.S. National Archives and Records Administration.

P107. https://en.wikipedia.org/wiki/San_Quentin_State_Prison#/media/File:San-Quentin-Prison-4.JPG

P109. https://en.wikipedia.org/wiki/Drawknife#/media/File: ZiehmesserTop.jpeg

P110. *The Canvas Tipi* (1982, Lodgepole Press), by Jaime Jackson; illustrations by Janet DeHaven. Out of print.

P114. https://commons.wikimedia.org/wiki/File: Buffalo_Boy_Canoe_headstone.JPG

P130. https://commons.wikimedia.org/wiki/File: Chevy_thriftmaster_1948.jpg

P161. https://en.wikipedia.org/wiki/American_alligator#/media/File: American_Alligator.jpg

P162. Tommi Stevens — who photographed my tanning in the early 1980s at my cabin property.

P167. https://en.wikipedia.org/wiki/Ku_Klux_Klan#/media/File: Ku_Klux_Klan_members_and_a_burning_cross,_Denver,_Colorado,_1921.jpg

P201. https://www.123rf.com/

photo_31732847

P251. https://en.wikipedia.org/wiki/
Jerome_War_Relocation_Center#
/media/File:War_Relocation_
Authority_camp_near_Jerome,
Arkansas(1942).jpg

P266. Own work, CC BY-SA 3.0,
https://commons.wikimedia.org/
w/index.php?curid=197235

P269. https://en.wikipedia.org/wiki/
Ouachita_Mountains#/media/
File:WestHannahMountain.png

P278. https://en.wikipedia.org/wiki/
Hand_pump#/media/File:
Ebenezer,_GA,_US_(06).jpg

P293. The author, late 1970s.

P309. Jason. https://en.wikipedia.org/
wiki/Boston_Mountains#/media/
File:Buffalo_national_river_steel_
creek_overlook.jpg

P321–324. Tommi Stevens

P334. Tommi Stevens

P336. J. Jackson Archives

P342. Public Domain

P346. https://iloveancestry.net/post/
68117479759/phillip-deere-
muscogee-creek-1929-1985-no

P348–349. https://en.wikipedia.org/
wiki/Coyote_Hills_Regional_
Park#/media/File:
CoyoteHillsView.jpg

P352. Norm Kidder

P355. (above) https://en.wikipedia.
org/wiki/Bison_hunting#/media/
File:%22 Rath_&_Wright's_ buf-
falo_hide_yard_in_1878,
_showing_40,000_buffalo_hides,
_Dodge_City,_Kansas.%22_-
NARA-_520093.jpg

P356. (below) https://en.wikipedia.
org/wiki/Bison_hunting#/media/
File:Bison_skull_pile_edit.jpg

P357. (**Above**) Tommi Stevens

P357. (**Below**) Jaime Jackson

P368. Jim Hansen (*The Natural Horse:
Lessons From the Wild*).

Milton Keynes UK
Ingram Content Group UK Ltd.
UKHW030246190324
439698UK00014B/741